No Fight, No Glory

The early beginnings of Chinese adoptions, and the inspiring personal story of this missionary family's ministry in China.

By Randy Ryel

Dedication

To God be all the praise and glory! This is written for my dear wife Ruth and our children Adrianne, Stephanie, Erika and Emily, and to all our many precious grandchildren. It is also in memory of my mom and dad, Charles and Ann Ryel, as well as my brother Richard Ryel. In memory of my wife Ruth's mom and dad, Charles and Mary Manley

To all whose love and sacrifice were integral parts of this testimony, Ruth and I recognize in our story some key individuals which God used in a great way to direct us, and some who directly facilitated what God accomplished in and through us. My best friend Charles was so important to us in adoptions. Once you read the book you'll also realize, Mr. Y played a very important role of our story. I will call him by this initial in order to protect him and his family from any consequences for what they were involved with 36 years ago in service to God and to me.

We also want to recognize the ministry influence of all the members of the Alvin and Rhoda Cobb family, including of course their son Kendall, who greatly impacted our ability to stay sane, and our efforts and effectiveness on the mission field. Their names are mentioned because I've been given permission to do so.

Another important part of our lives and ministry I refer to in the book only as SC. SC's value and testimony still challenges us today. Some, who were not engaged in activities the Chinese government would find in anyway offensive, are at least in part, referred to by their real names. Many others I will mention either by their English nick-names if they used one, and/or their Chinese first or surname.

Couples who adopted through us I will refer to by their first names only to honor their privacy since it is impossible for us to contact all of them directly.

Table of Contents

Chapter 1	Preparation for Battle	page 6
Chapter 2	Slow Boat to China	page 18
Chapter 3	God Calling	page 27
Chapter 4	We're Here! Now What?	page 41
Chapter 5	Snake Mouth	page 53
Chapter 6	My Name Is Li En Tian	page 68
Chapter 7	Mount Shekou	page 83
Chapter 8	The Three-Self Church	page 90
Chapter 9	Puzzle Pieces	page 99
Chapter 10	The Testing of Our Faith	page 108
Chapter 11	The Battle Rages	page 114
Chapter 12	Tiananmen Harvest	page 120
Chapter 13	Friends and Neighbors	page 129
Chapter 14	Divine Appointment with Caleb	page 130
Chapter 15	Culture Shock in Reverse	page 147
Chapter 16	The Orphans	page 153
Chapter 17	Witness to the Miraculous	page 163
Chapter 18	You Need to Come With Us	page 173
Chapter 19	Comin' Round the Mountain	page 185
Chapter 20	Christmas in Kansas	page 201
Chapter 21	How Do You Say It in English?	page 211
Chapter 22	More than the Mind Can Bear	page 219
Chapter 23	It's Not Your Fault	page 234

*List of the first names of our Adoption Couples and their babies.

Preface

For many years my family and friends have asked me to write this book. Even strangers I've met have mentioned it knowing nothing about me. One man I hardly knew referred to my story as "God's beautifully colored tapestry", even though he had no knowledge of my life story. Whether or not we call Jesus our Lord, each one of us are a tapestry of some design created by God, ourselves and others. It might be mostly beautiful. For others it might be mostly dark or disturbing. For mature Christ followers I must believe they are mostly beautiful. *"We are God's masterpiece created in Christ Jesus" Ephesians 2:10a NLT.*

These tapestries I speak of hold all the colors we can imagine, but all the shades of gray and black are also there in significant quantities. As in most of our world's works of art, the greatest sense of beauty can be seen in its many fine details. I pray that you'll be able to see the beautiful details God created on the canvas of our lives and give Him praise. The closer you look at the details of your life's tapestry; you should delight in what God has done in and through you. Like the apostle Paul, you may find for yourselves that even in your suffering and weakness God gave you His grace. His strength is made perfect in our weakness. Perhaps you'll see the glory which comes after you are challenged by suffering, hardship and spiritual fights. These are to lead you to the obedient completion and perfection of your faith.

At the end of the book I will share how a traumatic event in our ministry left me with deep seated guilt which made it impossible for me to write my story till now- 36 years later. You may find it puzzling as to why I have always been ashamed to write it, look at pictures or videos of it, think about it, or even read the many letters of thanks we received at that time. Only in the last few years has God revealed the much bigger, clear truth I speak of in this book and it set me free. My mom would say it like this, "you must take the bad with the good." Job told his wife "Should we accept only good things from the hand of God and never anything bad?" Job 2:10. As still others might say, "No pain, no gain." To illustrate the principle in this book, I will endeavor to tell my family's somewhat unique missionary story while highlighting the events and discussing scriptures which reveal the underlying truth I hope to convey.

Perhaps this book will for some be a guide for your own missionary faith journey. I do feel confident in saying it can absolutely be a testimony to help enlighten Christ followers to God's ways and give them boldness in their spiritual battles.

Before I begin, I want to lay the groundwork for its title by giving you very brief scriptural foundations of why I call this precept "No Fight, No Glory", a spiritual truth. If you're anything like me, once you start to see truth in scripture, examples will begin to leap out of every significant story of the bible. Scriptural evidence abounds if you examine Jesus Himself and all the heroes of the faith. A quick example of some of our heroes of the faith is found in Hebrews chapter 11. I will do my very best to tell our story with complete accuracy to the very best of my recollection, but primarily relying on our newsletters and the hundreds of letters we wrote to our family members while on the mission field. I will be very careful to not exaggerate what occurred in any way, but neither will I whitewash, marginalize or diminish what God did in and through all who are mentioned in this book because He alone is worthy of praise for all He has done.

Our beautiful family just before we moved to China In 1988 - Beginning on the back row, left to right - Stephanie, Ruth, Adrianne, Randy, Emily & Erika Ryel

1

Preparation for Battle

Let's begin our story with a description of where Ruth and I were in life and the years leading up to our call to the mission field. Perhaps you will see some similarities present in your own life journey. The year was 1986. My wife Ruth and I had been married nine years and had four daughters of our own: Adrianne age six, Stephanie age four, Erika age two and Emily who was still a newborn. By God's leading, we also took on legal guardianship for Chrystal age ten, and Angel age eight who needed a temporary home. We lived in the small suburban community of Valley Center north of Wichita Kansas where I worked for AT&T. First let's take a step back to look at what led up to this point in time.

After graduating from Arkansas City, KS high school in 1972, my first semester of college was not working out. I was too committed to spending time with my girlfriend over lunch instead of going to my Calculus class. After a few months of small jobs I applied for and received a position at AT&T in Wichita, Kansas in March of 1973. I was hired to be the first male, long distance operator in the state of Kansas. An "honor" I have often boasted of in jest over the years. The social/political climate demanded that large companies such as AT&T needed to hire females to fill traditionally male jobs and males to fill traditionally female roles. It certainly was not my ideal job, but thought it would be a "step in the door" with a great company which I could develop into a more satisfying and lucrative long-term career. After nearly four years working two inside jobs, I landed an outside technician job as a Cable Splicer. Ruth and I were married April 16th, 1977 and we moved into our first little house in Maize, Kansas. Our realtor was a nice lady by the name of Joann. In the future, Joann would play a valuable role in our lives and in God leading us. Ruth worked in the office at Prairie View retirement home for a couple of years. We then had our second home custom built in 1979 in Maize, and welcomed our first daughter Adrianne with immense joy in October of 1980. As newlyweds God planted us at First Assembly of God in

Wichita. There we made our start assisting with and leading various lay ministries. After four years however, we were feeling an urge to move to a church closer to where we lived, and God led us to a church in Valley Center, KS in 1980 to be a part of the local Assembly of God there. This was a key step in God's plan for our lives. I learned early in my walk with God how important it is to be an active part of the fellowship of believers God wants you to be in. The people He surrounds you with will be instrumental in a variety of ways in His plan for you. Perhaps like us, you have suffered hurt being part of a local church. Maybe you've given up altogether, not wanting to be hurt anymore. But you need to remember that establishing the Church was God's idea. They are not perfect by any stretch, but the local church is vital to a believer both in receiving from God, and in your role of service to others. He leads and trains us using the people He surrounds us with. This principle has proven true many times in our lives. Largely due to our close friendships in Valley Center, we made plans with two other couples in our church to help each other build our own custom homes on three adjoining cul-de-sac lots directly behind the church we attended. It's worth noting, none of us had ever done such a thing before.

  The next couple of years were difficult for all of us. Together, as well as with the help of others in the church, we completed construction of our three large "dream" homes. The fellowship and ministry in Valley Center was very sweet. We developed precious relationships that have lasted more than forty years. Quickly we began working with various lay ministries such as kid's ministry, teaching Sunday school, youth ministry, worship leading, and I served on the church board. Later, as God was leading us on to do greater things, I realized whether or not you have a degree in Christian ministry, to be faithful in the little things *(Luke 16:10)* is the most important building block for developing your ministry. If churches are rightly about the business of making disciples, Christians can learn much about ministry by simply doing it. God gives us gifts of ministry and it is up to us to humbly exercise them. Of course, nothing can take the place of your own personal study, prayer life and walk with the Lord to prepare you for what God's plan is for your life. For me personally, the last few years before our call to China were the most powerful of any period of time in my life. My prayer life was on fire as was my personal bible study. I'd made it a habit to start my day at 4:30 for an hour of study and prayer. One of my most lengthy studies was on how God wanted me to be a good disciple with my finances which at the time were a big mess. I was able to get completely out of debt in just eight months with only one exception - our home mortgage.

Warriors preparing for battle must rid themselves of material or worldly things which would tie them down or hold them back. *(Heb 12:1)* Oh, how much this principle would come to be applied in our future. Our marriage and love of family were thriving. Life was very good, secure and stable. Those qualities of life are great, but like He did in our case, God may want to call you to a different front line of spiritual battle. Perhaps His plan for your life is not secure comfort. Did God save you for such a cozy life, or was it to be a soldier or ambassador to advance His Kingdom? Perhaps, it is bold living, risk taking, faith walking miracles He's calling you to. Every believer needs to ask themselves on a regular basis 'what is God's desire for me?' Then seek the leading, inspiration, and boldness of the Holy Spirit.

In 1986 I had a fulfilling job working as a Cable Repair technician in Wichita. Our work, church and family lives were busy and in a period of growth. Ruth and I found great joy spending time raising our beautiful girls. The girls were such a joy to us. To earn a little extra to pay bills, Ruth opened a very small daycare in our home. Life was good!

Our church was blessed with excellent leadership. Terry and Ruthanne Hoggard were our pastors. Joe and Connie Voss were our associate pastors. Our church was growing in numbers and spiritually. So, what a surprise it was when Terry announced they had accepted a missionary assignment to Rome, Italy. Joe and Connie then became our lead pastors. Our youth pastors Bobby and Beth Massey became our associate pastors. Another man in leadership, whom God used in our lives, was our mission's coordinator Dave Cundiff. He had made a few trips to foreign mission fields. His enthusiastic passion for foreign missions to reach the lost and build God's Kingdom was absolutely infectious.

One Sunday morning Dave announced to the church he had been communicating with a man in the United States who often led construction teams to South American countries for the purpose of building churches and schools. This man's next project was building a bible school in Quito Ecuador. Dave asked the church to consider joining him and some others from around the country to go with him to build this bible school. God prompted me in my spirit to go since I now fancied myself as somewhat of a builder since completing the building of our own home a few years earlier. I was very excited and began the process of getting my passport and saving money for my first mission trip. Ruth originally planned to go but as the mission date got closer, Ruth felt strongly that she shouldn't go to Ecuador. She had just given birth to our youngest daughter Emily so we agreed it would be best for her not to go with us at that time.

Several brothers and sisters from our fellowship committed to going on this mission trip. The anticipation was building in us much like the days leading to Christmas. The whole church was alive with missionary fervor. Those who were not going were financially assisting those who were. I recall how mission trips seemed to always spur significant spiritual growth and move of God's Spirit in our fellowship. They became one of the focal points of our church's overall vision for ministry.

THE FIGHT - The week before leaving for Ecuador I had an encounter with what I thought at the time was Satan himself, but perhaps it was just one of his many minions speaking to me. I was driving home on a beautiful afternoon and I had just turned down Dover to my house at the end of our cul-de-sac. I was thinking about my upcoming trip when all of a sudden, a voice in my head shouted, "you're going to die in Ecuador." That was the first and only time I have heard such a voice and known that kind of instantaneous fear. The memory of this encounter has been etched in my mind ever since.

THE GLORY – After a grave and lengthy pause my response I know for certain did not come from my natural mind, but from deep in my spirit. "It would be worth it!" The dark heaviness that had launched the attack on me instantly left. Indeed, I thought building a bible school for the training of pastors and missionaries who would then reach thousands of South Americans with the gospel for many years to come would most definitely be worth my life.

Perhaps one of the reasons our spiritual enemy thought he could scare me away was due to a string of life events leading up to this devilish word from the abyss. I believe my spiritual enemy had tried and failed to kill me several times throughout my life. At aged twelve I was invited by my neighbor Alice to her Baptist church revival. My faithful Methodist background had not prepared me for 'hell, fire, and brimstone' preaching. I trembled to the altar and was led in a prayer of salvation. However, due to lack of discipleship, I returned to becoming a foul teenager seeking mostly girls and cheap highs. I must say though that for six years, I never thought God abandoned me. Anytime my mind was in a quiet, humble state, I felt God's presence. I heard His still, small voice calling me to follow Him. At age 18 I made Him the Lord of my life.

THE FIGHT – Earlier at age 18 while working a summer job at a local oil refinery, one of my daily assignments was to sweep out emptied tank railroad cars of remaining petroleum and rust. Typically, the type of petroleum was a one of low odor and toxicity, and I never had much trouble with it. One day however, I was assigned a tank car which contained pure Benzene. Benzene is a sweet smelling chemical which is a highly toxic carcinogen. Lately Benzene has been in the news due to leaching into the ground water at Camp Lejeune and the subsequent class action lawsuit. It is used in small amounts in paint and varnish remover. In short, as I descended the ladder into the tank car, I instantly felt drunk, and within seconds I began hallucinating. My supervisor was up top turning an old wooden, hand crank oxygen supply pump to my air mask and holding the other end of my safety rope harness. Of course, this man of small stature could not have pulled me out of there by my safety line if his life (or mine) depended on it. Because he didn't seem to realize how much trouble I was in, he just kept turning the little air crank without trying to alert anyone. I was down there for about 10 minutes or more before I miraculously became sober. I was shaking like a leaf, wanting to get out of there, but I couldn't. My safety line and air hose were tangled around the ladder and steel tubes that connected the top valve wheel to the shut off at the bottom of the tank. I unbuckled my safety harness, took off my air mask to get free and shakily climbed out. Since I was known by my supervisor to be a "long haired hippie", he simply thought I had taken some drug that morning, or perhaps my long hair prohibited my air mask from making a good seal on my face.

When I took my lunch later I thought I might want to use that stuff for a cheap high, so I tapped a bit of it into a plastic medicine bottle and put it on the back floor board of my 1968 Mustang. When I got off work, I went to grab it, but all that was left was a dark greasy spot where the medicine bottle had been. I decided at that point it was probably not in my best interest to be sniffing it for a high. ☺

THE GLORY - The next day I reported the incident to the refinery's safety coordinator and showed him the mask and hose I'd used. After testing the equipment he reported back to me that he stopped after counting 100 holes in my air hose. Obviously I had directly breathed pure Benzene for the entire time I was in the tank car. After completing his investigation he learned the hose had been hidden from OSHA inspectors by an "unknown" employee who knew it was defective. The safety coordinator therefore had it destroyed. My mom took me to the doctor for an exam but he didn't find any obvious health problems. By any measure of logic, it must have been God who saved my life that day. He had different plans. Now at the age of 70 I have never been diagnosed with anything which could be linked to my Benzene exposure.

THE FIGHT - In 1976 I took my first AT&T vacation and drove to Phoenix, Arizona to visit my best friend Steve Manley. When Steve got out of the Army months earlier, he got a job in Phoenix at a lab which tested soil samples to determine what amount of water was needed to achieve maximum compaction for various construction projects such as bridges, dams, buildings, etc. Steve had bought a new Jeep CJ from money he'd saved while in the army and we had a blast wandering around the desert there. We even made a trip out to Los Angeles to visit friends and the then somewhat famous Calvary Chapel in Costa Mesa. We also went to Disneyland for their "Night of Joy" which had many of the contemporary Christian music groups which were popular at the time. I had such a wonderful time with Steve. So much so, I didn't want to go. We stayed up much too late the night before I was to leave. After maybe four hours sleep I started back to Wichita. My lack of sense and planning made it so that I needed to drive 24 hours straight through to get back home for my girlfriend, Ruth Manley's (Steve's sister and my future bride) 19th birthday. She was attending Wichita State University at the time.

Heading home the only thing I ate were snacks and drinks I purchased when I stopped for gas. Passing through Flagstaff, Albuquerque and then Liberal Kansas in my little gray 1974 Dodge Colt, I was getting very weary. Just east of town I pulled over and got out to walk around trying to revive myself. I rolled down the window, turned up the radio and I was off to see my sweetie. It was midnight, May 5th with only four more hours to go. Since I thought I was invincible, surely I could make it.

THE GLORY - I got back on the highway driving 60 mph and that was the last thing I remember before waking up three hours later. In my life I've had many instances where I fought to stay awake while I was driving. In my drowsiness I would nod off, but then quickly awaken to swerve back in my lane. This was not that. This was like waking up from a long, deep sleep. I was wide awake like I'd had a good nights sleep, driving through downtown at 20 mph. I didn't have a clue what town I was in though! I looked at my watch and to my great surprise it was 3:00AM. Wait! What? I'd been sleeping for three hours? I was in shock, but again, where was I? I frantically looked around at the surrounding store signs for clues as to where I'd ended up. Finally, I spotted a sign on a business that revealed I was in Kingman, Kansas. I could not believe it! I'd travelled down 54 Hwy through the towns of Kismet, Plains, Meade, Fowler, Minneola, Bucklin, Mullinville, Greensburg, Haviland, Cullison, Pratt, and Cunningham before my arrival in Kingman without a single, solitary remembrance of any of it. Keep in mind 54 Hwy at that time was a dark two-lane road which did not bypass any of these small to mid-size towns. Also, the highway in a couple of these communities was not a straight shot through downtown. There were a few turns in them a driver had to make to stay on the highway. One turn I had actually missed when I travelled through there wide awake on my way out to Arizona. At about 4:30AM I arrived safe and sound at my little studio apartment at 1910 S. Broadway in Wichita. Before going to sleep, I calculated that had I been awake, it would have taken me approximately three hours to drive from Liberal to Kingman. I could only conclude that I'd had an angel driving my car. He'd given *"His angels charge over me"*. *Psalm 91:11*

THE FIGHT - My third lifesaving miracle occurred in 1985 while on the job as a Cable Repair Technician for AT&T. My job this one particular day was northeast of Park City, Kansas on Hillside with the purpose of repairing enough pairs of phone wires so new customers farther north could have service. The day before I'd measured nearly all of the wiring defects to the vicinity of a single span of our aerial cable. Of course, I couldn't be sure, but I suspected that our cable had been shot with a rifle by someone in that area trying to shoot birds or squirrels off our cable. My challenge was that our phone cable was exceedingly high and stood about 20 feet east of the road, over a dense row of hedge trees. Hedge trees in the plains states like Kansas were planted by farmers after the dust bowl days of the 1930s as a means of blocking the wind so the topsoil was not blown from their crop land. This extremely hard wood grown in very dense rows was known for its long thorns and green bumpy hedge apples. Because our own company bucket trucks did not extend nearly high enough to reach where I needed to go, my only option was to arrange for one of our tree-trimming contractors to bring out their double arm bucket truck for me to use.

The contractor's 18 year old son, whom I knew from previous jobs, met me there on north Hillside. After showing him where I needed him to go, he pulled the truck up as closely as he could to give me a chance to reach the cable in question. There was a wide, somewhat deep drainage ditch which separated the road from the hedge trees and cable. This bucket truck we used was as far from state of the art as you can get which meant of course, it did not have outriggers to support the truck from turning over. The bucket itself had a simple mesh wire floor and one inch welded square steel tubing. It did not have any type of protective cage, neither did it have working controls in the bucket to maneuver it. The only working controller was on top rear of the truck at the base of its double arm. I got my tool belt and test equipment and climbed aboard.

THE GLORY - The young contractor began controlling my bucket to raise me up to get a closer look. Just as I was coming within about six feet of the phone cable, I had the unwelcome sense that my bucket was going down, not up. So, I looked down at my companion and saw pure terror on his face. The entire truck was starting to turn over due to the bucket arm being extended so far out, no outriggers and the truck being parked onto the slope of the ditch. I closed my eyes and the only thing I could say was "Jesus!"

This was by no means the first of this type of accident in AT&T history. I recall listening to my supervisor reading an accident report of this same type of incident happening about a year prior whereby the man in the bucket was slammed to the ground with such force that he was killed. As for me, I didn't slam to the ground nor was I decapitated by or impaled by a tree branch. I went crashing down into the outside edge of the hedge row, stopping horizontally three feet off the ground. The potentially dangerous hedge row became a "hedge of protection" for me. The trees caught the giant arm of my bucket and stopped it rather softly. While I was trying to figure out what "condition my condition was in" (quote from an old Kenny Rogers/First Edition song), my young companion followed the truck bed down, jumped off and was tearing through the hedge row trying to get to me to see how I was. His clothes and skin were a bit shredded by the hedge thorns in the process. With his help, I managed to crawl out sideways from the bucket. As I walked away from the fiasco, he and I were inspecting my body for injury. Shockingly I had not gotten a single scratch or bruise on me. The absolute only evidence of my accident was a one-inch L shaped tear in the right leg of my jeans. *"For He will order His angels to protect you wherever you go. They will hold you up with their hands, so you won't even hurt your foot on a stone."* Psalm 91:11-12 NLT

    We went to a neighboring house to call his dad Chet for help, and to compose ourselves from our traumatic ordeal. About forty-five minutes later here came dad with another helper speeding down the road toward us before skidding to a stop in his old winch truck. Chet was a respected contractor for AT&T, and normally quite chill. But certainly not that day! He jumped out of his big truck and lit into his son like the poor kid had just assassinated the President of the United States. Curse words of all shapes and sizes were shouted at the top of his lungs for five solid minutes. Chet was frantic, realizing of course that potentially he could be sued. At the very least, his livelihood was threatened since AT&T was by far his primary source of income from tree trimming, backhoe work and buried cable placement.

    Once Chet settled down, he began hooking his winch line to the overturned bucket truck in order to pull the truck back on its wheels. As he did, he explained to me that his son's mistake was pulling the truck into the ditch at an angle rather than into the ditch parallel to the cable. Once the truck was back upright, Chet operated the arms of the bucket in every direction to be sure it was still operable, which it was. He asked me if I wanted to try again to look at the cable. After a minute of consideration, I said yes. I still needed to verify whether or not the cable was damaged by bullets or just from lightning. Chet maneuvered the truck as he explained earlier. In my opinion, the truck did not look like it was at all safe because instead of just the nose of the truck being parked at a downward angle, the entire truck sat on the significant slope. Three primary thoughts, other than the need to finish what I started, crossed my mind as I determined what I should do. First, I trusted Chet. I'd worked with him for several years and knew him to be very knowledgeable about all his equipment. Secondly, I trusted Jesus. He delivered me before, so He could deliver me again. Third, I figured if I didn't get back in the bucket truck and overcome my fear in that moment, I would never be able to get back in another bucket truck for the rest of my career. I refused to let fear control my life, so I climbed back into that bucket and up I went a second time. Though I was able to get close enough to the cable to verify the bullet holes, it was not close enough to work on it. I ended up putting the entire job on hold and reported to my supervisor all that had transpired. He asked me if I wanted to press the issue regarding the accident. I said no. Together we decided to simply turn the entire mile length of the in-accessible cable in for emergency replacement.

After a few years, I looked back on the timing of these three miracles and realized something which left me in awe. Each one occurred only a short time before major spiritual events in my life. The first miracle came only one month before I made Jesus the Lord of my life. Before I showed God my love, He demonstrated His love for me not only by sending His Son Jesus as a sacrifice for my sin, but also by miraculously saving my life. The second miracle occurred a month before I asked Ruth to marry me. And the third, a few months before God called me to be a missionary. I knew without any doubt that I had a spiritual enemy. I also know that great are the plans God has for us. Those plans shall not be thwarted by any of the devil's destructive schemes. These faith building lessons I learned early on, were the foundation for all the difficult trials and battles which lay ahead.

The mission to Ecuador was tremendous. Quito is often called the city of eternal spring. The days are always very warm which yielded to cool nights. Since the elevation is 9350' above sea level, the sun is very bright and hot to the skin. I was surprised not to see the plethora of flying and crawling bugs I was accustomed to in Kansas. I loved it! The bible school's foundation had just been started by the crew preceding ours. Our assignment was to finish the concrete footings, construct the rebar column structures which we would then fill with hand mixed concrete. It was arduous work, but very fulfilling. In the evening we took part in some local church meetings which was a great thrill. The lively music and singing were extraordinary. Late in the evenings, I always liked to look out my hotel window and watch the busy, nightly social life. People were always out on the streets, visiting, laughing and eating together. I was very drawn to their simple lives which held such close relationship with those around them. These beautiful people had a type of richness in their lifestyle I had not experienced. Their only great lack was spiritual. I'm likely to mention various songs in this book. Music has played a large role in my life. God has often used the testimony of Christian music to lead and inspire me. The 1984 Steve Green song *"People Need the Lord"* was playing in my head as I looked out at the mass of people.

The reason we were in Ecuador was to do our part in filling the great need in the building of a bible school. The exciting sense of being where God wants you to be, doing what God wants you to be doing is spiritually intoxicating. Once you get that level of purpose in your life, it's so very hard to be satisfied with less. In a way, it can simply ruin you for what most might consider a normal Christian life. In my early morning quiet time, I would sit outside my hotel room in the hall, pray and read the book of Isaiah. God always met with me at that time and the fellowship with Him was sweet. It wasn't long after I went out into the hall that others of the group would join me for reflection on God's word and the trip in general. Often, I would pull out my guitar and lead in a couple of worship songs. It was a sweet time of fellowship indeed.

I was drawn to the people and their happy, joyful relationships, even amidst their physical poverty. I wrote a letter to Ruth while I was there saying "we're moving - just sell everything and bring the girls here to Ecuador". Not that I was completely serious, but as you might imagine, the idea did not go over well with Ruth. So, back home to Kansas I went. That entire experience did however plant a seed in my heart which eventually led to us becoming missionaries. Our group came back "on fire" for God which, as it usually did, spread to the rest of our church. It wasn't long before brother Dave had a line on another missions' project in Togo, West Africa. This mission was to again be one which involved construction, only this time, it was to build a rural church building. Once Dave presented the trip to the church, several of the congregation jumped on board. I was hungry for more, but Ruth had never been interested in going to Africa. Besides, the cost for just one to go was about $2200, which seemed to be impossible for us both to raise. I told Dave to "count me in".

No crucifixion, No resurrection!

2

Slow Boat to China

Our group to Togo was small compared to the one the year before. Except for Dave and I, the people planning to go had not gone on the Ecuador trip. We were happy to hear that our beloved Pastor Joe was going with us this time. We were all busy saving our money and preparing everything we would need for the excursion into the West African countryside. Dave reported to us we would need to take a variety of hand tools with us in our luggage, but he was having trouble getting a list of what we would need from the missionary who was to coordinate our project. As weeks rolled by, and the date for the trip drew close, Dave was getting nervous. He simply could not reach the man who would give us our final instructions. Finally, Dave had to make a decision. He called a group meeting and told us that we would regrettably need to cancel our plans to go to Togo. It was three weeks before we were to leave, and Dave was losing confidence he would hear back from this missionary. He called the meeting to explain his dilemma, and told us that if we were agreeable, he felt God was redirecting us to China.

Dave's announcement to consider changing our mission trip to China took a bit to fathom to say the least. Similar to your dad promising you one thing, but after several months of getting excited about it, he changes his mind to something else. But, as we were starting to process the idea, Dave began to explain his thinking. He pointed out that during the preceding weeks while we were waiting on the Togo contact, we had a young man come who shared with the church on a Sunday evening about his trip to Hong Kong. He had recently gone on a two week trip to assist a Hong Kong ministry to smuggle bibles into China. In 1987 Hong Kong was being governed by the British and had not reverted to Chinese control. This short term missionary had worked with Revival Christian Church in Hong Kong which was very active in their efforts to supply bibles to underground churches deep in China. These fellowships of underground believers were exploding in their numbers of new believers but suffered a great lack of bibles to teach and train them.

Another recent contact Dave had which he discussed was a letter he'd gotten from an Assembly of God ministry called China Radio, located in Hong Kong. By the end of our meeting with Dave, our group was totally on board with moving in that direction, but we had less than three weeks to put it all together. Dave tasked me with contacting China Radio, and he was going to get back with the young man who came to our church in order to know how to contact Revival Christian Church.

Since the destination for the mission trip had changed, I proposed to Ruth that she should come with me. As we quickly pondered the idea we discussed the needed finances. Once we got home we continued to discuss this new information. Ruth opened the envelope Pastor Joe had slipped into our hands that morning. Money being transferred between people in the congregation through Pastor Joe's hands was not uncommon, but we'd never been given any. To our complete amazement, she pulled out five one-hundred dollar bills. It was what I imagine winning the lottery would feel like. As we sat there stunned, we began to calculate what we would need for us both to be able to afford the trip. We both concluded the gift was a prompting from God that we should both go to China. Also, China would actually be considerably less costly than the Africa trip per person. So we felt led to move in that direction. There were other considerations as well. We contacted our parents to see if they'd be able and willing to take care of our girls while we were away for two weeks. They said yes! But that left one last hurdle. Ruth had no passport!

The next two weeks were a rush and full of unexpected twists and turns, like a roller coaster you'd never been on. We put a rush on getting Ruth's passport. We needed to get plane tickets, and contact the ministries in Hong Kong. Dave was never able to get in contact with Revival Christian Church, but I was successful in calling a missionary with China Radio by the name of Jimmy Gafford. Jimmy explained that China Radio did not have guest houses and really didn't have a bible courier ministry but went on to tell me about his good friend Alvin Cobb who did. He gave me Alvin's phone number and I called him to explain our situation. He was thrilled with us contacting him. He had housing, and bible carrying opportunities for us to take part in. Eureka! I relayed the info to Dave and the others, and we were all set and once again, very excited.

The final number of our group was six, which included Pastor Joe, Dave, Steve, Kenny, Ruth and I. Time passed very quickly in those three weeks. We scheduled to meet together one last time at Pastor Joe's house to go over the final details before we were to purchase our airfare that next day. I showed up at that meeting with all the excitement and trepidation of a first day of school. I reported on everything I had learned and gotten set up with our new contacts in Hong Kong. I was quite proud to have played a small role in setting up the trip. However, I was not prepared for what followed. I was to receive one of the greatest shocks of my life.

THE FIGHT - After I shared all the details I had gathered, Pastor Joe sheepishly told the group that he was certain that God was telling him he should not go on this mission trip to China. As we sat there with our mouths open, Dave likewise shared that God had spoken to his heart the night before that he was not supposed to go either. Wait, what? The rest of us could not believe it. We questioned them saying perhaps we should call the whole thing off. The thought was expressed that perhaps we weren't spiritual enough to hear from God and that something terrible would happen on the trip. Was God saving them from a plane crash or being high jacked by terrorists? What were we missing? Yikes! Dave and Joe calmed us down the best they could. Both were confident we were in fact supposed to go, and that I was to lead the group. What? Why me? As the expression goes, 'you could've knocked me down with a feather'.

Well now, that put an entirely different spin on things. I went home and told Ruth, and she of course expressed the same thought mentioned at the meeting. "Well, is the plane going to crash or get high jacked?" she asked. We definitely had a serious conversation, but within minutes Ruth and I rejected that fear and established a new determination of faith in our hearts to embrace this surprising challenge. We were going to lead the "Ryel Expedition" to China to smuggle bibles.

The few days before our trip were filled with last minute details. Ruth got her passport, our girls were scheduled to go to our parents, and Steve and Kenny were still on board to go with us. I was the only one that had been on any mission trip, and if I recall correctly, it was Steve and Kenny's first trip out of the USA. A small group from the church was there to pray for us, and see us off. After about a 21 hour flight, we were finally approaching the airport.

The anticipation was similar to the moments before a bride comes down the aisle of the church on her wedding day. All of a sudden we dropped beneath the clouds, and there it was in all of its splendor. Hong Kong was laid out beside us neatly tucked in among the mountains with all its many miles of fully lit skyscrapers. It was a true marvel, and we were totally in awe!

THE GLORY - Alvin Cobb's son Kendall met us at the airport and drove us to the house we'd be staying at during our stay there. Normally, bible couriers would stay in rather simplistic apartments with only basic furniture, such as bunk beds, but not for us on this trip. They put us into a beautiful home in Taiwai, New Territories across from the train station. This was the home of a YWAM missionary Mick Marshall, and his wife. A few years later, Mick would play an important role in what God intended for us to do in China. The Marshalls were back in the states on furlough and Alvin was given charge over their home to use it for bible couriers. Also staying with us was our hosts, a great couple from Tulsa, Oklahoma by the name of Mike and Jackie Farrell. The Farrells were short term missionaries and, had already been in Hong Kong a few months.

After a night plagued by jet lag, we spent our first day with the Farrells. Mike and Jackie were everything you would want to have for guides. Very sharp, knowledgeable and committed to the mission of supplying bibles to the Chinese believers. They took us as tourists, to Kowloon peninsula where the majority of tourists went to shop. Of course, we needed to stop by one of the many money changers to exchange our American dollars for Hong Kong dollars. The exchange rate at that time was seven point eight Hong Kong dollars to one American dollar. We felt rich with them giving us so much money back. We learned that Hong Kong was a country which was divided into three areas. Hong Kong Island, the Kowloon peninsula which lies directly across Victoria Harbor from the island, and the much larger area of New Territories which lay on the opposite side of Kowloon divided by a small range of mountains. Each of these areas contained a number of cities. Our day trip with the Farrells took us from Taiwai, under Lion Rock Mountain to Tsim-sha-tsui at the tip of Kowloon peninsula. The main mode of transportation was the train system which was very impressive to us Kansas folk. Then of course there were the monstrous skyscrapers. Mike told us the population density in one particular square mile in

Hong Kong was the largest anywhere in the world, about 35,000 if I recall correctly. It seemed as though there were thousands of these sky scrapers everywhere we went.

One of the sights that intrigued us was the scaffolding on the great many buildings under construction. It was made of bamboo poles lashed together with a heavy plastic twine. This scaffolding would extend more than a hundred feet in the air from the ground, covering entire faces of the structure. Again, this was very amazing to our small town group. All the confrontational beggars were also a bit unsettling. One man of about 55 years of age at the boat dock was particularly interesting. His hair was completely filthy, long, and knotted in what one would guess were at one time, braids. His clothing was absolutely nothing more than plastic bags of all sizes tied together and wrapped around him. In many cases like his, we were thinking demon possession was a great possibility and yet mental illness or drug abuse could have also been the cause.

Once we returned to the house, we began packing some large nylon bags with bibles and other Christian materials because we were given great news. A trip into China had been planned for that evening. We were to join with a larger group, and go to the night boat port on Hong Kong Island and board what they jokingly referred to as a "slow boat to China". We all boarded a mid size 1940's vintage passenger boat. Our tiny berth slept the four of us in bunkbeds plus a small adjoining toilet. The Farrells explained to us that we'd be going to sleep in Hong Kong and sailing a few miles up the Pearl River to Guangzhou, historically known in America as Canton. After boarding and getting our gear settled in, we went out on the deck to look at the gorgeous lights and skyscrapers which towered over us as we sailed out of the famous Victoria Harbor. We were completely mesmerized by the beauty of it all. There was absolutely no comparison to anything we had ever seen before. Pretty exhausted, we all climbed into our bunks as the boat gently rocked us to sleep.

THE FIGHT - The magic moment arrived. We awakened and quickly realized the boat was not moving. Like a bunch of kids on Christmas morning we were so ready to be smuggling in our bibles. We really had no idea what to expect, but boy howdy were we excited. We hurriedly got ready and lined up with all the others in our group of nearly 20. While it was still dark, we disembarked onto the dock and filed into the Chinese customs building at the port of Guangzhou. To our great shock, the Chinese customs officers, dressed in their intimidating green uniforms came out at once and stopped our entire group before we even got our bearings. It was almost like they were expecting us. They lined us up in front of a long metal counter while several of them stood behind it instructing us in Chinese to put our bags up on the counter for inspection.

THE GLORY - One by one we complied, except when it was my turn, there was no room on the counter for me to place my bag, and so I just carried it along out of their view until they simply waved me on. I could only guess they thought I had already had my bag inspected. Every one of our large group had their bags of bibles confiscated except for me. Later when I was asked to give the Farrells an accounting of how many bibles I was able to get in, I told them 66 full Old and New Testament bibles. The thought occurred to me with a bit of a smile that it was ironic since there are 66 books in the bible. A numeric detail which would later play a role a few weeks later when God called us to China as full time missionaries.

Of course, we were filled with questions about what had just transpired. The pros in the group explained that it happens that way sometimes, but not to worry. The customs officers occasionally spot familiar looking people or bags which were very much alike from previous groups who had crossed at that border. We were relieved that all the confiscated materials which were taken from us would be picked up later by other couriers and taken back to Hong Kong. Then they would be carried back to China by subsequent groups. Our little group of four was able to take a few more trips into China with bibles and be successful getting them across the busy Shenzhen train border as well as a second boat trip farther inland.

One very special evening the Cobbs and the Farrells gathered with us simply to get to know us and share their heart for missions. Their stories of great adventures were so inspiring to all of us. One thing Alvin said which struck an immediate chord with me was that "the passion for missions is not taught, it's caught". It's a fire which cannot easily be quenched. Either you submit, or continually deny it till it gets buried beneath the cares of this world. Pastor Joe and Dave didn't lead our group, but I soon became aware just how important it was in God's plan for me to be the leader on this trip. It gave me greater boldness, a totally different kind of engagement with these missionaries, as well as greater responsibilities which I would otherwise not have had.

One of the other trips we took which I want to tell you about was when Mike took the four of us on a boat trip much farther up the Pearl River to the city of Wuzhou. The thought was that such a trip would be more likely successful since basically very few bible carrying groups ever went that far up into China from Hong Kong due to the added expense and time it required. However, the customs officials would be less likely to scrutinize us as closely. Another down side was that this city was far less western than what we had witnessed up to that point. The expression 'culture shock' would soon become very real to us in Wuzhou.

The boat we boarded on this trip was pretty nice, and much faster than the slow boat to China we had gone on before. Once we arrived in Wuzhou, Mike took us to the best hotel in the city. We all looked at each other with the same puzzled look. If this was the best, what did the worst look like? Time to eat! We were quite hungry after the long boat trip and looked forward to some tasty Chinese food at the hotel restaurant. The five of us became the center of attention in the restaurant that evening. We guessed few westerners ever came to Wuzhou. When our order was brought to us, the confused reaction on our faces was likely evident to all the gawking eyes in the room. Kenny and Steve were especially unnerved, first by the quality of the hotel and now by the food they served us. We were eating at the best restaurant and the best of what they offered turned out to be a watery soup with sparse green pieces of vegetable, small pieces of chicken and bone, along with a large pile of rice. Kenny and Steve could not fathom staying any longer and suggested that it would be best for them to return to Hong Kong as quickly as possible.

The next morning, the two were still anxious to leave and Mike agreed to accompany them. After checking out of the hotel, we grabbed some snacks from a street vendor and bought tickets for Ruth and me to take a boat back to Hong Kong that night. Upon seeing Mike, Steve and Kenny off at the train station, Ruth and I decided to go exploring to see what Wuzhou was all about. Mike had told us we should take a tour of their snake depository, so that was our first stop. The city's claim to fame was as the second largest snake depository in the world. I believe now in 2023 it is the largest. What is a snake depository you ask? Chinese medicine as a whole, utilizes more things directly from nature than we westerners do. Various parts of the snake for instance, particularly snake bile, is very popular for treating various health maladies and is in fairly high demand. In fact, one of this city's popular exports was its snake bile wine. No, we didn't try it! Well of course I had to go visit this exotic destination. We arrived at what I refer to as Snake Mountain, and at once we were greeted by some of the lead staff there. With no warning, they came up from behind us and promptly adorned our necks with thick, six foot long snakes. Needless to say, my sweet, snake hating Ruthie completely froze. She was doing her very best to be brave, but it wasn't long at all before she and her new friend had to part ways. Of course, this was the staff's favorite stunt, so they could hardly stop giggling.

Snake Mountain contained what seemed like miles of manmade, dimly lit tunnels wherein lay countless woven bamboo baskets stacked along each wall and crevice. These baskets would each contain several of one type of snake. Nearly every variety of snake in the world was brought there as inventory for harvesting parts of each snake's anatomy. As we walked through the long winding tunnels, the friendly snake handler guide and his translator would explain many of the special snakes on the tour and what type of remedy a part of that snake might produce. They would occasionally take out one of the snakes for show and tell, enjoying our reaction. He seemed diabolically gleeful as he referred to this snake or that snake as being extremely deadly.

That evening we returned to Hong Kong on a boat much different than the faster one we rode going to Wuzhou. This boat was another night boat, but instead of sporting the private berths which we enjoyed on our first trip to China, this one had a very large sleeping room with three long tiers of slender bunk beds. Half were on one side and half on the other. Each of the two inch foam mattress beds were basically two inches from the one on either side it. Now picture 300 Chinese with all their belongings packed into such a room, all sleeping together for the duration of the night. Yes, it was truly a night we shall never forget. The great redeeming factor of that night was Ruth and my first opportunity to witness to a Chinese person. This precious young Chinese girl of about 20, who lay next to us, was a special opportunity. Though her English was quite poor and our Chinese non-existent, I believe we were still able to plant a good seed in her open heart. By faith I believed at the time we would someday see her in heaven.

Soon after returning from our Wuzhou experience, it was time to return home. All in all, our bible smuggling efforts were fruitful. Although I don't recall the exact number of them our small group of four was able to take across the border, I believe it was definitely in excess of 2000. We were utterly thrilled to play a role in supplying God's Word to hungry new Christians across China. As we headed back home, Ruth and I pondered how meaningful the trip was, and thought we should go back sometime. Little did we know what kind of life challenges, tests, battles, miracles, and victories God had in store for us.

No battle, No victory!

3

God Calling

We were very happy to be back in America, united with all our girls, family, and friends. The morning after we returned, I reported to work with my crew at our AT&T garage in Wichita. I had a somewhat difficult job as a cable repair tech, but I felt like I had the respect of my supervisors and crew as an effective technician. I had recently been chosen to be one of only two techs in Kansas who were first selected to go to Houston, Texas for training in fiber optic technology, which at the time, was in its infancy. It was very cool! Because I had the top position in seniority on our crew, I got first pick for my three weeks of vacation each year and the newest bucket truck was mine. My career was very fulfilling. I could absolutely say that my spiritual life, a family life full of joy, my church ministry as a worship leader, and church board member were all great. Financially we were doing well, with no debt except for the mortgage on our house. We loved the five bedroom three bath custom-built dream home we had built next to our very good friends just a few years prior. Life was good, better than we could have ever expected or dreamed of. Christians speak often of how God divinely shows up in the middle of difficulty, which is true. I will often shed light on that truth in this book. What we do not often discuss, is what God might show up and do when life is at its best, then in a sense, wreck it for His higher purpose and glory. You could say that this is what happened to us. *"Then Peter began to speak up. "We've given up everything to follow you," he said. "Yes, Jesus replied, "and I assure you that everyone who has given up house or brothers or sisters or mother or father or children or property, for my sake and for the Good News, will receive now in return, a hundred times as many houses, brothers, sisters, mothers, children, and property -* **along with persecution***. And in the world to come, that person will have eternal life." Mark 10:22-29*. I'd long thought this was God's promise that in this life I would see Him replace the house I gave up with an even better house. I'm convinced now this teaching is in error. God truly has given back to us all we gave up. As you'll see in this book, He provided many houses for us to stay in and families to be a part of.

Walking into my crew room my first morning back felt so normal, even after the great adventures I had just experienced. The room was filled with the usual sarcasm and teasing among the crew. A couple of them asked about my trip, but no one was particularly interested except for Joe who I had helped lead to the Lord not long before. I was back to being Randy the cable repair tech in Wichita, not Randy the missionary to China. Promptly at eight o'clock, our supervisor, Chris Deeker, began going over a few mundane company issues and dismissed the crew to go to their first jobs. As the other guys were leaving, my boss called me over to his desk to tell me about a new development.

THE FIGHT - Chris needed to inform me of a recent company action. He began explaining to me that there were a couple of Cable Repair Technicians in Bartlesville, Oklahoma who were in the process of either losing their jobs or being assigned a lesser job. The company had more cable techs in Oklahoma than they could use and needed to cut back. Therefore, the powers that be in Oklahoma approached those in Kansas with an idea. If Kansas could find a couple of Cable Repair Technicians who would be willing to accept a "buy out," Oklahoma would pay the cost of those buy outs and transfer the two willing Oklahoma techs to Wichita. So, Chris asked me rather jokingly "would you like to give up your career with AT&T for a big payout?" As most guys might do in this situation, I asked "how much money are we talking about"? He said he didn't really know. It would be based on my time on the job, etc. He then told me he could find out if I wanted him to. I said no, but that I would talk to my wife, think about it, and get back to him. Of course, I had no real intention of taking the silly offer, so I didn't give it much thought. I did however remember to bring it up with Ruth later that evening. We had a bit of a laugh and dismissed it. Little did I expect a divine wrecking ball would hit everything in my life that night?

THE GLORY - It was early November 1987. Still suffering with jet lag, I was wide awake at 2:00AM but Ruth was somehow still asleep. Not wanting to wake her, I just lay there wide awake as God through His Spirit began talking to me. "Read Isaiah 66." "What?" I asked myself. "Read Isaiah 66!" "What? I don't even know if Isaiah has 66 chapters." "Read Isaiah 66!" 'I don't want to get up God, I want to go back to sleep.' "Read Isaiah 66!" 'I don't want to wake Ruth up. Can't I do it in the morning?' I just could not shake it. "Read Isaiah 66!!" I began to recall the incident at the Canton customs when I slipped by the security officers with 66 bibles in my bag. My spirit began responding to Gods' early morning prompting. What could I do, but get up and go to my prayer closet. Four years earlier I had designed our "dream house" with a large walk-in closet which included a small built-in vanity for Ruth to use. Ruth never wanted to use it as such, so I had taken it over as a small study desk for my early morning rendezvous with God. That morning it was where I went to see what in the world was so urgent to God regarding Isaiah chapter 66. As it turned out, it was not as much 'WHAT in the world', but WHERE in the world I now recall with a smile. The first thing I noticed when I opened my New American Standard bible was that indeed there were 66 chapters in the book of Isaiah. It was actually the last chapter. I'm thinking, 'maybe I'm not crazy, and God really is trying to say something to me.'

Before I edited this book, I included the entire book of Isaiah 66, but I decided to remove it. If you'd like to, read it for yourselves. The words which enflamed my heart that early morning will not likely stand out to you. But did for someone who had just returned from a land filled with worshipers bowing to altars of idols and incense. But even more than God's Word, it was God's Spirit moving on my heart is such an unmistakable way which was so impactful. This strange culture faraway whose primary source of meat was pork, (swine's flesh), one which in fact ate dogs, cats, mice, rats, and every detestable thing imaginable, was what I had just experienced.

Let me be very clear before I continue. In no way did I think at the time nor now that this prophesy applied to me in any significant way. Although I'm no scholar in prophesy, it seems pretty clear that the prophet is primarily speaking about Israel in its continuing in sin, its coming judgment and destruction, and the remnant which would be saved. What I do believe, and was convinced of at the time, was that God was using portions of this scripture to turn my spiritual eye toward China. From that point I can only describe the next three hours that night as a powerful, non-stop, spiritual conversation with my Father. One like I had never experienced before or since. I had in my prayer closet, several study books which I could have utilized to search out relevant scriptures. But for this one and only time I simply flipped through pages of my bible. Each page I turned to quickly revealed verses which pointed me to an immediate call to China to be a missionary. I can neither tell you the scriptures the Holy Spirit led me to, nor the exact number of them. I can only say that each one was as powerful as the others. With every verse, God was shouting louder and louder within my spirit, "Go to China NOW". When God's spirit finally released me from my page turning, I started to reason out why I could not or should not go. All our money had been spent on the previous trip. I would need to raise a lot of cash and a significant amount of monthly support for my large family to live on. I had not been trained or prepared to be a missionary. China was closed to missionaries. Just as God shut the mouth of the lions Daniel faced, he quickly shut my mouth by dropping HIS plan into my heart and mind, piece by piece. First, He said that He would supply all my needs according to His riches in glory. I also recalled the great quote "Where God guides, He provides". Second, He told me to rent out the house we were planning to spend the rest of our lives in because there was no time to sell it. Third, God told me to donate my 1976 GMC pickup to Bob Massey (associate pastor Bobby Massey's father) who I'd heard needed it to make trips providing clothing and other basic needs for people in Mexico he was ministering to. Fourth, I was to donate our 15 passenger Ford van to our church for bussing children to church, or for youth ministry. God was showing me that if we were to sow what we had into these ministries, we would reap support for our ministry. After all, we were there to do our part in building THE Kingdom, not simply provide for our ministry. Fifth, I was to sell or give away nearly everything else we owned. Sixth, upon arriving in China, I was to study Chinese, then preach the Gospel and make disciples. Seventh, GO NOW! We were not to spend months in making rounds to multiple churches raising cash or monthly support. We were to simply give our testimony, take an offering, pass out prayer cards and tell those who listened that if God led them to support us, to send their donation to the Valley Center church. Our church might then forward it to us each month. That's it! My only response to God was "Yes! But God, you're going to need to convince my wife Ruth."

    By six that morning I knew beyond all doubt, God was calling me and my family to be full time missionaries to China for an indefinite length of time. Ruth was beginning to get ready for the day, but before we got all the girls up, I approached her with what had happened to me that night. I'm not sure, but she might have gone into shock because she struggled to respond. I asked her to pray about it and said I thought if I was truly called, God would speak to her heart as well to give us confirmation. After three days, Ruth came to me saying that every time she prayed and sought God about it, He just told her heart that I was her husband and that she should follow me to wherever He called me. She had a peace about it, as did I. We scheduled a meeting with Pastor Joe and Connie to tell him what we felt God was doing with our lives. I explained everything God said, including the part about sending donations to the church and that they could perhaps be responsible for sending them to us once each month. I also felt that our church should act as a spiritual and financial covering for us. One way I suggested was for us to submit a monthly finance report of everything we received as income and every expense we incurred. Their response was very encouraging. They prayed with us and Pastor Joe gave us both his blessing, and the backing of the church. The next day I went to work and really shocked my boss. I explained to him about the trip I had gone on, and how God was calling us to go back to China. I was never sure where Chris stood in his faith, or lack thereof. He did however seem to respect me and the decision we had made. He promised to send my request for a buy-out up the chain of supervisors. One of my co-workers who worked out of a different location in Wichita had his job bought out rather quickly. While we waited on the phone company to give me my approval and buy-out amount, we began to follow Gods' specific instructions. We advertised our house for rent, and had an "everything must go" garage sale.

A nice couple answered our "for rent" ad within one week. He owned a sign company and I seem to remember she helped him with the books. They had no children or pets, which was good but it seemed a bit odd they wanted to rent a five bedroom, three bath house for just the two of them. After working out the lease, we agreed to be out before the end of December for them to be able to move the first of the year. Ruth and I got busy going through everything. We needed to get our entire household down to twelve brightly colored Walmart foot lockers, and six carry-ons. One vivid example of what we were dealing with, was when we went through all the shoes our six girls had. As we gathered the ones they would not be taking with them to China, we neatly lined up the pairs in one of the unfinished bedrooms in the basement. When we had collected them all, we were shocked and a bit ashamed that the entire 10 foot by 11 foot floor was completely covered with little shoes laid out in tight rows. We sold and gave away stuff like crazy over the next several weeks. It was nearing Christmas and I still had not heard from AT&T about my buyout. By late December we had emptied everything except a few boxes of special memory items such as some pictures and keepsakes. These things we were invited to put under the basement stairs at the home of our dear friends from church, Gary and Deby Taylor.

During this period of time, we set up a couple of opportunities for us to share our calling and upcoming mission to China with two churches. One was with our own church. The other was at the Assembly of God church where Ruth grew up. At this point of our story, we were still living in Valley Center waiting on AT&T, so what we shared with these churches included the financial gain from the buy-out we would be able to use to get us to China and enough to sustain us there for a while. Our church was supportive, maybe even inspired, but there was understandably no real urgency for them to support us financially. Joann Westfahl, the realtor I mentioned in chapter one who sold us our first house, and whose brother built our second house, had been attending our church for some time. She approached us after my message to the church that Sunday evening. We were not expecting what she had to say. Something we couldn't really wrap our head around at the time but would become a major part of our ministry in China. She privately explained that she had a vivid dream the night before where she saw Ruth and I surrounded by Chinese children. She sincerely said she felt we were to have a ministry with Chinese orphans. Well, that was news to us. God hadn't said anything of the kind the night he called me to go. So, how should I respond? Ruth and I looked at each other and simply said "Wow"! Children had been our love and passion all our married lives. We went on to say to Joann that though God had not given this direction to us, we would certainly say yes to whatever God wanted to do with us.

One of the best Christian friends God has ever given me was a man by the name of Nolan Gorham. For a few years God used him over and over to speak truth into my life. More than anyone, his impact always led me to think outside the religious church norms. He was constantly challenging me to press into a deeper connection with God and walk in the Spirit. Soon after the day of my calling to China, Nolan and I had an opportunity to get together and share. As I explained the details of God's plan for me to go to China, I began talking to him about an idea I had to start a Bible study course offered by the Assemblies of God. I thought that I could continue it in China till I was at some point able to be licensed through them. Nolan had just one word for me - "Why? Did God tell you to do that?" "No" I said. "So then why?" I fumbled for an answer, but I didn't have one. After all, God didn't tell me to train or to study, only to go. Nolan reminded me that if God felt I needed more of anything, he would not have told me to "Go NOW!" So, I abandoned the idea. Throughout my life I have reflected on my dear friend Nolan. What would Nolan say or do in this situation? His words, his smile and, his joyous chuckle still live on in my life. What affected me the most however, was his love for me. He taught and demonstrated so many things, but often it was about the freedom we have in Christ. I haven't had anyone else in my life like him till very recently. My current pastor Richard Harrison, is now my soul brother for sure.

Since our new renters didn't have enough furniture to fill the big house, and because we didn't really want to part with these somewhat important parts of our lives, we agreed to leave them our living room furniture, our dining room furniture, the bedroom furniture that I gave to Ruth as a wedding gift, and our breakfast table and chairs. We thought we could trust this pleasant, professional couple but we could not have been more wrong. Since God had not told me to keep any of our possessions, we would learn a hard lesson, and later regret leaving the items instead of selling or giving them away as God instructed me. A word of advice - follow ALL of God's instruction.

It was Christmas Eve, 1987. Our precious girls were one, three, five and seven. God provided a new home for Chrystal and Angel to live with their aunt who lived nearby. Our plan was for me to stay with our friend Kenny who had gone with us to China, and continue going to work at AT&T until my buyout came through. Ruth and the girls would stay with my mom and dad in their small two-bedroom home in our hometown of Arkansas City, Kansas.

Ruth's mom and dad also lived nearby and were going to help as well.

We got an unexpected visitor from China, who happened to be in the general vicinity of Valley Center and stopped in to see us. He was a good friend of the Cobb family, his name was Dwyatt Gantt. We had the opportunity to meet him when we were in China a month earlier. Dwyatt was a charismatic speaker who had been ministering in China for a number of years. His rather large ministry was that of placing Christian men and women from the United States to go teach TESL (Teaching English as a Second Language) in various cities across China for the purpose of sharing the Gospel. He and his network of contacts worked out placement contracts with various schools in China. The schools would tell Dwyatt how many teachers they needed and where. He would then select one of the teachers who had applied with him, and place them in that school. The Saturday he came to visit just happened to be when a men's breakfast was scheduled at our church, so I asked and was given permission to have him speak. He gave a very insightful and impassioned description of ministry in China. He described Jesus as the "Captain of God's Armies" who was calling men and women from all over the world to the front lines of His great harvest in China. The men were very moved that morning. I felt at the time it was something of a flash point for our church to have an even greater appreciation for why we were going there. That was not the last of my contact with Dwyatt. He was to become instrumental in our future ministry, and I in his. As I said at the beginning of this book, God has divine appointments laid out along the path to which He calls us. Such appointments are one of the ways he bolsters our faith and directs our paths as we carry out His mission.

SEASON OF FIGHTING - Christmas Eve 1987 is one we will never forget. Even after all these years we can picture it like a home movie clip playing over and over in our minds. Our family of six walked out of our beloved home for the last time and walked across the street to say goodbye to our dear friend and neighbor Cindy Bogle along with her children Kevin and Tiffany. As we stood there at the side of our cul-de-sac, the most penetrating thing any of my children has ever said to me emerged from my sweet, nearly two year old princess, Emily. She said in a very sad and confused voice, "I want to go home now." Ruth and I simply lost it! All of a sudden, the reality of what we were doing smacked us right in the face. Till then, we were called of God to be missionaries to China. But in that moment, we were just a dad and mom who were tearing our little girls away from the only home any of them could remember. What we were sacrificing suddenly became very real to us, and all Ruth and I could do was cry. Now, 36 years later as I write the story of that day, the emotion remains just as real. Ruth and I again broke down with intense sobbing as we read these words together.

At the time we didn't know what lie ahead of us. It was only faith which comforted us and kept us focused. It would be worth it all, wouldn't it? Something I just realized the significance of us leaving our home on Christmas Eve. In a sense, it was something of a dim reflection of the sacrifice God made when sent away His Son from His home in Glory on the first Christmas Eve. God was sending us, just as He has thousands of other men, women and children throughout the ages who came to a point in their faith when they declare *"He is no fool who gives up what he cannot keep for that which He cannot lose." Quote by missionary martyr Jim Elliot.*

My mom and dad opened their small two bedroom home to us and we enjoyed a very full Christmas Day. Mom and dad couldn't have been more thrilled about us being there, nor be more dismayed we were soon taking their little girls so far away. I want to take this moment in the book to talk a little about our parents, who were also making a great sacrifice. Charles (Bud) and Ann Ryel raised my older brother Rick and me, but mom had always wanted a daughter. My parents were the best people I've ever known. They were loving, kind, gentle, generous and faithful to each other and to God. Needless to say, our four girls were the joy of their life. The thought of us taking them to China was to say the least, heart breaking. Had it not been their own faith, and willingness to make this great sacrifice for the Kingdom, it would surely have devastated them. Ruth's parents, Charles and Mary Manley, were faithful Christ followers as well, and were similarly affected. We counted ourselves very blessed to have the Ryels and Manleys not only as parents, but as faithful supporters with prayer and finances.

After Christmas I returned to Wichita to continue working and waiting for word about my buy out. Early in January 1988 I finally got the call we were waiting on, but it was bad news. While I was on the job my boss called to say that it looked like the buy-out was not going to work out. So now what? I was on a major cable failure assignment (with Chet from chapter 2 by the way) at the time and really didn't have time to process it.

Here I want to pause our story and address something very often said in Christian circles which I believe to be misleading at times. I'm speaking of the idea that if something is God's will and direction for your life, He will open the door. If it is not, He will close the door. Although this may be the case for young Christians, it is not what you typically see in scripture among the heroes of the faith such as Joshua and so many others. As mature Christians, I believe God allows obstacles to what He calls us to do. *"We walk by faith and not by sight." 1 Cor. 5:7* God tests our faith in what He directs us to do. *"So be truly glad. There is wonderful joy ahead,* **The Test:** *even though you must endure many trials for a little while, these trials will show that your faith is genuine. It is being tested as fire tests and purifies gold - though your faith is far more precious than mere gold. So when your faith remains strong through many trials, it* **The Glory:** *will bring you much praise and glory and honor on the day when Jesus Christ is revealed to the whole world." I Peter 1:6-7 NLT*

When I got an opportunity a couple of hours later from what I was working on, I called Ruth to give her the news. What does this mean?" she asked. I responded in faith alone because of what God had done in me. He had made me so very certain of our calling, we were ready to bust down any gate of hell to get there. "This news doesn't change our calling Ruth, it only changes the way God was going to provide for it." I said. Then Ruth, in the faith God was building in her, agreed. We were going to China; we just didn't know how we could pay for it. You are not going to believe what happened within an hour of me calling Ruth with the bad news. I got a second call from my boss. Surprise! The buy-out was approved after all, and the amount would be more than $23,000. I immediately called Ruth back with the news. We rejoiced of course! But we were still waiting for a decision of what day would be my last.

One Sunday evening during this waiting period, we were invited to speak at the church Ruth grew up in. Pastor Steve Dow, and the church as a whole were very passionate about missions. After sharing our testimony and calling, the church gave us a significant offering. Adding this to our own money, plus what we were able to raise by selling so much of our stuff, and the offering we had received from our home church, we had enough money for all the nearly $3000 one-way airfares plus about $1000 to sustain us for a while after we got there. Things were working out pretty well we thought.

While at work the last week in January, I decided the long wait was not making sense, so I called my second level manager Mr. Larry Beal directly. When I asked about my buy-out, he apologized that I had not been informed. He told me that my buy-out had been rejected and began to explain what had happened. My immediate supervisor, Chris, had gotten a call in early January from the fifth level manager who was the final say in the state of Kansas asking if I still wanted the buy-out. Chris replied, "Yes! Randy's already moved out of his house and will be leaving with his family to be missionaries in China as soon as the buy-out goes through." The top guy thanked Chris for the information and hung up. Of course, Chris was trying to help me to get it pushed through. However, the top guy took the info and decided to cancel the buy-out. If I were leaving anyway, why pay me. I thanked Mr. Beal for the information and asked what I needed to do to turn in my resignation. He told me to call Chris, and he would get it set up. Once again I got Ruth on the phone to give her the news and let her know I was going to resign that afternoon. Bless her heart, she was still in agreement. In a later chapter of this book, I'll specifically spend time to identify and honor in the best way I can, the challenges and sacrifices women make when as mothers and wives they endure the types of tests they are faced with when preparing for and being on the mission field.

There is a part of our story I only recently learned from my sister-in-law Cheryl. During this period of waiting my brother Rick and I were talking on the phone about my upcoming adventure to China. My brother was a great American; a Senior Master Sergeant in the Air Force military police stationed at Randolph Air Force base at the time. His duties were in military intelligence. He was a patriot who served his country with honor and distinction. More than any other human on the planet, he was my greatest hero. As we talked, Rick raised his concerns about our safety. The concern he expressed was one he'd raised before we went the first time. Since we'd be involved in smuggling bibles, he worried that we'd be used as drug mules. What he didn't express to me however was that, given his position in military intelligence in the squadron he was part of, he had to report my family's move to China to his superior officers. This of course raised a red flag since my family could perhaps be used by the Chinese to extort classified information from my brother. Unbeknownst to me, this meant Rick could not stay in intelligence there in San Antonio. His commanders determined he'd have to be transferred to a different base and moved out of intelligence. When Cheryl revealed this to me I was stunned and ashamed that my actions negatively impacted my dear brother's military career. The look on my face must have concerned Cheryl because she said "no, no don't feel bad! It was a good thing." So she began to explain that because he was no longer in intelligence, he was no longer going to be stuck at his rank of Senior Master Sergeant. After the reassignment his new commanding officer in Del Rio, Texas saw he was struggling with alcohol abuse due to the traumas he experienced in Southeast Asia. She made sure he connected with an Alcoholics Anonymous group there. In addition, because he was an excellent leader of men, his commanding officer, Captain Debra Borio soon awarded him the rank of Chief Master Sergeant. This was a great financial blessing while on duty, but also giving him better retirement benefits. Once Rick retired from the Air Force, he began a 28 year mission to sponsor other men and even led A.A. groups in San Antonio where he retired. In an unexpected way, our calling to go to China had a significant impact in my brother's life and family. Relationally and financially it was a blessing, not even mentioning the great number of men, women and families he was able to help in unfathomable ways. It is conceivable even that his significance in God's Kingdom may have surpassed mine because of our simple decision to obey God's call on our lives.

  The time for waiting was over. We were going to China as quick as we could get tickets and leave. Talk about a roller coaster! Obeying God does not always lead you on a smooth journey. Once again, just consider the primary characters in the bible. I called Chris about resigning. He had known about the buy-out cancellation for a few days, but since he felt responsible for it falling through, he couldn't bring himself to tell me directly. I told him I understood he was only trying to help us. Let me interject at this time 'the rest of the story' as Paul Harvey used to say. Twenty years later, I actually went back to work for AT&T as a Customer Service Technician. After working six additional years and bridging my service with my previous years on the job, it gave me a total of 21 years service. I was able to retire with full benefits at the age of 60. What would have been a $23,000 buy-out in 1988, became an amount many times more than that in 2014 as my retirement benefit. Yes, God is so good! Even when we don't see it, feel it or understand it, He's working. *"And we know that God causes everything to work together for the good of those who love God and are called according to His purpose for them." Romans 8:28 NLT*

We purchased our one-way plane tickets to Hong Kong and finished packing our multi-colored footlockers and carry-on bags. It was February 2, 1988, and in the wee hours of the morning we went to the Wichita airport. We were quite a sight. A large group of our friends were there to pray with us and see us off. Everyone's emotions were highly charged with excitement. We made our way to the ticket counter to check in. As we stood there watching the ticket agent review our tickets, we got the huge shock of learning we couldn't use them because they were one-way tickets. Hong Kong didn't allow anyone to fly there without a return flight ticket. Needless to say, the wind went out of all our sails in a heartbeat. I was very embarrassed, like giving a public speech then later realizing your zipper was down the whole time. We would have to pay nearly $5000 for round trip tickets. Of course, we didn't have anywhere near that amount of money. Pastor Joe stepped up and told us not to worry. He would get on the phone and see what the church could do to help us. Meanwhile we went with our friends Gary and Deby Taylor to wait once again. It wasn't long before Pastor Joe called to give us the news that the church had purchased the return trip tickets for us. Note: After we got to Hong Kong, Pastor Joe was able to cancel our return trip, but the church was not able to get all the money returned from our tickets and the return Hong Kong to Wichita flight. Pastor Joe told us not to worry about the difference, that the church would cover the loss. What a blessing Pastor Joe and the entire church was to us. We were called independent missionaries, but we weren't really. Just like the Apostle Paul, we had the backing of our local church. If any of the readers of this book are considering becoming missionaries, be sure that even though you may not be part of a formal missions program, it is very important you have backing of some type of group or organization from your hometown to submit to. When you arrive to wherever God has sent you, you will need someone there who is experienced and geographically close by who you can submit to as well. It is essential that you have a spiritual covering. Lone wolves, like loose cannons, are often dangerous on the mission field, both to themselves and to others.

The next morning, once again we showed up at the airport in all our glory. The crowd of people to see us off, was understandably fewer for this departure, but still enthusiastic. We flew to Denver and then arrived in Seattle only to find out the planes there were all grounded due to nasty winter weather. "You've got to be kidding!" was our flustered response. So, off we went to a hotel to spend the night. We were thinking, the devil sure doesn't want us to go to China. The lesson we were beginning to learn was that if we didn't have the faith to press through obstacles to follow God's calling, we weren't worthy of that calling. God allows trials to test our faith. We were nowhere near the end of the testing which was to come, but we were very convinced of God's calling on our lives. We would not be stopped. That next morning Ruth and I realized that the layover in Seattle was actually a great blessing. United Airlines had put us up in a nice Holiday Inn and gave each of us an $18 voucher for food. After all the drama we'd had in the days leading up to our flight, we truly needed the rest. The next day we were back on an airplane bound for Hong Kong. Our girls basically slept most of the 13 hour trip which was a blessing. This time we would be arriving during the day. As we approached the airport, our girls were bouncing around with joy. After so many changes, sacrifices, and so much waiting, we had finally arrived. Was it the end of our testing? No, it certainly was not, but *"Now glory to God, who is able, through His mighty power at work within us, to accomplish infinitely more than we might ask or think." Ephesians 3:20 NTL*

No hurt, No healing!

4

We're Here! Now What?

We gathered our three large carts of luggage and awkwardly made our way to the Hong Kong customs desk, dreading how they might treat our large brood. Surprisingly, we got another foretaste of what traveling with four beautiful, blonde-headed little girls in China would be like. Their playful spirit and wide smiles charmed even the most stoic customs officials, and, pretty much every other single Chinese person we would ever come in contact with for the entirety of our time in Asia. No matter where we went, if we stopped for any reason, it was an opening for the Chinese to take pictures and if they could get away with it, stroke their fair skin or long golden hair. A practice the girls would soon learn to cringe from quickly.

Our first apartment

THE GLORY - As we came out into the greeting area at Tai Kok airport in Kowloon, there was our smiling friend Kendall Cobb. He had borrowed a van big enough to carry all of us and our luggage. What a blessing! As a doting dad of young girls himself, he and our girls hit it off right away. Then, when he broke out the bags of candy he brought for them, well let's just say they were part of Kendall's fan club for life. He even brought our family a box of groceries to get us started in the apartment he was driving us to. It was quite a long trip from the airport to the city of Fanling, located near the Chinese border in the New Territories. As a reader, are you getting the sense that though the testing is quite long and difficult, God interjects immense blessing along the way and this trend continues through all of our nearly five years there.

We were very thankful to have a place to stay, but the accommodations were bare (see previous photo). It was one of the apartments I mentioned in chapter two which was used by local ministries to house bible couriers. They were meant to be short term accommodations for large groups of people sleeping mostly in bunk beds with only the minimal requirements for cooking or laundry. This particular apartment was operated by Tim and Sis Kimbril. They were a nice couple from Alabama with four boys Daniel nine, Joseph seven, Samuel six and Andrew three, plus a six month old daughter, Grace. One look at our girls and it was love at first sight. Keep in mind that these boys rarely saw blonde girls their ages, so they intended to play with them every moment we and their parents would allow it. For the weeks we spent in that apartment until we left, we didn't see much of our girls. Ruth very much appreciated Sis who was also a home school mom and a pro at missionary family living. The Kimbrils had moved to Hong Kong after years of living in India. They, as well as the entire Cobb family, would become and remain our dear friends, even now 36 years later.

Let me say right off, Hong Kong in February is the worst possible time to come. Our sparsely furnished apartment had no heat, but hoards of mosquitoes and a fair number of very large roaches. Ruth was doing her best to save money and prepare our own meals, but cookware and utensils were few. The small kitchen sink didn't have hot water, so Ruth had to carry hot water in a bucket from the shower to the kitchen to do dishes. As many of you know, a young family of six produces a great deal of laundry. The tiny washer we were provided with needed to be filled with a hose from the kitchen sink. Then Ruth would manually turn on the agitator. Once you felt like the clothes were clean, you would turn off the agitator, drain the tub and fill it with rinse water. Then she would agitate again and turn on the spinner to drain the tub. In February it was simply next to impossible to get all those clothes dry. We had no luck at all putting them out on the balcony or roof since it rained at least part of nearly every day. And since the humidity was in the 80s and 90s for the entire month, it was nearly impossible to get them dry. We then tried hanging them all over the apartment to dry. Whether inside or outside, we would always be praying "Please Lord, don't let them sour." which would mean washing them all again. Ruth was quite exasperated with it all to say the least.

There is a limit to how many mosquitoes we could listen to buzzing in our ears while trying to go to sleep, and how many bites we were willing to suffer before becoming homicidal. I reached that limit about midnight our first night there. Between the jet lag and the mosquitoes, we hardly slept that first night, so I laid awake considering what I could do to annialate all those thirsty little blood suckers. First chance I got, I made the ten minute walk down a narrow path which crossed multiple vegetable gardens and a very smelly open sewer, to reach the main road to do some shopping. I wanted the most powerful insecticide on the planet, and I found it. The labeling was all in Chinese, so I didn't bother to understand exactly what it was. That evening I was ready. After everyone went to bed, I was up spraying mosquitos and managed to get the lion's share of them. The next morning I awakened to a sight which looked like a killing field. In addition to the scores of mosquitoes, there were more than two dozen large roaches on their backs all over the floor in every room in various stages of death. Oh my! What was in that stuff I sprayed? I had no idea we had that many two plus inch roaches in the apartment, and I had not even sprayed it on the floor at all. I thought I should take a closer look at my death spray. As I scanned through the Chinese characters, to my horror, I came upon the letters D-D-T. I recognized those letters. If you are not familiar with this chemical, it had been banned in the United States as a seriously bad carcinogan. I had just poisoned my family with a dangerous pesticide!

Well, 'Mr. Know It All' who never asked anyone for help, directions or advice (that's me) was totally ashamed and therefore sought advice. "Pif-Paf!" was what I was told we needed. Well back to the shop I went, in search of this modern day Asian marvel which would magically repel or destroy my fiendish enemy. The device was a simple five inch round, rather flat heater which you plugged in. The user would simply put a small, pressed paper wafer which had been treated with a mosquito repellent onto the metal heating element. As the wafer heated, it gave off an effective, yet invisible vapor force field, without killing everything and everyone else in the house. It was a miracle!

Without a doubt, life was sure easier back in Kansas. Of course we were dealing with culture shock. We were "out of our element", or to use a popular phrase first made popular in the mid 1980s, we were out of our "comfort zone". Everything was so strange to us and every aspect of our lives was so difficult. However, each day that passed, this crazy new life slowly became our new normal.

We found ourselves waiting once again. With all the detail God gave me when He first called us, He didn't tell me specifically what city in China we were supposed to study or live in. I did as much research as I could. I asked nearly every American I met, where the best place for me to study Mandarin Chinese was. The consensus was that the city of Xiamen in Fujian Province. Xiamen was located just up the coast and supposedly had the best program in south China. I was occasionally told not to study in the Cantonese speaking Guangzhou province which bordered Hong Kong, because teachers there could not speak the national language of Mandarin properly.

Two other situations had us stuck in Hong Kong. The first was it would take a little time to get our Chinese tourist visas, but the primary problem was that it was Chinese New Year. It was a great time to see fireworks, but a terrible time to cross the border into China. Everyone in Hong Kong who could, traveled to China to visit their relatives for several days. The borders were absolutely overwhelmed with travelers for days. When I had the chance to visit with Kendall about where I should go to study the language, he suggested that I accompany him just across the border to Shenzhen University to check it out. He had a few friends who were studying Chinese there or teaching at the university. There was a young man by the name of Tim who was there with the Youth With A Mission (YWAM) organization. There was also SC who lived in the area. I agreed with Kendall's assessment, so we set a date after the holiday for us to go check it all out. I would finally go in to China and see if God would give me the guidance I desperately needed. I always find God often leads us by simply going to a place to see what the Holy Spirit impresses on us. As is often said, it's impossible to steer a ship that isn't moving. Start moving then God can guide you and when you arrive in the right location. The Holy Spirit will confirm it to you with peace and inspiration.

In the meantime, we needed to move out of the Fanling apartment to allow some bible couriers to come in who had booked it before we were known to be coming. But, we were given the opportunity to move into Alvin and Rhoda Cobb's apartment for a little while. Although it only had one bedroom, it was very nice and spacious with several modern appliances. Also, it was located in the middle of Kowloon, which was great for shopping. Living in Fanling made it difficult and expensive to travel anywhere to do anything. We would also be closer to Revival Christian Church where we were very blessed to attend. Pastor Dennis Balcomb and his precious wife Kathy were, and still are, among the most respected American pastors in Asia. His decades of dedicated and far reaching ministry in Hong Kong and China are without exaggeration, legendary. Without this amazing man of God, the underground church in China would have lacked most of the growth, attention and support they've received all these years.

THE FIGHT - Of primary concern to all missionary families is of course, the safety and wellbeing of their children. Ruth and I continued our home schooling each day and we discovered Rhoda had left behind a large collection of Christian bible and missionary story cassette tapes. The girls were enthralled with them. They were such a great blessing to our whole family, so much so, that for all these many years the girls recall fond memories of listening to them. As adults, they don't remember much of anything about our time in China, but they remember listening to those amazing missionary stories. Christian parents, you have many resources today from which to draw. These can unlock the imagination and spiritual inspiration of your children, so take time seek them out and use them. As I mentioned in my introduction to this book, one of its purposes is intended as an historical and spiritual account of our years in China for our daughters. It's a significant piece of their life story. Ruth and I pray that the book will be a blessing and testimony which will act as an anchor to their faith and to the faith of their children for generations to come.

During the time of our relocation to the Cobb's apartment, ALL the girls began getting hit with lice and chicken pox. With everything else going on, this was certainly difficult due to having limited health resources, but not as bad as the next affliction. In Asia they don't typically use hot water tanks for dispensing hot water, but use electric or propane tankless, on-demand heaters. We weren't at all familiar with these appliances and discovered them to be a blessing and a curse. Our seven year old Adrianne had always loved long, leisurely baths since she was little. One morning she found a small bucket and her ingenious plan was to fill it full of extremely hot water which she could later use to heat up her bath water. Problem was, she placed the bucket on the flat edge of the tub. At one point, the inevitable happened. The bucket of super heated hot water fell on top of her tender thighs. We rushed in hearing a level of screaming which every parent recognizes as being something very serious. Our precious daughter had severely burned herself from her stomach down to just above her knees. Nightmare! Each leg quickly developed huge blisters, causing us all to gasp. It was Sunday in a strange city, in a strange country half way around the world from everything and everyone we would normally turn to in this type of crisis. We prayed as we gathered some towels soaked in cool water, then laid them on her poor little stomach and legs, then prayed some more. We called Kendall's wife, Gina for advice about local medical care. She recommended a doctor whose office was not too far from where we were living, but of course we would have to wait till Monday. Adrianne finally calmed down a bit that day, but had difficulty sleeping through the night. As soon as we could the next day, we got on the phone with the Doctor Gina told us about and made an appointment for that afternoon. The doctor was reassuring with his pleasant and professional demeanor as he examined our brave little girl. He gently drained the very large blisters, applied what looked like zinc oxide, and wrapped up the injury.

THE GLORY - With burns, infection is always a danger, but we did all we could to care for the wounds properly. The rest was now up to God. As the week progressed, Adrianne seemed to have less and less pain, but after four days we felt we should unwrap the bandages and check the burn for any sign of infection. To our amazement, all signs of the burn were gone. Adrianne had nothing but beautiful pink skin where the huge boils had been. Yes, God was, and still is, our healer. As western Christians, we have become accustomed to having the luxury of having things like insurance, great medical care and credit cards which allow us to be less reliant on God. Here is a quote from Ruth in a letter to her mom and dad on March 15th, 1988. "We have really been through the ringer health wise. God must have something great in store for our lives for Satan to attack us so viciously." By God's grace, our faith remains intact. You might find it interesting to note that this was the only time in the nearly five years of living in Asia we ever needed to seek medical care other than dental. God placed a hedge of protection around all of us and gave His angels charge over us. Here is a quote from our March newsletter. "Two things have come to mind as Ruth and I have sought God concerning our lives here. First, we awakened ourselves to the extent of the spiritual battle to which we have engaged with the Buddhist worship going on all around us. And second, a simple flame is easily blown out by winds of adversity, but burning coals are made more fervent."

"We're still waiting for your divine direction Lord." I wrote in my March newsletter. The following describes our mindset at the time. "A couple of weeks ago in a church service at Revival Christian Church, I was encouraged by a prophecy spoken forth which said, "You ask my will. Voices from the north, south, east and west tell you many things, but don't listen. Know my will. Obey, listen and do not doubt, and I will make you a man that My blessing will rest upon. You will heal the sick and cast out demons." I continued to write, "This would not have been so significant to me personally, had I not been greatly discouraged that very morning with all the waiting, and doing what I considered to be so little for the Kingdom, all the while, receiving the loving support of everyone back home. The Spirit witnessed to my spirit that this timely message was for me and I was greatly encouraged." The following week, I was at a different gathering when another public prophecy was given. "To obey is better than sacrifice. Behold I have laid a path before you." It was only a few days later when God would reveal His path for our lives.

Doing whatever I could to stay active, Kendall took me each week to a Friday morning men's bible study on Hong Kong Island where I met some awesome, influential men from several different countries doing ministry in Hong Kong and China. Kendall asked me to help him remodel a Christian brother's apartment. Also, I was called upon by my new friend Jimmy Gafford to build two portable, four by eight foot sound dampening barriers for the China Radio recording studio. They needed to lessen the echo they were getting.

In addition, they were having trouble with their air conditioning vent creating wind noise but which was also causing the radio announcer to continually develop colds. I was very happy to donate my time to do whatever I could to be a blessing and serve the local ministries while I waited on ours to develop. If you ever find yourself waiting on God for your ministry direction, you should look around and see how you can bless the ministries around you. It might just be that the relationships you develop during those times become very important to what God wants to do in you to fulfill your ministry.

THE FIGHT - It was early March, and we once again needed to move back to Fanling. Alvin and Rhoda Cobb were returning from their visit to the United States. Earlier I mentioned that the church would be collecting all donations made to our ministry and forwarding them to us. The person who would be taking care of this for us was Ruth's best friend, Deby Taylor. Deby was the church secretary the entire time we were in China. She also volunteered to copy and mail out our newsletter, which I mailed to her each month. We had no idea how much to expect on our first support check. I must admit, we were as nervous as we were excited. We knew we had spent literally all of our initial $1000 during the first month we were there for our rent, food, transportation and miscellaneous expenses. Therefore, if God was going to supply our needs, we were thinking our support check would be somewhat close to that amount. Imagine our surprise when we opened our letter with a check for $284. After the month of challenges and trials we'd had, we couldn't help but be a bit disappointed. By faith we knew though that God's provision would be enough, and what's more, it will always be on time.

THE GLORY - But then God! Just as we completely ran out of money, our $4500 IRS tax refund came in the mail. I cannot explain why, because it's the only time in our lives it has ever happened. We failed to anticipate and pre-plan spending our tax refund. A friend from church prepared it for us and I guess with all that we were dealing with that year, we simply forgot. What a blessed surprise! This money would be exactly what we needed to make our anticipated move. It sustained us through the next few months until our monthly support rose to an average of $1000 per month the entire time we lived in China. At first you might think this was no miracle. After all, it was a IRS refund check. But I assure you, given our circumstances it was a timely miracle to us.

Finally the Hong Kong - China border over crowding normalized, so Kendall and I got together to make our planned trip to Shenzhen University. The locals refer to it as ShenDa, short for Shenzhen Daxue.

Before continuing to give the details of our all-important fact finding tour, I want to interject some history about Shenzhen you may find interesting. In 1988, the city of Shenzhen, of which Shenzhen University and towns such as Shekou were a part, was only nine years old. I discovered that when the Chinese government wants to build a city, they simply pour all the money, resources and people necessary into the area to make it happen. Before 1979, Shenzhen was just a fishing village of about 13,000 people on the border with Hong Kong. In 1988 the Shenzhen economic zone was home to a million people. Clearly the Communist Party of China was embarrassed with the way their most important border city appeared when foreigners came across. Therefore they quickly built a modern looking city. Today the metropolis is home to more than 13 million people.

Shenzhen, along with Shanghai were the first two of many economic zones which exist today. Contracts made between China and foreign companies would require those manufacturing companies to provide the experts and their all important proprietary technology for the business/factory, while China was to provide the land, infrastructure, buildings and workers. The foreign experts were responsible to train all the Chinese workers over a period of a year or two, and then eventually pull out for the Chinese to near totally operate the business. These zones were more loosely controlled by the Communist Party government and the great benefit was that the foreign companies would not be taxed nearly as much as they had been in the past. China would retain 51% controlling ownership in the company while the foreign company would own 49%. This has continued for several decades now. One recent example people now know well, is the Wuhan Economic Zone, which has recently been the subject of scrutiny with its Institute of Virology lab which was originally a French joint venture facility, and its connection with COVID 19. Currently, it doesn't appear that the lab is being operated as a joint venture, but it is clear that America, and Canada has been educating its doctors and technicians as well as funding their research. It seems we have played a very significant role in the medical experiments conducted there. I wanted to provide this background knowledge so you can better understand not only China in recent history, but the various ways these joint ventures still play a role in our lives today. In the 1980's the Chinese were in the throes of planning that in 1997 Hong Kong Island, Kowloon and New Territories would all be reverting back to Chinese sovereignty after a period of nearly 46 years of British control. Today Shenzhen is a major export hub for goods such as clothing, shoes, bicycles and electronics manufactured there and shipped all over the world. Shenzhen Economic Zone was among the first of over 30 which would be created over the coming years. Their purpose was to entice western companies to invest and share their knowledge and technology in China, in exchange for having access to the huge Chinese market for their goods and services. Major foreign businesses and manufacturers such as America's PPG (Pittsburg Plate Glass) and Canada's Nortel (Northern Telecom Company) made their home in the Shenzhen Economic Zone. These two, as well as many others, including eight oil companies, had businesses in the Shenzhen Zone. Each one had entered into "joint venture" agreements with China. This was the beginning of the slow, persistent leakage of western technology and know-how to build China up to the economic and technological behemoth it is today.

The amazing Kendall Cobb

Kendall and I crossed the Chinese border that first day, with many "kibbles and bits", which at the time was comedic code for bibles and tracts. We then hopped on the mini bus bound for Shekou. This city in the Shenzhen economic zone was located strategically across the bay from Hong Kong. Its location made it very easy and convenient for foreign residents, business executives and their families living there, to go by boat to Hong Kong for business or shopping. However, Kendall and I would be getting off about twenty miles down the road at Shenzhen University. Our first stop was the university cafeteria to meet and visit with Tim Obendorf. Tim was a charming young single man from Oregon who was temporarily in China with YWAM- Youth with a Mission. It was a joy to meet him and gain from his insightful understanding of ministry in the area. Tim had only been at ShenDa a short time, but the impact and level of ministry he had achieved in the area was very impressive. I later discovered that in addition to his dedication to ministering to students, he had started two bible studies which he conducted in the nearby city of Shekou. One, to a group of Chinese and Filipinos who worked there, and one to a group of American expatriot couples who worked for PPG and other companies. Also, he was there at Shenzhen University to begin Chinese language study which was to start in the coming weeks. Of course this information was of particular importance to me.

After an interesting lunch of rice, stir fry vegetables and pig intestine with Tim and some of the Chinese students, I was invited by one of those students named Oliver to see his dorm room. We enjoyed visiting about our lives, and particularly his life at ShenDa. I was the first person to ever share the Gospel with him, and he seemed very engaged. I left him a Chinese New Testament which he greatly appreciated. That moment became a pivotal divine appointment. I felt a peaceful comfort drawing me to Shenzhen University. I knew, without any doubt, I was in the place God wanted me to be. I later reconnected with Kendall to meet SC who also had ministry in the area. I loved and deeply respected SC from the very start and we later become great friends. All in all, it was a great visit. We didn't go to Shekou that day, but later discovered it to be the best location for our family to live because living on campus would put us under a microscope with their foreign affairs office. On the journey back to Hong Kong, I couldn't wait to tell my family the good news. No more waiting!

Birthdays are, and have always been an opportunity to have a party in the Ryel household. Just because we were now in China, there was all the more reason to keep the tradition alive. Erika's fourth birthday was March 19th and mine was on the 21st. There was a large mall in the nearby city of Shatin, Hong Kong. Their McDonalds at the time was known to be the busiest one in the world. This was the location for Erika to have eleven of her new, young friends to come celebrate with us. Per Erika's request, Ruth baked a cherry cake topped with white frosting and fresh strawberries to go with all the ice cream sundaes the kids ordered. They all had a wonderful time, and Ruth and I were so thankful to all our new friends and the sense of normalcy the party brought to our precious girls. My party was having thirteen of our new friends over to our Fanling courier apartment for a small celebration. Once again, Ruth baked a cake to add to ice cream, nuts, candy, popcorn, shoe string potatoes, Koolaid and hot tea. If you should take your family to a foreign country, please don't set aside your family traditions. You may need to alter them a bit, but in your zeal to embrace your new country and ministry, your family needs some sense of continuance of feeling "at home".

    Once again, my dear friend and mentor Kendall, as well as many others during those years were a continued blessing. It cannot be overstated what an impact these families, and the Cobbs in particular, had on our lives and ministry. Never underestimate the impact people God puts in your life can have. But also how important it is that we be ministers ourselves in their lives and the lives of those around us. I'm reminded of the scripture *"Walk with the wise and become wise; associate with fools and get in to trouble." Proverbs 13:20 NLT.* It was only a few more days after my, and Kendall's initial trip to ShenDa when I moved into a dorm room with my new friend and classmate Tim. It was a temporary move to allow me to start language class with the others. I was also waiting to secure an apartment in Shekou for my family to move in to. I got the opportunity to follow up with my previous witness to Oliver and also led a physics professor with the English name Charles to the Lord and began to disciple him as well.

No trial, No freedom!

5

Snake Mouth

Let me describe a little more about the area and people God had called us to. The entire ShenDa campus was quite new in appearance, with bright white modern architecture, outdoor sculptures and a grand fountain. However, the interiors were quite stark and gray by western standards.

Young Chinese, especially college students, were always eager to practice their English with native speakers. We often heard it said there were more Chinese learning English in China, than speak it fluently in the rest world. In school they learn English grammar quite well, but their teachers are not able to speak it with any confidence. They rarely had the opportunity to speak with a native speaker which is the only way they could ever improve. Although most were embarrassed to speak, there were those who were surprisingly bold. In many of those cases, their eagerness to learn English was to further their education and careers in international business. Of course this entire dynamic provided a great opportunity for those who wanted to share the gospel. In most Chinese cities a particular area of large campus' or city parks would be referred to as "English corners". English speakers would go on Sunday afternoons to parks and Universities to engage with several students and young professionals. My family would soon make use of these for sharing the Gospel.

A SEASON OF FIGHTING - We needed to find a home to rent in Shekou. We checked out a place in Nantou, a small agricultural village in the Shenzhen zone. It was large, but more money than we thought we could afford. At that time, our monthly income was quite low. We could not be certain what we could expect in the future. The town was also a bit too primitive for our family to be comfortable. It was increasingly clear to us as we explored the area around ShenDa, that the small city of Shekou (pronounced Shur-ko in Mandarin) was ideal. Shekou, which translates "snake mouth", was a port city so named for the shape of the peninsula it is located on. On a map it looks like an open snake mouth.

    We were totally lost in our effort to find a place to rent. We didn't know anyone in Shekou. Our friends at ShenDa did not have the connections or social reach to be of any assistance because their sphere of influence was only at the university. We were totally in God's hands. SC and Tim introduced us to a friend of theirs with the English name Isaac. He was a fairly mature Christian originally from Shanghai whose English was very good. It wasn't long before Isaac found a place he could recommend. It was a third floor apartment in a building which was owned by a sweet, elderly Christian couple who was also from Shanghai. They didn't speak any English of course, but seemed very friendly and accommodating. They were thrilled watching our little girls prance and dance around. Furnishing the apartment was the question at that point.

    Our friend Alvin Cobb was the embodiment of missionary zeal for supplying the underground church in China with bibles. Alvin likely spent a portion of every day praying and planning ways to make that happen. To further that aim and help us at the same time, Alvin came up with a grand plan. His idea was that he would follow up on classified advertisements in Hong Kong for those who were moving back to their countries of origin. In the past he had been able to purchase some nice furniture at a good price. Once he was able to acquire several pieces, he would then hire a Hong Kong moving truck to transport the furniture and our possessions across the border. To his knowledge, the moving trucks were not thoroughly checked by customs at the border. Of course this was in addition to the even more important purpose of smuggling more than 2700 (100 cases) Chinese OT/NT bibles which would be hidden within and behind the furniture and footlockers. Of course, the very real risk Alvin was taking was his investment in the truck rental, the furniture cost which he wasn't going to charge us for, and the valuable bibles. Our risk was that if the bibles were discovered, the reaction of the Chinese customs officers would surely be swift and severe. The Ryel mission in China could likely be over before it even began. By faith in God and also in Alvin's judgment, bathed in a lot of prayer, we came to the conclusion of agreeing to Alvin's plan. It was a go! Our family of six from Kansas was moving to China.

After making arrangements with our new landlords via Isaac's translation skills, we moved. We only took what we needed across the border and into our new four bedroom apartment. This was the first opportunity Ruth and the girls had to see our, gray on gray "palace". In all my excitement for God's provision of an inexpensive place to live and location for our ministry, somehow it escaped my observation of what a truly bare and ugly place I was moving my precious family into. Suffice to say, Ruth was in a complete state of shock when she walked in. The girls, however, only envisioned an opportunity to roller skate all over the bare concrete floors of our new digs. To this day, Ruth WILL NOT let me commit to living anywhere without her seeing it first. I can't say that I can blame her for that. Can you?

I will try to describe our apartment to you, but no matter how many adjectives I use, my description will most certainly fall short of how sad this apartment was. Every wall and ceiling was made of slightly white washed, cracked, and red dirt stained concrete. Every floor was bare, gray concrete. Every room, except the bathroom of course, was equipped with one ugly 220 volt electrical outlet. The rooms had a single bulb for light in the center of them, but no fixture. The kitchen had a white ceramic tiled, three inch concrete counter about eight feet long, with two huge concrete, tiled sinks in it. The first was for washing dishes, etc. Instead of a typical plumbing to drain waste water away, one sink had a hole busted out of the corner of it. Waste water would flow out, down the corner of the room below the sink into a make-shift cement open trough on the floor. The water would then run down to a hole busted out of the adjacent corner of the room. Water flowed out of the kitchen wall and into a vertical pipe which was positioned on the outside of the building. The second, larger sink was used as a cistern to sustain us through times when the water would be turned off. No cabinets, shelves or drawers of any kind existed. The bathroom was just barely big enough to walk into. A wall mounted sink was positioned next to a western style toilet (but not a squatty potty praise the Lord). The shower head was directly above the toilet and sink so that you could actually take a shower, wash your hands and sit on the toilet at the same time. For such a big apartment, you'd think they could have made more space for a larger bathroom was Ruth's thought.

There was neither a heater nor air conditioning. The worst part was that there was no hot water for showers and not a stick of furniture. As difficult as it was to live in the Fanling apartment, Ruth was longing for it in exchange for what she walked into that afternoon. All you ladies would echo Ruth's absolute disdain for what came out of my mouth next which was "But Ruth, it's very spacious and only $90 per month rent!" Randy, sometimes you're a real dummy. One true benefit to our apartment though was that it was on the third floor. Because nearly all apartments there had no screens on the windows, we learned that living on upper floors resulted in far fewer mosquitoes. We also learned it was very bad luck to live on the fourth floor. In Hong Kong especially, the buildings didn't even have a fourth floor. Elevators magically jumped from the third floor to the fifth floor. The pronunciation of the number four was the same as the pronunciation of the word for death- pronounced "si" with a short i sound. Also a benefit was that the outside door of our building was only 60 feet from the main street of Shekou where many shops were. All the mini-buses would travel down this street as well, so transportation was now easy to access.

Usually when we quote the scripture *"forgetting those things which are behind, and reaching forth unto those things which are before"* from Philippians 3:13 KJV, we don't think in terms of leaving good things behind. Typically it's leaving negative things behind for great things. Ruth was leaving a beautiful life for what was in the natural, a very ugly one. Our brave little band of missionaries was determined to make the best of it though. Only by God's grace, we absolutely would make it, and it would be glorious some day.

Ruth and I made a list of some things we would need to make it until our furniture arrived several days later. We all made our way out to the main street to see what the local shops had to offer. Though all such shops were very small, they provided quite an inventory of needed goods. Our girls were such a joy and blessing to us, especially in the difficult seasons of life. Now our girls were spreading their joy to a new place and quickly reached celebrity status in Shekou. It seemed they were the talk of the town with their playful demeanor everywhere they went. As the girls were spreading happiness, Ruth and I did our best to communicate with the shop keeper what we needed. Since we had no beds whatsoever, we at least had to have mattresses for the floor. The only mattress available at the shop was a three inch thick, three by six foot foam pad, so we bought four of them along with sheets and blankets. We purchased a small, square folding table, six small round folding stools as well as a few recognizable food items. The total cost of course was surprisingly cheap. We got it all taken up to the apartment before going back down to see if we could find someplace to eat supper. We were famished! After having a pretty good meal at a nearby restaurant, we decided to tour the surroundings of our new home. We were delighted to learn that Shekou was a tourist spot. It was kind of like the feeling you get when someone unexpectedly gives you a very nice surprise gift for no apparent reason. As we walked by the shops along a street which followed the coastline we came upon what they called "Sea World". It was an old ocean liner which had been permanently docked and converted into a tourist destination. It had a great many shops and meeting rooms on it. We also went down to a nice walk way along the seashore to a very impressive building and grounds called the Nanhai Hotel. All these discoveries were certainly the highlight of our day. We finally returned to our dimly lit apartment to figure out our sleeping arrangement. We spread out our thin mattresses, tucked them into our new sheets and blankets and collapsed. Of all the memories our daughters have carried with them all these years about our time in China, they still remember this, and it causes them to smile as they recall it with great fondness and clarity. All of us were snuggled together sleeping on our thin mattresses lying on a bare concrete floor, but to them it was somehow the finest bed on the planet. You often hear these days of families doing wonderful things to 'make memories' for their families. By pure happen stance, it seems this nightmare for mom and dad has exceeded most our family memories, even above the more purposed memory creations

we would ever try to make. Once again, God took what was an awful circumstance, and created a beautiful, lasting memory.

It would take about two days before Ruth's shock waned, but then the sobbing began. Perhaps you ladies can put yourselves in Ruth's place and cry a bit as well. All the circumstances surrounding this memory I will never forget. I'd gone out that particular night to a bible study which Tim Obendorf (on previous page shown on top row, third from the left) led in Shekou. Also taking part was dear Hilda, studying Chinese with Tim and I at Shenzhen University. One young woman (shown in front row, second from the left) came with a Buddhist idol which had been in her family for a couple of generations. At the end of the meeting, she took it out of her backpack and wanted us to celebrate and witness its destruction with her, which occurred the night this photo was taken. By this act, she wanted to declare her commitment to God. It was extremely moving and I was on cloud nine in seeing this profound level of commitment and sacrifice.

When I returned home to tell Ruth all about my exciting evening, I found Ruth and all four girls completely overcome with weeping. The initial state of shock had worn off and had given way to a reality which brought a flood of tears. Ruth had no interest in what great things I'd experienced. She was in full-on crisis mode, and was absolutely ready to return to her life in Kansas. All the girls were totally empathetic, crying right along with her. I had failed my family! I had not provided Ruth a proper "nest" for her to nurture our precious babies. And to make matters worse, I'd gone out in pursuit of my glorious ministry and left her at home with absolutely nothing there but emptiness and despair. Life at that point was unbearable for them. I didn't know what to do, so I cried with them and cried out to God for help. He would indeed fix it, but it would again take prolonged patience and perseverance. I wrote to my mom and dad the following: "Ruth constantly battles utter discouragement. She is so frustrated because she doesn't have what she needs to care for her family. She is washing clothes in a bucket, no hot water, no beds, no furniture, no school materials, no tub, no cooking utensils, limited food supplies, etc. But God has given us some precious Chinese friends who have brought us much food, shopped for us, and loaned us a bed with mosquito net for the girls. They've been so giving; we were tempted to turn them away. It's very humbling when people you are called to give to, are giving to you instead". God is so good to encourage and sustain us through any and every battle. He is *"a friend which sticks closer than a brother"*. Proverbs 18:24

After a week of living in our bare apartment, we got news Alvin had gotten several pieces of nice furniture together. He hired a moving truck company which had a permit to cross the Chinese border. He would get it all picked up, and the truck would soon bring it to us. For two agonizing days we waited for the truck to be processed through the border, praying all those bibles would not be discovered. The day was Saturday, April 15th, 1988, and our 11th wedding anniversary was the following day. We got the news that the truck would be at our apartment that afternoon. Praise the Lord! The bibles were not discovered by customs. When the truck arrived we started the unloading process. Of course, this was quite a sight for the locals. Most of their moves are made on the back of bikes or motorcycles. All the interest in what we were doing resulted in a couple of dozen onlookers and a dozen strangers wanting to help us. We of course welcomed the help, but were concerned by their questions regarding the one hundred identical, heavy boxes. "What's in them?" they asked repeatedly. We just responded that they were study books. It was obvious they weren't buying it, but thankfully their English was too poor to further investigate.

Just after starting this challenging task, Isaac came to us with a very alarmed demeanor. He had just talked to the elderly owners of the apartment we were renting from, and learned they had been visited by the PSB (public security bureau, aka, the local police) that day. The police told them they were unknowingly in violation of a new ruling which stipulated that foreigners were not allowed to rent from Chinese private citizens. Isaac further explained that the police were coming that very night to be sure we weren't there. Talk about a scare! Our fight was not over; not by a long shot. Our truck had to return to Hong Kong. We had no place to take all our stuff and no way to get it there if we did. What could we do but continue unloading the truck. Isaac told us the owners welcomed us to store some of our furniture and appliances in their downstairs apartment till we could find another place to live. Once everything was taken inside, Ruth and I began unpacking bibles to hide them out of sight. We stacked them under the big bed which our landlords had loaned us and emptied most of our twelve, footlockers to store bibles there. I then went to the university to hopefully find someone in the foreign affairs office on a Saturday to beg them for a couple of dorm rooms for my family. After much persistence we were able to secure two adjoining teacher dorms.

When I returned to the apartment a few hours later, it was nearly dark. As the mini-bus neared our apartment, I looked down the street, shocked to see all my sweeties sitting on the corner curb of that busy street. They were all crying, frightened to be in the apartment for fear the police would show up at any minute. I was very sad to learn they had been sitting there for nearly two hours. We all went up to our apartment and gathered as much as we could carry to get us by for a couple of days, and made our way back to ShenDa on another mini-bus. We arrived at the dorms completely exhausted. We wearily made the beds and collapsed. The girls were out like a light, but Ruth and I were well aware that the police would possibly find all those bibles. Not only we ourselves, but the future of our ministry was again at risk. In addition we were concerned about the sweet elderly landlords who had been so kind to us.

We rose that Sunday morning with a great temptation to fear. Prayer was lifted up with as much faith as we could muster, but still we battled with the "what if" questions which were bouncing around in our heads. Had the police indeed come that night? Had they discovered the bibles? Would they be waiting for our return in order to arrest all of us? It was time for church, so as I dropped off Ruth and the girls to an unofficial Christian gathering. I then took the bus to our apartment to see what our fate would be. Had God once again shut the mouths of the lions on our behalf? In faith THE GLORY lie ahead, but all we knew at the time was THE FIGHT!

THE GLORY - When I arrived at the apartment, I discovered it to be just as we had left it. Later I would learn the police did in fact come at midnight, but when they didn't find us there, they left without searching. Hallelujah! The fact that they did not conduct a search was a great miracle in itself. I mean, why wouldn't they? We knew it had to be God. So I needed help getting those bibles moved to someplace safe. I looked for and found a pay phone and called the only man I knew who would know what to do- "Kendall the Magnificent". It was Sunday morning, but I was able to reach him. He quickly sprang into action. He was able to put together a team of several guys to come to my rescue. After waiting a few hours, they all showed up in a rented mini-bus. In a very short time, they had all the bibles loaded up in bags and took them on to

Guangzhou for storage until they could be moved further inland. While I was in Shekou dealing with the bibles on our 11th wedding anniversary, Ruth was with the girls praying with a few of our friends. 'What happened to Randy?' 'Was he arrested?' This test was truly difficult for my precious family, but all we could do was keep depending on God; keep trusting Him, and keep fighting.

Early that afternoon, I returned to my family. They were never so happy to see me. It was truly a day of rejoicing for all God had done to give us this small victory, even though we still didn't have a real home. A family of six living in two teacher dorm rooms was actually easier than the apartment we had stayed in. We had an air conditioner in each living area, which contained two double beds and one desk in each. Each unit had a bathroom and each one had a refrigerator, clothes washer, and hot water supply. We used one bathroom for washing and bathing ourselves and one we used for washing dishes in the tub. Ruth created a make-shift kitchen with an electric burner on one of the desks. All the chaos and trauma finally abated. We actually started to settle in as I carried on with my Chinese study. Our friendship with nearby SC grew strong. Their wisdom was a great well from which I could, and often did draw from.

I continued to get opportunities to witness to and disciple students on campus, and continued to go with Tim to the weekly meetings in Shekou to minister. It was a joyful time of rest from the intense spiritual fight we had been engaged in for so long. Near Ruth's birthday in early May, we all went with SC and a number of Chinese friends to a nearby beach. It was a gorgeous bay of crystal clear blue water on the South China Sea. We had such a wonderful time playing all afternoon but discovered too late we were badly sunburned. Though the battles were tough in April, we played a discipleship role in leading 20 Chinese young people to the Lord. The glory filled victories were mounting so it gave us the sense of purpose we longed for; victories which made the fight worth it. We were very thankful May began with fewer battles and greater rewards.

A hurtful surprise came in May however. I got a call from Dave Cundiff one day to inform me that he and Pastor Joe received a letter from Paul Greisen, the highly respected head of the Assembly of God ministry known as China Radio. I talked about China Radio earlier in this book, speaking of my efforts to bless them by building a couple of portable sound proofing panels. The letter Paul sent to my church stated he was concerned with our "rogue" ministry. His fear was that we would get ourselves in trouble and could bring his ministry unwanted, negative attention from the Chinese government. Paul closed by telling them they should absolutely recall me back to the states. Dave said that their reply to brother Greisen was to thank him for his concern, but that we were under their covering, and were not making it known that an Assembly of God was sponsoring us. In writing about this incident I absolutely do not mean to disparage Paul Greisen or China Radio in anyway. They had operated a very effective radio ministry to China for a great many years. Brother Greisen had every right to protect what God had placed him in charge of. In fact, I continued doing all I could to assist them in their ministry from my side of the border in the months to come. In the coming chapters I will detail how we worked together, but for now I just wanted to point out to those considering being missionaries that not everyone, including other ministries around you, will accept what you are doing. However, if you are obedient to the Holy Spirit, and humbly doing what He has called you to do under the covering of others who are overseeing you; I'm confident you and your ministry will likely be vindicated with at least most of them. Warning: do not let bitterness take root. Bitterness will absolutely kill your ministry. Pray for them and take whatever opportunities God gives to both honor and bless them.

The foreign affairs department of the university was charging us $14 USD per day ($420 per month) for staying in their dorms, which put a strain on our budget. In addition, they planned to move us to two student dorms which had no appliances of any kind. It seemed we would need to move once again. At that point we had many more contacts in Shekou due to the meetings we were having there. We put out the word that we needed a place to live in Shekou.

Just a few short days later we learned of a two bedroom apartment in a section of Shekou where there were many homes built for westerners. This part of town was a district most of the foreigners working for the joint venture companies lived in. This fully furnished apartment was being rented by an expat from his joint venture company, but we would be allowed to sublease it while he was out of the country for two months. It was small, but nicely furnished with all the amenities westerners were used to having including air conditioning. It even had a beautiful teak wood parquet floor. The cost was more than we were paying for our dorm rooms, but by this time our monthly donations had climbed to nearly $1000 per month. We felt God's prompting to make this our new home, even though we knew it would again be short term.

You can bet with all the relocating we did in those first months, we were beginning to feel like nomads. Even with all the moves we were making, we still felt very blessed to have such a nice place. The girls were particularly thrilled with the neighbor across the street from our apartment, a Park-n-Shop. Their excitement was not unlike that of a miner who struck gold in California. Park-n-Shop was a small western owned chain of markets in Asia which carried a large selection of western food items. Some of their western grocery items included candy bars and other snacks we often got hungry for while living in China. We were very familiar with Park-n-Shops from our time in Hong Kong where they were a tasty oasis for foreigners such as ourselves. Our little Emily was only two at the time. She was so demonstrably elated; I made up a little jingle about it. "Emily likes to go, to the Park-n-Shop! Oh, Emily likes to go, to the Park-n-Shop. Let's go! Let's go! Come on daddy let's go. Let's go! Let's go! Come on momma let's go." The girls slept in a small bedroom with a bunk bed which had a double bed on the bottom where our three youngest slept cross ways and a single size bunk on top for our oldest, Adrianne. The move went smoothly and we settled in once again with a big sigh of relief.

There was another Christian couple I wanted to mention from this period of our lives. Their names were Scott and Tina Marcassi from Pittsburgh, Pennsylvania. They had two sweet little girls our girls loved to play with. This family was always a part of our birthday parties. Scott and Tina were living in Hong Kong as missionaries. They were some who partnered in the ministry of Revival Christian Church. One day that May they invited our family over for a getaway. They were so generous to let us make six phone calls back home to family and friends. Respites like these were so valuable to us. They were part of God's sustaining grace in our lives. Families like the Cobbs, the Marcassis the Kimbrils, SC and others made all the difference in whether our ministry would survive the intense trials we were facing during our time in China. We were of course important to each other for the morale support we gave each other, but they also were our mentors. Others would join them in the course of our ministry, but none were as important as they during those first few turbulent months.

I'm not able to relate in this book every instance when I, or we as a team, led someone to Christ. I do, however, want my readers to have a sense of the spiritual hunger which existed during our time there. The fields were absolutely white unto harvest. Just as it is in America, we weren't always able to follow up with all of them though. The students and local workers we ministered to were in many cases, quite transient. We sowed into those God gave us, and trusted Him with ones we were not able to baptize or disciple. There will be some in our story, however, who for various reasons are stand outs. I will take time to shine a light on their stories. For now I want to take a quote from a letter I wrote my parents on May 19th, 1988. "Our ministry continues to progress. I just came back from our Thursday night bible study after praying with three young men and another one who was about 40. They received Jesus as their Savior. I believe six prayed for salvation altogether that night. We need to plan a lot of baptisms (about 20-30) for the near future." I also read in a letter written by Ruth that month that she got the opportunity to lead a young woman to the Lord. I was very thrilled when she got this chance. It was just what she needed to begin feeling and filling the role of a missionary. The part Ruth played in our ministry to the Chinese was vital the entire time we were there. Of course she was an amazing wife and mother under some very difficult circumstances, but she was also a very effective minister of the gospel. So as you read this testimony, I want you to never get the idea that I alone was "the missionary". We have always been partners in life. The ministry we had in China was perhaps the best example of that. I went on to write in my letter, "Last month Ruth also began learning to speak some Chinese from one of our Chinese friends. It's difficult, but she's learning enough to travel and shop at the open markets and the many vegetable/fruit street vendors. She became quite good at negotiating prices with them." As I mentioned earlier, we knew our move to the furnished two bedroom western style apartment was temporary. June 10th was when we had to be out. We had continued to be on the lookout for "the place" we knew would be everything we needed. It should have a spacious living area we needed to hold church in. It needed to have at least three bedrooms and be located in the vicinity of ShenDa University and Shekou. Our Chinese friend Isaac who had found the first apartment came through with just the ticket. It happened to be in the same general area as a Christian couple with the last name Lewsetter. This family had two pre-teen sons and a daughter who had worked with the Cobb family, but were abruptly forced to return home to the states. Kendall knew the Lewsetters had left some furniture in storage near where we were going to be living, so he contacted them to see if they wanted to sell it. God was providing for us once again. The building with the apartment we were moving to was owned by the local government run electric company and used as their living quarters. They didn't need all of the apartments, so they had an apartment we could rent from them. We brought over our pieces furniture which were still being stored in the elderly Christian couple's apartment we'd first rented. These pieces, along with what we bought from the Lewsetter family, gave us a good start on the furniture and appliances we needed. This time we were able to take a little more time moving. Finally we arrived at the place God had for us and we would live there the remainder of our time in China.

This second story unit was by no means, a western style apartment, but it was fairly new, and tailor made for our needs. It had a large living area for our meetings, a large dining room, and three large bedrooms. The kitchen and bath area were a nice size as well. The apartment had two large balconies, one off the kitchen and the other off one of the bedrooms. Rather than the typical bare concrete, the floor was a nice gray, green, black, and silver terrazzo. It was also very affordable for us, just $265 per month.

The girls laced up their skates once again. They loved skating from room to room. We were able to put two sets of bunk beds in largest bedroom with the balcony, which they also loved. I've been prompted occasionally to include in this book, excerpts from our letters home which describe a bit of what our home life was like. In a letter written in June of 1988 to her parents, Ruth reveals a little of our family dynamic. "Emily, at two years old, is so cute! Every time something goes wrong for her she exclaims, "Oh gracious!" I'm sending you a picture of Stephanie without one of her front teeth. Isn't she cute? She is really proud that her permanent tooth is coming in. The other front tooth is very loose, but she won't let us pull it. We offered her money for it, but so far she values her tooth more than money! I guess the thought of pain is too much for her. Adrianne is really a good helper. She helps dress the little ones, and she really knows how to clean house. I am so thankful for my darling daughters. They are such a blessing to me. Erika (age four) has gone into a "time for a fit stage". Whenever anything doesn't go her way or even if one of her sisters doesn't do things her way, she throws herself on the floor and has the biggest fit I ever saw. Of course I spank her (more like a love tap), put her in her room and tell her to come out when she can act human again. In about ten minutes or so she would collect herself and come out acting as if nothing ever happened."

Shekou apartment with Stephanie on the balcony

We were very happy with our new home. I was able to provide Ruth with a few good pieces of furniture and appliances all for a relatively low price. Some may wonder why we had to move so often. As I sought God on the matter, He reminded me that after David was anointed King he slept with sheep and in caves running from Saul. After Joseph's dreams as a youth, he was thrown in a pit, sold, and went to prison at different times before God's plan was fully manifested. Daniel was separated from his home and family, made a eunuch, betrayed, and thrown in a lion's den in the midst of serving God. It was only a week or two before we were able to start having church and bible studies in our new place. Life and ministry in China was taking shape. We became enveloped in God's grace and glory. It was a season which would last nearly uninterrupted for the next two years. As I close this chapter I want to share a scripture and a quote which was a great source of my passion, even in the most difficult times. *"Accordingly I set a goal to preach the gospel, not where Christ's name was already known, so that I would not build on another man's foundation; but as it is written (in Isaiah 52:15), They who had no news of Him shall see, and they who have not heard shall understand" Romans 15:20-21 Amplified Version.* A quote from China missionary Hudson Taylor's book about his China Inland Mission was also very inspiring. *"What right does anyone have to hear the gospel twice, when there are those who have not heard it once?"*

No guilt, No mercy!

6

My Name is Li En Tian

With my family finally settled in a long term apartment, I could begin focusing more on my language study. Ruth could also focus on catching up on our girls' home school learning. I want to take a minute to tell you about my Chinese language class. Our Chinese teacher Mr. Tang, was a 48 year old friendly man from Shanghai. He was patient and kind to his small group of students. One day he opened up to us about his past. He grew up in the horrible era of the Communist Cultural Revolution. I won't elaborate in this book, but if you're not familiar with it, I'd recommend studying it if you're interested in Chinese Communist history. Mr. Tang went on to talk about nearly being sent to Vietnam. Vietnam? I asked abruptly. He explained that during the 1960's China sent soldiers to Vietnam to fight. Of course it was kept from the international news, but it did happen in very significant numbers. In order to keep this news quiet, the Chinese soldiers were never allowed to speak, ever! So they were simply called the "silent soldiers". Mr. Tang was a good teacher, but I'm afraid I was not the best student. I was so focused on saying the words correctly, I never became very good at just speaking fluently. Reading and especially writing the language was extremely intimidating. After the six months of study, I would eventually give it up.

Li En Tian was the name Isaac gave me soon after he met me. It was the name I typically used when introducing myself to the Chinese. The name Li (Lee) is a common surname. En (Un) was my first name and it means "grace". Tian was what you could use as my middle name and it means "heaven". So my name was in essence a testimony for why God sent me- Grace from Heaven. I received raised eyebrows every single time I introduced myself. Ruth and all the girls would later be given their own Chinese names. Ruth was Lu En Na (spouses usually continued using their family's surname), Adrianne was - Li Ya Qin, Stephanie - Li Ya Fen, Erika - Li Ya Li and Emily- Li Ya Mei.

These type shops were typical behind our apartment at that time.

To give you more insight to our home life during this period of time, I want to quote some excerpts from a letter Ruth wrote her sister Susan on June 24, 1988. "We have a nice table with six chairs and a buffet. God also provided us a refrigerator. I think I have one of the only home ovens in SE China as well. People here do not bake things, only steam or stir fry them. I could probably make a mint here if I wanted to sell baked goods. But of course I have neither the time nor the desire to do such a thing. Our family will get lots of good out of our oven though. We have a nice large living room. We bought a small stereo, and someone gave us a TV so that we can get the little bit of Hong Kong English broadcasting. It doesn't work now, but we are having it repaired. It gets very boring around here in the evenings without Randy around (he's doing ministry a lot). So, the TV is really important to have just for our sanity. Some nights I think I'm going crazy with loneliness and boredom. Don't get me wrong, I love the work here, but I don't want to paint a false picture for you to lead you to think everything is just wonderful for us here. I think many people have the idea we live an exciting, adventurous life, but I promise you, apart from the excitement of ministry, things get mundane here just like anywhere else. After the newness wears off, things are much the same as always. Life here is just much harder because we have to go through so much. We have to catch a mini-bus to travel just to go anywhere at all. Things just aren't handy in this country. I usually try to bring our groceries from Hong Kong, so I have to bring them back to China on a small two wheeled luggage cart. It gets rather heavy by the time I finally get home. Are you feeling sorry for me yet? (Hah!) It's really ok. I'm just having a much harder work day than I did in the States. Hanging out clothes is another chore I'm not used to. I really miss my handy dandy clothes dryer."

    To her mom she wrote on June 29th "It's another day in hot China! The lychee season is in full swing. Pineapples and plums are in abundance also. I saw the first of the local grapes in the market yesterday, but they are too expensive to buy yet. There are watermelons at every corner. We are enjoying this fruit season. Our family is feeling very comfortable in our new apartment. I am waiting for some curtains right now. Rhoda Cobb in Hong Kong is making them for us. She is such a sweet person. Right now we kind of live in a fish bowl. Everyone around can see in to our apartment. We had a bible study last night and another young lady came to Jesus! PTL! It thrills our hearts to see the hungry Chinese being filled with the love and truth of Jesus. I sure miss my sweet family. This is the longest we have been away from home. Oh how sweet our reunion will be someday. There are days when I think my heart will break from being so homesick. Jesus always comes and strengthens me with His love and endurance. I can assure you, it's His call that keeps us here! This is not exactly my ideal spot in the world. There is such a huge need, and so few workers. We feel so inadequate most of the time, but we will keep plugging away doing God's work of leading souls to Him. There are so many who have never heard the good news. Adrianne has really become especially close to me. She helps me so much around the house, and with the younger girls. I thank God everyday for my lovely daughters. They are such blessings to me. Emily and Erika are so cute together. Their favorite game to play right now is Deby and Cindy" (my friends and former neighbors Deby Taylor and Cindy Bogle). They put on heels and play for the longest time. Adri and Steph play a lot together too. So glad they all have each other."

    In writing to my mom and dad on June 24th I said "We had some of our friends come over to our apartment the other night.

Ruth fixed Taco Chicken, homemade rolls, green beans, fresh vegetables with Ranch dressing, apple pie and chocolate chip cookies. We all enjoyed it thoroughly. Ruth's oven works great. It runs off propane." July 1st 1988 I wrote them "Most of the students are going back home now so things are changing a bit around the college. We are trying to get addresses and keep contact with people. In the future we want to visit a few of them. We have made friends from all over China. From Xian (home of the Terra Cotta Soldiers), Inner Mongolia, Shanghai, Wuhan, Guilin, Beijing, Changchun and all over our province of Guangdong. We have standing invitations to nearly every major city in China, and many small ones. We now already have friends in Malaysia, Indonesia, New Zealand, Singapore, the Philippines and various cities in Australia. It's been a marvelous experience! Last Tuesday my Chinese teacher put on a Lychee festival party for several Chinese students and teachers. They asked my family to bring some songs. This is a traditional Chinese custom to have those who come to the parties to bring the entertainment. They call it Jie Mu. I played guitar while the girls sang "Jesus Loves Me" and "This is the Day". Then we all sang together "For God So Loved the World". We were a big hit. Ruth and I mused we should develop them as a singing group. They would likely be the only young group of four blonde singing sisters in all of China. They are quite an attractive novelty."

With all the public attention we were getting, the local police (which we call the Public Security Bureau, or PSB) felt the need to investigate. We were beginning to have fairly large "bible parties" in our home. People were being saved and we began having many water baptisms in a local duck pond a couple of miles down the road as well. We weren't surprised to learn some of those coming to our meetings were undercover Public Security Bureau (PSB). They don't carry guns but do have wicked cattle prods on occasion as they patrol the streets. We would soon learn that many of these undercover police spies were getting saved and baptized themselves. Over the course of time, I can't say how many of the police became Christians, but I do want to highlight one of them as a thrilling example. This young man of about 30 went by the name Joe. Before we realized he was a spy, we knew him to be one of most on fire and water baptized converts we had. Joe frequented a fellowship at the university as well as our meetings occasionally. He veraciously read his bible, and could simply not get enough of Jesus. The last time I saw Joe he had brought three young ladies to our bible study and testified of what God was doing in his life. A few months later Joe was able to get a visa to travel to Australia where he enrolled in a bible college in Melbourne. Another similar story was of a young man who went by the name Waldo. Before he began coming, he was a secretary for the Chinese communist party youth league. We later discovered that many of our converts were party members. To be a Party member was the way to get ahead in China if you were a bright young person. Like Joe, Waldo was on fire. When he was offered a promotion in the party, he turned it down. Upon witnessing to his fiancé about Jesus, she broke up with him and said he was crazy. He moved back home with the intention of preaching the gospel. "Where's Waldo" you ask? Like so many, we never saw him or Joe again. We just had to put our trust in Jesus and the power of His Holy Spirit to continue in these young men what He had started.

Our calling and approach to preaching the gospel in China was different than other most of the Christian teachers in China. One such Christian teacher visiting from another part of China sternly warned us and others there we should be aware of the PSB. We said to them that the PSB better beware of us, because we were turning their ranks into Christians. Our thinking, but more importantly what God was telling us, was that it would be better to be bold and courageous to win many over a short period of time, than to be fearful mice and talk to only a few. On the one hand we felt our approach was teaching our converts to be bold and courageous. On the other, it would be teaching them to be fearful. We were taught to believe that God will deal with our enemy if He has an army who will step into battle with a song of praise on their lips and the anchor of faith in their hearts and minds. Better strength of faith, than fearful excuses. Because we actually live in China though, we felt it best not to risk being arrested and asked to leave because of us bible smuggling which was being done by so many other ministries. Therefore, beginning in the middle of 1988 we began expanding our synergistic planning and making it known to various bible ministries out of Hong Kong that our apartment was available for them to drop off, and later pick up their bags of bibles, Christian books and tracts. It gave us more contact with Americans to befriend and testify to what God was doing in China. These couriers much appreciated it since it was rare for such couriers to meet those actually living and doing the work of the ministry in China.

Now let me introduce you to my best friend in China. Mr Y was a young Chinese man of about 18. Looking back, I can say for certain he was one of the reasons my family needed to go to China so quickly. By divine appointment I met him at ShenDa in April that year where he was studying international business and trade. He was actually in a program where he was told he had the promise of marketing computers in China for Hewlett-Packard. We were divinely drawn to each other, and I led him to Jesus. Over the course of this book, you'll learn much about this extraordinary young man. He came from a small village in the countryside of Guangdong Province but he was absolutely the most charismatic and talented Chinese person I'd ever met, but at the same time quite humble. I could say with confidence that Mr. Y could become anything he wanted to be. He was intelligent and bold in faith. Apart from God Himself, he was the key to much of how God would use us in China. As I began discipling him, he simply captured my heart. Ruth embraced him as well, making him more like a son than a typical disciple. He had very little clothing so Ruth bought him some things in Hong Kong. In July His father was very sick with pneumonia with no medicine available. We found out what he needed and were able to get him medicine in Hong Kong to make him well. Charles was ferocious in learning English. When I met him he was already quite good, but within a couple months he was quickly becoming excellent. Within several months, he was one of the best I'd ever heard while I was in China.

As I mentioned earlier, my Chinese language training began in March and ended in July of 1988. Of course from the beginning of our ministry, I needed a translator in order to preach the gospel. Our friend Isaac filled that role in the early months. However, as Mr. Y's English and his understanding of the gospel improved, he and Isaac would take turns translating. Both were a great blessing to our fellowship of about 35 to 40 each Sunday morning. A great many were being saved and baptized as a result. Now I introduce the irrepressible Jerry Zhang! Jerry was already a believer and was born and raised in Shanghai where he worked for a factory as a mechanical engineer. His wife and son had to remain in Shanghai so Jerry was a precious part of our family and another prominent part of our ministry. He spoke good English, but whether in English or Chinese, Jerry was always in high gear. His raw enthusiasm knew no end. Once in one of our Sunday morning services while we just stood in a large circle singing and worshipping, God led us to pray for the sick. Jerry felt God heal him of the cancer he'd been diagnosed with. I thought he was would simply fly away with joy. Jerry knew God touched him, which he later confirmed with his doctor. He visited us in Kansas a few years ago. Jerry remained cancer free all these years. Our disciples Jerry, Mr Y, Isaac and a couple of the women like Karen and Jane, would often follow up with those asking questions about God. In my opinion this is where the real ministry took place. Being handicapped by my inability to be fluent in Chinese, I depended on them to drill down and bring those who were touched by the message to a place of repentence and salvation. Sometimes I'd lead them in prayer, but usually I encouraged my disciples to do it. During a period when I lamented my inability to speak Chinese, it occurred to me that by relying on translators, I was effectively training them to share, preach the gospel and lead others to Christ. I stopped lamenting and began rejoicing in my weakness.

Moving our attention back to our family life, swimming was at the top of our daughter's list of things to do. One of the very best things about living in Shekou was the NanHai Hotel. The NanHai was an absolutely gorgeous joint venture hotel. Although their water fall, fountains, foyer, restaurant and rooms were excellent, the very best thing about that hotel was their swimming pool. To date, it ranks as one of the most beautiful, idyllic pools I've ever experienced. With the majestic, concave shaped ten story hotel as a backdrop, you looked through a convex formation of a long, palm lined portico area which separated you from an unrestricted view of the South China Sea. You could easily see the skyscrapers of Hong Kong on the horizon most days. When we learned we could get a family season pass to the pool, it was like we had been given our own pool. My family spent a great many summer afternoons there.

On Stephanie's July 6th birthday we gave her a purple BMX bicycle we bought in Hong Kong. SC and Mr Y joined us at our apartment for a party of bologna sandwiches, cheese curls, corn chips, deviled eggs, cake and ice cream. After lunch and some play time, we headed out to XiLi (pronounced she-lee) Park about 15 minutes by bus from our house. We had heard about it, but had never been there. It was a great park with many attractions, including of course, a wonderful pool. The pool had slides and some spring diving boards, an Olympic size platform board, and a cable slide. About two hours in, Adrianne and I had a bad collision on the big slide when I ran into the back of her head. It cracked the bridge my nose. Bummer, but we still stayed a couple more hours and had a great time. XiLi Park even had a small amusement park with a merry-go-round, a cage with monkeys, and a 12 story pagoda we could climb up in. All this was surrounded by luscious green mountains. We were definitely not in Kansas anymore.

Having just mentioned Stephanie's new bicycle which was bought in Hong Kong, please allow me to share what you quickly learn if you were to buy a typical bicycle made in China for the Chinese to ride. These "bicycle rules" may not apply currently, but at the time, they were very well known and closely followed. Rule #1: the first thing you need to do when you buy a new bicycle is to take it to the shop to get it repaired. Rule #2: Once you get it repaired and all the parts have been tightened and adjusted, you need to leave it out in the rain a couple of times so that the parts can rust into place, otherwise you'll quickly start losing nuts, bolts and other parts off of it. Rule #3: Should you happen to still lose something off your bike, you don't need to go to the bicycle repair shop to replace it. Simply walk along one of the primary bicycle routes and pick the part you need off the pavement. Now I know to you this all might seem like I'm making a joke, but believe me, it's the absolute

Our four beautiful ballerinas

truth. Everyone who had ever bought a Chinese bike in China at that time knew it well.

As summer was half over, we visited the Chinese elementary school to see if it was possible to enroll one or more the girls there. It was our understanding they would be able to learn the language much easier than adults if they were somewhat immersed in it. We discovered that yes they could all enroll on September 1st. As the day drew near, we made the decision to enroll Adrianne in first grade even though she was actually ready for third grade in her home school studies. The school thought it would be easier for her to pick up Chinese at that level, rather than go into the third grade. Stephanie's education was a different situation. As smart as she was, her reading was not progressing as it should. We decided to keep her home for more work on her reading skills, but also it was clear to us that Stephanie's aptitudes were more in line with taking a clock apart, than telling time. Also, she had extraordinary vocal music skill we wanted to encourage and develop. Erika and Emily enrolled in kindergarten together for two hours each morning. When they all started Chinese school in September, what an interesting time that was. Adrianne was in a class of 50! Although her classmates were a bit of a terror outside the classroom, the teacher had their full attention in class. Ruth and I were so thrilled with the Chinese songs and dances she learned while she was there. As I mentioned, Adrianne's little five and six year old classmates terrorized her relentlessly by pulling at her hair, calling her names and laughing at her. After several months, based on Adrianne's mood and demeanor, we began to realize that it was not working out. Though it wasn't as bad for the little ones, we pulled Erika and Emily out as well and simply went back to home schooling them.

Ruth had been looking for some help with the housework and watching the kids when God gave her Frieda. She was about 45 with limited ability to speak English. She worked three days a week for us at a cost of just $.85 per hour. Ruth loved her girls so much she would regularly take all the girls to Hong Kong to get away from the hum-drum of our apartment, and to see their friends. Keep in mind this was both very difficult, and expensive. I would also go when I could, but often it was Ruth by herself. Every mom knows what a chore it is to take little ones shopping, even with the ease of American transportation. Living and shopping in a third world country without private transportation was a great deal more challenging. I beg your patience in allowing me to help you understand what a typical shopping trip was like for Ruth. Apply this scenario to the great number of missionary families you might know who are currently living in third world countries, unable to afford a vehicle or be able to send them to an international school. This should help you pray for those families. If you are considering going on the mission field, this may be useful information for your planning and preparation.

Typically Ruth's long planned shopping days would begin early. She would need to get herself, and our girls ready, who at the time were ages 2, 4, 6 and 7. She would need her two wheeled luggage carts (at least one) complete with large red, white and blue rice bags, and the extra large purse every mom needs for a group of that size. Ruth and all the girls would each need their passports, fanny packs complete with a fresh package of tissues for bathroom use (no toilet paper in public restrooms in Hong Kong or China at that time), back-packs with snacks and perhaps an umbrella, poncho, rain coat or jacket. Now it's time to walk ten minutes out to the main road to stand and wait for a bus going to the Shenzhen-Hong Kong border crossing. Then there would be nearly an hour of travel time to get there. Going through border customs was a challenge of patience and our youngest girls were very active, so keeping them somewhat corralled was difficult. Depending on how crowded the border was, it might take 20 minutes or it might take two hours to get through Chinese and Hong Kong customs. Thankfully, as the girls got older and more used to the process, they became more easily managed and helpful.

Once through customs it was just a matter of waiting a short while for the train back into Hong Kong to arrive. The train was by far our favorite part of the trip. It was very sleek and modern looking, and ran through lots of countryside with rice paddies and such, scattered throughout the New Territories of the country of Hong Kong. After several stops in each of the cities along the way we would arrive at our primary destination- Shatin Mall. The train station was actually located in this huge, three story shopping mall. Shatin Mall was perhaps our favorite place on earth outside of home of course. It was as close to an American feel as we could see in Asia. This mall had the newest stores with all the latest fashions in one glorious place. Our first stop was always our PO Box to check the mail. If a check arrived, we would then go to an ATM to deposit it. By then it was time for lunch! Of course that meant McDonalds. As I mentioned before in the book, this busy McDonalds was an experience you had to see to believe it. Of course there was a line of about eight to ten at the counter in front of its six registers. The actual dining area was not really much larger than your typical large McDonalds in America. Therefore each table had one or more groups of people standing next to it waiting for the ones seated to finish their meals and leave. That took a little getting used to. Of course no trip to the Shatin Mall was complete without watching the huge music and light fountain show once or twice. It still stands as one of the best fountain shows we have ever enjoyed. Occasionally we would meet up with friends, which was always fun. Of course, if there was a birthday in our group of friends, a party was a big part of the day. There was a nice park area outside the mall we'd often play at or have one our famous birthday parties in. Ruth would occasionally need to buy presents or clothing at the mall, but there would always be a trip to Park-n-Shop. It was much better stocked with a greater variety of foods than the one we had in Shekou and the prices were better. Ruth would always wait till it was near time to return home before doing her grocery shopping. No need to get the groceries and lug them around unnecessarily. Back on the train to go through customs on each side of the border, then find a minibus to make the one hour journey back home. Of course the long trip back home was always borderline miserable. Everyone was hot and exhausted. The girls were beginning to get cranky which meant Ruth was strongly tempted to do the same. They would get home in the early or at times, late evening completely exhausted.

  Let me close this chapter relating a couple more things which happened in our family. I mentioned earlier a fruit called the lychee. Lychees are a big deal in SE China. During Imperial times, lychees would be transported north to the Emperors who enjoyed them very much. We were told how some of the trees not too far from where we lived have been there a very long time. Lychees from these trees would sell for nearly $50US per pound, but we would usually pay one to two dollars per pound on the street for the typical lychee. In summer, locals would have an annual Lychee Festival. Our family developed a ferocious appetite for these golf ball size delicious citrus fruits. On one occasion we all sat down and ate ten pounds of them in one sitting. Not good for our bodies, but they were just so very good. It seemed that only every other year was a good crop with very few if any worms. One thing we learned the hard way was that lychee groves were somewhat famous for being inhabited by demon spirits.

Saturdays were usually the day we got together with friends for lunch at our house. One Saturday that summer all the kids were out running around our apartment complex fully engaged in some serious hide and seek. A few hundred feet from our apartment was a dense grove of lychee trees. At some point our six year old daughter Stephanie got separated from the others while playing hide and go seek. The other children had already returned home but Stephanie was looking everywhere for them, which included searching the lychee grove. She soon came running up the sidewalk and into our apartment completely frantic with terror in her eyes. The following is the story she told us when she finally calmed down. As she was walking out of the grove, she heard her name being called out in a disturbing, low voice. Expecting that one of her friends was just playing a trick on her, she quickly spun around, but no one was there. In fear, she started running back home, but the voice kept repeating her name over and over getting closer to her as she ran. She and the voice didn't stop till she arrived at our building. Needless to say, all of us began praying fervently to rebuke this evil spirit. We pled the blood of Christ over her in spiritual warfare. Naturally though, we all steered clear of the lychee grove from that point on.

Late that summer, Ruth had an interesting encounter with one of the street vendors near our apartment. There was a nearby location where a large number of vendors lined up to sell their fruit and vegetables. Ruth's Chinese language skill was very basic at that point and Ruth had not been shopping there long. She was just getting used to dealing with them, and they with her. One particular day she was walking along trying to negotiate a good price for what she needed that day. One young lady quoted a good price to her and Ruth decided to do business with her. Each vendor had a rudimentary type of balance scale they used to measure out what they were selling. But it was quite easy for venders to cheat their customers by shorting them on product. Because Ruth was a savvy shopper, she could tell her vegetables were not nearly heavy enough. When Ruth questioned her, the vendor acted insulted and started getting agitated. So Ruth went over to the fair scale official to get a true measurement. Sure enough, Ruth was right. The vendor had cheated her by quite a bit. When the official realized what Ruth was saying about the weight, he went to the vendor and gave her a serious scolding. This vendor was in big trouble and deeply embarrassed to be so publically disgraced. The scolding and embarrassment impacted the vendor so strongly, Ruth felt bad about it. So, the next time and every time thereafter, for as long as we lived there, that same vendor was where she bought all her fruits and vegetables. The vendor and Ruth became great friends. Ruth always got a good price from the vendor, and the vendor always got a simple Christian message from Ruth.

One of Ruth's converts and good friends was a girl who went by Candy. We were having great turn outs at our meetings, even though many students had gone home for summer break. Candy came to a meeting where at least half were unbelievers who had been invited by many of our new converts. On this particular night, our friend Candy came to the meeting very sick with a high fever. She came expecting God to heal her. She was in so much agony; she couldn't even tolerate a cool cloth on her forehead. She even complained when someone blew on her forehead. When it came time to pray for the sick, Candy of course was first in line. We prayed believing in the healing power of God, and she was instantly healed. Not even so much as a headache. Later that year her mother became very sick, but did get better, but her father passed away. She was also struggling with her husband who lived and worked in Hong Kong. She wanted to divorce him, so we were of course counseling her, but at the same time she received word that she was accepted and given a visa to attend a university in Sydney, Australia. We stayed in contact with Candy over the next year and she was doing well.

Ruth's helper Freida quit after just one week. It wasn't a good fit for her or us as it turned out. However, God brought us Sincere, a precious girl from northern China. Her, and her husband were forced to live separately. Sincere was with us for many months. Later in the chapter 9 of this book called "Puzzle Pieces", I will tell in detail why Sincere was one of the many reasons God called us so quickly to China. Lastly, I wanted to relate a precious story about Donna, who was a Chinese convert who also helped Ruth for a time.

My mom and dad gifted us enough money to buy a small, electric clothes dryer. While Donna watched the girls, Ruth and I went to Hong Kong to buy it, pick up our support check and buy groceries. However, to our great surprise, the support check had not arrived. We only had enough money to get back home, so we left without the food we needed. Although we'd told no one about our need, Donna made a huge sacrifice and gave Ruth $10 after we got home which Ruth used for food to get us by. It was a tremendous blessing! On a humorous side note though, Donna was not overly watchful of the girls. She knew how sweet they were, but not how ornery they could be. We returned from another trip we made to Hong Kong when Donna was the nanny to find some bed sheets tied together in the girl's bedroom hanging down from their balcony. The older girls thought it would be fun to lower three year old Emily from our second floor balcony down to the ground. Poor Donna was pretty embarrassed but no one was hurt.

    Chinese wet markets have recently become rather infamous in our news media since we returned from China, so I want to relate one of my personal encounters. As I and a couple of my girls were walking through one such market nearby just for fun. We came upon one of the most intriguing sights I've ever witnessed. A vendor selling fish was standing at his table which had some fresh fish laying on it. As we walked by, I notice the vendor had taken a 24 inch fish and cleanly sliced it open from the middle of its lip all the way to its tail laying on his work table. This amazing fish however was still opening and closing one side of its mouth in sync with the other side of its mouth. Its gills were each opening and closing in sync as well. Remarkable!

    Though we'd only been in Shekou a few months, God was using this former telephone technician (me) to minister the gospel for His glory! This excerpt is from our July, 1988 newsletter. "Let me assure you the benefits and *"fullness of joy and pleasures" Psalms 16:24* far exceed any discomfort or sacrifice. Last Thursday night we had a precious time of worship and testimony. It was a beautiful time of loving one another in the Lord. Usually we had a strongly evangelistic meeting, but the Holy Spirit threw my studied presentation out and ministered a similar message, but in His own way. Thursday nights will often run 35-45 people, but most all the university classes have ended, so many of the students had returned home, leaving our meetings smaller. The 20 or so last Thursday were pressing in with praise and worship. Their testimonies were of a particular blessing to us. I greatly wished that I could have taped the meeting and sent it to you all. You would know the reason for our joy. God has brought a fruitful harvest and it appears the fruit is remaining and increasing. The depth of faith we are beginning to see in their worship and testimonies assures our hearts that the Holy Spirit is at work in their lives."

To end this chapter, I'll quote from a letter I wrote to my parents about a special dinner we received from our upstairs neighbors. Their apartment was rented by a state owned company whose directors used it as a kitchen and dining hall for all their staff. I don't recall what type of business it was, but these businessmen wanted to get acquainted with us and practice their English. They of course loved watching the girls play. "Chinese really take pride in their cooking and do prepare amazing food. If they want to impress you, it's not unusual for them to serve as many as 15-24 freshly prepared courses. Most of the dishes were what you might expect, but there were a few exotic dishes. One which most caught our suspicious eyes was a plate of what I can only describe as a Kansas June bugs. They informed us the price they paid at the market that day was $42.00US per pound; therefore we felt obligated to at least try them. They tasted somewhat similar to burnt toast." I don't want to bore you with stories about what food we ate while living in China, but from time to time I'll slip in a few stories which I hope you'll find interestingly entertaining.

No impossibility, No miracle!

7

Mount Shekou

THE FIGHT – I quote from a letter I wrote my parents on December 10th 1988. "The police pressure became worse while we were in Hong Kong a short time. The students were also warned to stay away from our meetings because the police were deciding what to do with us. We had two other sources tell us the same thing, so we've considered that perhaps we should end our open meetings and go more "underground".

Everyone who knows Ruth, sees her as an exceptionally happy, upbeat person. I want to expose a bit of what missionaries can face when most of what they've ever known is thousands of miles away. Here's an excerpt from Ruth's August 13, 1988 letter to her sister Susan. "I had a real battle with Satan a couple of weeks ago. He literally took me to the depths of hell, and didn't want to let me come back. I was totally depressed, and was so miserable to my sweet family. I talked about negative things all the time, and really wanted to die. I know that many people must have been praying for me, because on August 1st, the dark spirit just seemed to snap. From that moment on, I've been fighting to get my life back. I really feel I could have died had Jesus not put His hand on me. I really felt the darkness. I could hear what I was saying, but I couldn't really control it. I wanted to be happy and sweet, but there was no contentment in my heart. Finally, I just cried out 'God, You have to take this terrible thing from me!'

The view from the top of Mt. Shekou

THE GLORY - Immediately I felt a release in my soul, and joy and happiness started flooding in again. I really thought I was going to have a nervous breakdown there for a while. Poor Randy, he really did not know what to do. He was really sweet through the whole ordeal. I think Satan saw a weakness of discontentment in my spiritual life. He got in and started eating like a worm until I was out of control. I am learning to be thankful, no matter what situation I am in. Now I'm just keeping my eyes on Jesus, not on my circumstances. Whatever happens, He has the divine authority over all situations. He has given us His authority as well. Praise God! It's not easy being a missionary in a land where everyone stares or laughs at you, the food is so strange; the languages (Mandarin and Cantonese) are so strange."

Early in August 1988 I was facing some important decisions about continuing my language education as well as what educational path was best for each of our girls. Ruth had been struggling emotionally, and I was struggling as to how I could help her. Of course there were issues of how to best grow the ministry and, what if anything, I should do about the continued presence of undercover police in our meetings. It was time to fully engage in prayer and fasting. I considered my options of how I could get some alone time alone with God, but which wouldn't cost me money since we had none to spare. I decided I would climb Mount Shekou. At least that's what many locals I knew called it. Mount Shekou was a small grouping of mostly rocky hills which bordered the city of Shekou to the northeast. The plan was to spend the night up there alone and return the afternoon of the next day. I left my watch and only gathered up a light nylon windbreaker, a hammock and set out just after lunch. I walked from our apartment about two miles, then up Mount Shekou which took me another two hours. I climbed up and down a couple of the adjoining hills till I found what I thought to be the tallest one.

The view was magnificent! The city of Shekou, the South China Sea and the awesome country of Hong Kong was all laid out in full view. To my surprise, there was no meaningful vegetation up there, just small shrubs, big rocks and dirt. For some unknown reason there did happen to be a couple of metal poles planted into the rocks I could tie my hammock to. When I did, however, I found them to be too close together. I tried to lay on it, but it became more of an uncomfortable chair than a place to lie down. Oh well, I supposed I would just stretch out on a big rock to rest. I was very uncomfortable for sure, but I was determined to seek God with all my heart no matter the circumstance.

I had to get up a few times, to move around because I kept getting very stiff. The temperature was quickly dropping, and the wind picked up as well. I didn't realize how cold it could get on top the hill in late summer when temperatures during the day often reached 100 degrees Fahrenheit. I was so cold! I laid there praying until what I guessed was about one or two o'clock in the morning when I happened to open my eyes and saw a very large bird with an approximate wing span over five feet slowly gliding ten feet above me. At that moment my life truly flashed before my eyes, both good and bad for what seemed like five minutes. I didn't feel intimidated, but I was confused. At the time it seemed like God was giving me an accounting of my life, but of course I didn't know for certain. I did know my face was burned by the sun and wind. I was nearly as cold as I have ever been and could not stop shivering. It became clear I could not stay on that mountain any longer. But how was I to manage getting down from there in the dark. I hadn't brought a flashlight with me. Also, because I had never found a real trail to get up there, I had no natural hope of finding a trail to follow back down. After struggling awhile with the decision, I set off to get myself off that hill the best I could. It was painfully slow going. I slipped and fell many times along the way, but after what seemed to be a couple of hours, I finally reached the bottom.

Getting down was very difficult, but my difficulties were far from over. I came down the mountain in a far different place from where I began up the mountain. Until that early morning excursion, I had not realized Shekou had a prison. Upon reaching the bottom, I found I had stumbled upon the outside walls of a prison compound. Perhaps it was only a common jail, I didn't really know. What I did know for sure was that I didn't want to be discovered by any of the few security guards which were on the property in the middle of the night. As quietly as I could, I sneaked around their facility. By the grace of God I was not noticed, and at about five o'clock in the morning, I finally arrived home. Because I hadn't taken a house key with me, I had to knock on the door to have Ruth let me in. You should understand this was a very real scare to her because we knew that if the police were ever going to instigate a raid, it would be in the middle of the night. With great trepidation she came to open the door for me. After quickly explaining to Ruth what had happened, I was never before so happy to crawl into my warm bed and sleep much of that day.

Windy and Pat shown with our disciple Jerry Zhang

God did use my adventure to give me clarity on the things I needed answers for. First, I was to continue studying Chinese, but soon would also teach English in order to get my necessary Chinese visa when my Chinese class ended. Secondly, I was to prepare to do Sunday morning, Sunday night and Thursday night meetings in our home, but discontinue directly assisting any other local foreign missionaries on a regular basis with their ministries. Ruth was to begin having a weekly women's meeting in order to give her a more pro-active role in our ministry. Also, Stephanie and the other girls did indeed need to stay home to continue their education with Ruth.

The end of our language study for the summer meant that our friend and fellow missionary Tim Obendorf would soon be returning to Oregon, so he asked if I could continue the ministries he had started in Shekou. Of course I took on both of these ministries gladly. The first bible study would be moved into our apartment on Thursdays. The second would be one which Ruth and I would both do together in the expat's gorgeous villa. Of course both were a blessing, but being more able to utilize Ruth's love and wisdom into our ministry was a plus for both our disciples and for her own emotional health. This would give Ruth more of a purpose for being there apart from her duties as a mom and wife. The fellowship with other Americans would prove to be a great blessing to us personally, but as I will explain later, it would play a significant role in our calling to facilitate foreign adoptions. Ruth would later begin meeting just with the expat women every other Monday. That meeting would be a great blessing to Ruth and the other ladies. Although it was meant to be a bible study, the spiritual and emotional support it gave each of them was priceless as they each were able to share their daily fears and struggles. One lady had a couple of daughters near our girls' age so they all got together on occasion.

Early in our contact with the expats, they told us about a church building which the Chinese had built for the expat community in Shekou. They wondered if it might be possible for me to become the pastor there. We told them we'd love to see it, so they borrowed the key. It was a gorgeous stone building with cathedral ceilings completely ready to hold services in. When they pursued getting permission to use it however, the answer was no. I don't recall why. So many pieces of our calling to China were falling into place though. We were beginning to see great fruit from how God was using us. Like all of the friends we had there in China, we were "nobodies" God was using for His glory. I want to take some time here to tell the stories of a few we came to know in our first year in China as an example of what I meant about us being nobodies God was using in great ways.

I mentioned earlier that Hilda was a 78 year old widow woman who because of her love for God and unreached people, felt called to China. She had just retired from 40 years of being a postal worker in the small town of Dubbo, New South Wales, Australia, northwest of Sydney. Hilda's spirit was quiet, sweet, joyful, and endearing; therefore she was much loved by everyone she met. The Chinese would flock to her for wisdom and guidance as she witnessed to them. She lived in one of the bare student dormitories at ShenDa. She climbed up and down four flights of stairs many times a day to her dorm. She washed her clothes by hand nearly every day just as the Chinese did. She ate very simple meals of rice porridge and sticky buns for breakfast, rice with veggies and pig intestine for lunch and dinner. She never, ever complained or seemed overly stressed by living there. Hilda was never able to speak Chinese well, but she was fluent in the language of selfless love which was understood clearly by all who had the pleasure of meeting her. She returned to Australia that first summer of 1988, but the impact of her short ministry in China on that university cannot be overstated.

Another single American, Pat Caspary, was in many ways the polar opposite of Hilda. Although their ministry styles were different, their zeal for God was much the same. Pat also endured the dorm life, he often made mention of how his life in China was so filthy from his "sterile" life in California. Pat was a self described "germaphobe", but he was perhaps the most bold and demonstrative of any Christian I have ever met. Before coming to China, Pat owned a grocery store, and was known for walking the streets and highways carrying a large wooden cross, witnessing and passing out tracts. He was a big believer in leaving gospel tracts everywhere he went, and was always a zealous minister of the gospel whether to one or many. I have never known anyone who produced a more interesting, diverse newsletter to his supporters about what he and others were doing in China. They were works of art! They were always full of pictures with humorous captions with no lengthy dialogue. Not long before his call to China, Pat suffered the devastating breakup of his marriage, but God had now given him a new purpose for his life. Later, God would also provide him a partner in life-long ministry. Pat married Windy, a smart, beautiful, humble, unassuming Chinese student at ShenDa. Windy was a fairly new believer with a quiet spirit, but when she translated for Pat, her passion and zeal for God meshed perfectly with Pat's own. It was clear to us God had given him Windy to fill not only his heart, but also to fulfill his ministry in Asia. Once they felt their ministry in China was complete, they moved to Macao for a period of time before later moving to South East Asia where they are to this day. Pat and Windy minister in and out of closed countries in support of making disciples and growing churches in those areas.

There was another American who came on campus to minister the gospel there. I'm choosing not to use her name because her ministry fell short of what we all thought she was capable of. Like Pat, you might say she came there with emotional baggage, but instead of excelling in ministry or joining in the efforts of other foreign missionaries, it seemed she fell into a carnal lifestyle. It was not long before she returned to America. I tell you this story only as one example of what happens to missionaries who have not put themselves under submission either to any in China or any in their home country. You might also argue she may not have truly been called, but acted on her own. I would not presume to say either way. I do know she was a great person who came with great intentions. However, given the demonic temptations and loneliness of missionary life, a missionary will not make it if they leave behind unresolved issues and then try to make it alone.

The end of August, we had a door open up with a worldwide missionary organization. They worked locally from a base in Hong Kong which, among their many other ministries, carried bibles into China. They were in need of place to store bibles temporarily until couriers were available to take larger quantities farther into China. We were excited to partner with this notable international organization to supply the need for God's Word in China. The fellowship we enjoyed with the various teams coming to our apartment was great. They were from a variety of countries, all having much zeal to make an effective difference in China's spiritual growth. I believe I mentioned before, we would do everything we could to further the gospel in China. Creating synergies with other ministries was part of that vision. As I'll disclose later in the book, these relationships would grow in power and effect all during our time in Asia. Allow me to take another quote from our August 1988 newsletter. "The body we share is the Lord's. The mind we share is the Lord's. The calling we share is the Lord's. The burden we share is the Lord's."

No hunger, No fullness

8

The Three-Self Patriotic Movement

Now I'd like to take time to interject some Chinese government and church history to help you gain a better understanding of the political and religious environment we found ourselves in at that time. If you are easily bored reading history, feel free to skip past the next five pages.

Beginning at a time in China when it was still under Imperial Rule, there were various denominations working to spread the Gospel in China. The countries of Great Britain, the United States, and others were importing many things from China, including Opium. The Chinese too often were themselves being corrupted by this highly addictive drug. From 1839 to 1842 the first Opium War was waged on the Chinese because they tried to put a stop to this trade militarily. The Chinese were no match for the foreign navies, so China was forced to give up areas of land in China as concession for their losses. In 1856 the second Opium war erupted, but again China lost and more of their land was given up. Within the cities of Shanghai, Canton, Macau and Hong Kong primarily, small, foreign colonies were established. This is in fact how Hong Kong came to be controlled by the British and similarly how Macao became Portuguese until 1997 and 1999 respectively. In the cities of Shanghai and Canton (now known as Guangzhou) there were fairly large areas which belonged to different foreign nations.

The missionary organizations as well as trade companies from various countries began to build their lavish homes, businesses and bases of operations in Hong Kong, Shanghai, Macau and Canton. All too often the Chinese people themselves would be barred from coming into these nice businesses. History tells us there were a few signs which read "No Dogs or Chinese Allowed", posted outside certain locations in Shanghai. As you can understand, this level of racism greatly inflamed the Chinese people against foreigners. News of this type of outrageous sign spread throughout China as did hatred of the pompous foreigners.

Sun Yat-Sen emerged as a revolutionary figure from Guangdong Province. He had for several years traveled to America and Europe trying to gain foreign support to assist him in overthrowing the Imperial rule in China. History characterizes him as a Christian, but this is widely disputed. Early on in his campaign, Sun befriended a Christian Chinese businessman known as Charlie Soong. Soong is a little known to most Americans, but he and his children were very influential figures in 20th century China.

Here's a little background on Charlie. As a boy he stowed away on a merchant ship bound for America. The Christian ship captain's family took him in. They paid for him to get a great education at Vanderbilt and Duke Universities in America. Nearly everyone in his life felt he should become a missionary and go back to China to preach, but Charlie had an eye for the college girls which led to much racial criticism. After being sent to China as a missionary near Shanghai, he was assigned the task of teaching Chinese children. Trouble was, he only spoke in a dialect used in his home on Hainan Island. He was greatly disillusioned with his missionary organization, but still seemed to have kept his faith. He abandoned his missions organization and began working with friends he had in the cotton industry back in America to produce clothing in Chinese factories. He opened many clothing factories in China and exported the clothes back to sell in the United States. As you might imagine, Charlie became extremely wealthy very fast. He then developed an interest in seeing China become a Democratic nation and prosper as America had done. This passion led to him meet Sun Yat-sen which led to Sun's marriage to Charlie's second daughter, Soong Ching-Ling who had graduated from an American university. It's believed by many that Sun put on the ruse of being a Christian in order to garner money from Charlie, and the wealthy in western nations so he could purchase weapons with which to overthrow the Chinese Imperial government. It was 1911 when rebellion rather accidently broke out against the Qing Dynasty. It was begun by a simple bar fight in central China. Sun Yat-Sen jumped in to provide weapons and motivational leadership to then step to the forefront as ruler over all of southern China.

Some years later, another leader named Chiang Kai-Shek married the third daughter of Charlie Soong who had also been educated in America. Soong Mei-ling acted against her parent's wishes just as her sister had done and married a non-Christian. Chiang came to power in 1925, again with the money and influence of the Soong family. Although Chiang's criminal history has been thoroughly white washed, it is well documented he had been a hit man of one of the largest Shanghai triad gangs before marrying and becoming Generalissimo of the army and the President of the Republic of China. Just like Sun Yat-Sen, he also put on the ruse of being a Christian to gain western sympathies. In addition, his sophisticated wife Mei-Ling, gave him powerful influence in the United States. Later, when the Japanese invaded China, their unbridled level of brutality was so horrific that the Japanese became, and to some small degree, still are, China's enemies. In fighting the Japanese, Chiang's power was greatly weakened during WW2.

    All this political brokenness, hatred of imperialist foreigners as well as their poverty readied the Chinese people to be drawn in by Mao Zi Deng and the socialist ideology which he'd learned in Vietnam. Such new ideas went against the deeply religious Chinese people who were known for their worship of Buddhism, Taoism, Hinduism, Confucius as well as approximately one million Christians. But based on the strength of his charisma and intelligent rhetoric, Mao won their hearts promising a better life for the poor. Once he amassed a huge, mostly peasant army, Mao pursued Chiang Kai-Shek all over China before finally driving him out. Chiang went on to set up his nationalist government in 1949 on the undeveloped island of Formosa, now known as Taiwan or the Republic of China. Chiang didn't run off empty handed however. He emptied as much gold and priceless ancient artifacts from Beijing, Shanghai and other locations as he could get his hands on. Since that time, the Chinese communist party claims that Taiwan and its riches belong to them. Because of Chiang and his wife who had been educated in the United States they were thought to be Christians, (again, a ruse) they gained the unwavering support of President Roosevelt and the great many powerful businessmen doing business with China at the time. The Times Media behemoth was a great help with propaganda. Thus to the American people, the Chiang's Republic of China was in no small way their great allie. From then till the present time, the United States has had an agreement to protect Taiwan from any Chinese takeover.

    Interestingly enough, Charlie Soong's daughter Soong Ching-Ling who was once married to the much older Sun Yat-Sen left China after Sun's death to travel to Berlin, Germany where she studied Marxism. She would later ascend to the number two position as Vice Chairman of the Chinese Communist Party under Chairman

Mao himself. As it all turned out, the family of this charming stowaway teenager taken in and educated by an American sea captain, played a key role in forming the last three governments of modern day China and Taiwan. Charlie and his wife, by most all accounts, had a very deep commitment to God. Therefore, I cannot help but think that had Charlie remained a Christian missionary, or had Charlie just kept his family away from politics, China's form of government, as well as our current global politics might today be completely different. If you would like to know more of the incredible story of Charlie Soong, I recommend you read "The Soong Dynasty" by Sterling Seagrave. It's a very powerful and incredibly well documented account of this part of Chinese history. This was the primary resource I used to write this portion of the book. This portion of history came up a few times in my conversations with students in China and they were very well informed about it.

So why tell you all that? To understand Christianity (and indeed global politics in general) in China, it is valuable today to know what has occurred there in this past century. Firstly, it is perhaps understandable for the Chinese to think of all influence by other countries as undesirable, since so much of what has happened to them has been questionable. Because they are a proud, highly intelligent and hard working people, they are slow to trust or be dependent on other governments. For many years they simply tried to eradicate westerners from China. Only in the last 50 years have they begun a long, calculated plan to take wild advantage of the west in order to successfully enrich themselves. Secondly, their approach to religion is based in atheism, but over time they began allowing various religious practices into their country, but only if they could control them. The minority groups in China are very resistant to CCP control. Therefore, there is continued conflict in those regions. When they see foreign or religious interference however, to be sure, they absolutely deal with it. Even though they have not been successful in eradicating religious "superstition", they stubbornly hope that over time they'll be successful.

Now to put a finer point on all this dialogue, I want to explain Christianity as it has existed in China for many years now. The Three-Self Patriotic Movement (TSPM), is under the auspices of the Religious Affairs Bureau and Public Affairs Bureau as I understand it. So the TSPM, as it is known, is the legal church in

China. To understand the name, I felt it needful to explain China's religious history with the western churches.

The TSPM, as its known, has three guiding principles: to be self-governing, self-supporting, and self-propagating. In other words, foreigners are to stay out of their religious affairs. We learned very quickly that there were four things which were illegal with regard to foreign Christians in China: water baptism, witnessing to anyone under the age of 18, public meetings, and speaking ill of the Chinese government or its actions. It is their government's intent that there be absolutely no foreigners playing an active role or influencing the operation of the churches in China. Each TSPM church congregation has a pastor and a Communist Party Secretary. The secretary is responsible for reading and approving all sermons which are to be delivered by the pastor to be certain there is nothing said which would be offensive to the Communist Party of China. Also, each church is often used for propagating information regarding local life in each community which the Party wants to communicate. You should know that bibles ARE printed in small numbers and distributed to Chinese believers, but only to those believers who are "registered members" of a TSPM church. Those registered Christians attending the TSPM churches number close to 40 million at this time. The much larger number of Christians (by some estimates 200 million) makes up the underground church and is reliant on bibles brought in by smugglers.

Now, on to the underground churches all across China where there is tremendous growth. Right now you might be asking "Why don't all the Christians in China simply go to the TSPM church instead of illegally meeting and seeking out illegally obtained bibles?" Well, there are several reasons. For one, they don't trust the government. They never know when a Chinese leader will decide that they are a problem and seek to oppress or "re-educate" them. Second, once they are listed as Christians, they seem to become second class citizens in the eyes of the Party. If there is a shortage of food due to flood or famine, it is reported they will be last on the list to get help. This in fact has occurred in some areas. Third, their careers, work opportunities, and other matters of importance in their daily lives are deeply compromised. Fourth, if they are lucky enough to get a bible, it is in an older translation (at least it was at that time) using old Chinese script, which younger people, have trouble reading. Bibles brought in by foreigners were new translations using simplified Chinese script. Sometimes English/Chinese New Testaments which were brought in which were popular with young people in China learning English. Fifth, the Chinese government has never actively allowed new churches to pop up in every community. Therefore, it is highly unlikely there is a TSPM church remotely near where they live. Enough history!

Our family was getting very excited to have visitors from home. Our first visitors were Bob and Aleta Hirschberg from the church Ruth and I attended when we lived in Arkansas City, Kansas. The Hirschbergs were an older couple who came not only to tell us hi and bring gifts from home, but were meeting some contacts deeper in China where Aleta's parents had been missionaries. It was great to see them. They made an arrangement between their contacts and us to begin funneling them large college level textbooks for advanced Christian study. I got permission to use a couple of them to start a Christian library for the believers in our area. In a later chapter I'll speak in detail about the library I set up.

When I retrace the steps we took, especially in those first months that moved us there, it seems surreal. And as I retell all the stories, my mind returns to that place and time. The feeling is

My mom and dad at the White Swan Hotel in Guangzhou

similar to the process of climbing a tall mountain. Midway, the climb yet above me looks like a small challenge, but looking back at where you were, it looks so far down you are tempted to fear falling. In climbing any mountain, day to day is similar in nature to our walk with God. With your eyes set on the peak, step by step will get you where you are supposed to go; no looking or turning back. What you experience along the way brings new and sometimes great difficulties, suffering, fights, distractions, and challenges. Learn from them like you would in climbing a mountain. And once you have conquered the one peak, rest, get your breath and ready yourself for the next one till your life on earth is done. *"Therefore, since we are surrounded by such a huge crowd of witnesses to the life of faith,* (No, they aren't watching you as you may have thought. They are witnesses to the greatness, goodness, mercy and faithfulness of God) *let us strip off every weight that slows us down, especially the sin that so easily trips us up. And let us run (climb) with endurance the race (mountain) God has set before us. We do this by keeping our eyes on Jesus, the champion who initiates and perfects our faith." Hebrews 12:1-2 NLT*

    Finally there came the day our family had waited for so long. My mom and dad were coming to visit. They were now retired and needed to make sure their baby granddaughters were happy and safe. They missed us very much, and no distance was too great to keep us from them. They arrived in early November 1988 to Hong Kong. We stayed there four days to let them rest and took them touring to our favorite spots in Hong Kong. We also applied for and obtained their visas to enter China as tourists. Once the visas were in hand, we led them on a trek to our home in China just a couple hours away. Mom and Dad had traveled a little since retiring. Just a couple of years earlier, they visited my brother at Mendenhall Air Force base in England where he and his family were stationed at the time. We took a few days to take them by bus to Guangzhou to see the sights there. On the trip there they got to witness a couple of interesting things. They saw rice being winnowed by hand and the Chinese version of road side restroom stops which were only trenches which we could squat over, cut into the dirt which channeled sewage to an open cesspool. The trenches were surrounded by 40" rock walls for "privacy". Before our roadside bathroom break however, Emily had "to go" bad. Momma Ruth did what she'd seen Chinese moms do in times such as these. She thought she should simply stick Emily's bottom out of the bus window for her to relieve herself. As soon as the bus driver saw in his side mirror a two year old white backside sticking out the window, he promptly hit the brakes to allow mom to take Emily to the bushes. My poor mom and dad weren't sure what to think. Life was so exciting in China!

The month we had with mom and dad Ryel was absolutely precious. The girls' reconnecting with grandma and grandpa was the highlight of our year. It was so good to have them come and see for themselves all of what we had experienced that first year. It was like the feeling you get when someone comes to help you push a car out of the road. You're struggling, and pushing so hard you don't know if you can make it, but once help shows up, it's perhaps as much a moral support as it is physical. We had missed them so much. Mom and dad greatly enjoyed being a part of every church service and bible study. Our disciples were also thrilled to meet them. The Chinese culture teaches young people to honor their elders, but our parents were shown even deeper love and care. It gave Ruth and me an even warmer bond with our flock of believers than we'd had previously.

Though in every letter she wrote to her parents, Ruth asked her mom and dad to come see us, but they never made it, so that hurt. A big part of the struggle of being on the mission field is the constant emptiness of missing everyone and not knowing for sure if they really care all that much. You get tempted to feel like you have been forgotten. Other than our parents, very few ever wrote us and most of our family and friends didn't support us financially. I mention all this, not out of resentment or to seek sympathy, but to give you insight as to the kind of real feelings which develop when you're so far from home. A prospective missionary has to be prepared to deal with this kind of disappointment. You must give your family and friends grace. Set your dependence and expectation on God and those close by you whom God has given you, otherwise bitterness sets in and your ministry is sidetracked and squelched.

To end this chapter, I am going to insert a clip from the end of our newsletter which was called "China Light", dated October, 1988. "Our health is good and God is faithful to protect our ministry. As people cross our path, I share God with them. We had a Chinese customs officer come to our home as a guest of a new convert of ours. I preached to him and his unbelief was broken down so that he put his faith in God. I'm just not too picky anymore. I made an agreement with God that evening in the park when I decided to go ahead and preach to the five police officers among the 140 other Chinese, that if He brings them to me; I'll preach the Gospel to them. It's up to Him to direct us, and be our shield and protection. He brought us here to preach, and God forbid I look for a basket to hide under. Pray for us! God is really bringing them to the Light. Never cease praying for us. Our local newspaper had an article which said that local authorities in our area would be cracking down on unregistered religious activity in August and September. *"Yet amid these things we are more than conquerors, and gain a surpassing victory through Him who loved us." Romans 8:37 Amplified.*

No sadness, No joy!

9

Puzzle Pieces

NOTE: THIS CHAPTER is not placed in this book chronologically. I determined that placing all these random pieces in the order in which they occurred would be utterly confusing. Therefore you'll notice many of these events spoken of are out of sequence with dates and names mentioned in other portions of the book which are chronological. Even in this chapter you may find the chronological order is in some cases a bit skewed.

For those of you who enjoy putting large jigsaw puzzles together, you understand that without a picture of the finished puzzle, it is very difficult to know exactly what it is you are creating. In the beginning, only the one who designed the puzzle knows. As we walk by faith in our Christian lives, we often don't have a clue as to the artwork God is creating from our daily walk and ministry with Him. With His direction and power, it will no doubt be beautiful. Especially in the beginning, we just don't know what it is. Like all great paintings, our walk of faith is wonderful from a distance. But I believe up close is when the intricate details are noticed. As is often mentioned, "The beauty is in the details". We know from scripture that He is the Potter and we are the clay. In my comparison here, He is the painter and our daily walk with Him becomes the painting. Some things we may never know. Some wounds suffered in the "fight" are lasting scars, indicated by dark strokes in the painting. We struggle to find meaning in them as they occur. Perhaps because of their strange, isolated circumstances and proximity to an intense war zone, the missionary will certainly deal with such battle wounds and questions of purpose. Near the end of the book I'll open up about the struggle I faced for a long time following our return from China. But for now though, I'm going to begin a new scene which lies within the puzzle of our overall ministry in China.

THE FIGHT - DIVINE PIECE #1: I'm going to now step away from recounting our ministry in a chronological format as I mentioned, so as to better relate piece by piece at least the outline of this large, but very detailed part of our puzzle. It actually begins with my 1986 mission trip to Quito, Ecuador where I was accompanied by many from our church. Chuck and Karen Case was one such couple which decided to go, except there was no room on the trip for Karen. That is, until Ruth, pregnant with our fourth daughter, decided to bow out and stay home with our three girls. While there, Chuck and Karen together fell in love with the people and culture. They had two sons, but had always wanted a daughter. They began inquiring about adoption and felt strongly God was directing them to move forward. Upon returning home, Karen began researching adoption agencies which could help them. Chuck, Karen and Karen's sister Deby (who was our good friend Deby Taylor) some months later began communicating with a lovely lady in Redmond, WA by the name of Sharin Moznette. Sharin operated an adoption ministry called "Open Arms". This ministry had expertise in foreign adoptions, particularly in India and Korea. Later, Sharin

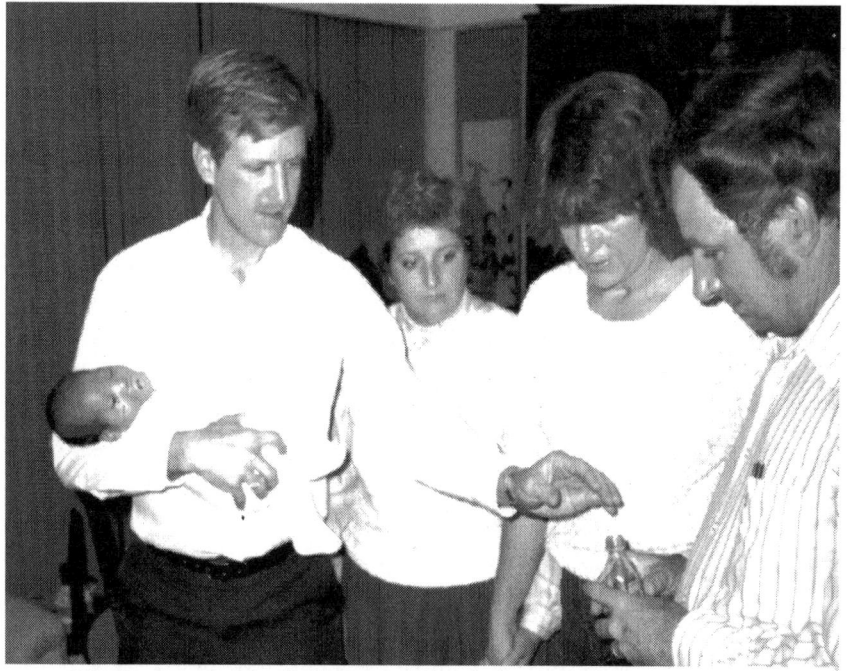

My first and only dedication of an adopted Chinese orphan

was to become my United States mentor and facilitator for the adoption ministry God would soon be leading us into. Had Ruth not stayed home, allowing Karen to go with her husband Chuck, my connection with Sharin might never have been realized.

DIVINE PIECE #2: Before I go further, I want you to recall the name Joann, from chapter three of this book. She was the realtor who sold Ruth and me our first home in Maize KS. You may remember that at the time of our calling to China, Joann said she believed God was going to use us in an adoption ministry. At the time, this had not even crossed our minds, but we thanked her, and "put it on a shelf" so to speak. We would not think about it again until 18 months later. Had Joann not received this dream and spoken it to us, we might not have been so certain about stepping out in faith to facilitate adoptions.

DIVINE PIECE #3: One of the couples who were a part of our expat bible study was a gentle unassuming couple named Elliot and Cathy. Elliot worked on an oil rig in the South China Sea for a drilling company based out of Louisiana. They were childless, but desperately wanted a baby. Elliot's General Manager there in China happened to be married to a Chinese-American lady. This lady was deeply empathetic to their plight and wanted to assist them in pursuing the adoption of a Chinese orphan. She happened to have relatives in Shanghai and with their help, secured a Chinese attorney who they thought would assist them. I dare not go into the sensitive details of their process, but in January of 1989 I performed my first baby dedication of Esther. This miracle baby was at a Shanghai hospital ready to be terminated because she was a second child. However, six hours before she was to be drowned, Esther was saved. She was a bit premature but healthy. After a while, she was adopted by Elliot and Cathy. Had Tim not introduced us to this couple and had they not pressed through a great trial to save Esther, we would not have been so encouraged to move toward adoption ministry by her miracle story.

DIVINE PIECE #4: In chapter six I introduced a young woman who was helping Ruth by the name of Sincere. She was a sad and burdened young woman. Her and her husband were not able to live together, because like nearly all Chinese couples, her husband worked for a government owned company which provided him a 12 person dorm room. This living situation was very common in China. It often took many years for an apartment to become available suitable for a married couple to live together. Since these couples were always living far from their immediate families, extra marital affairs were common place. Sincere had made Jesus her Savior and gotten water baptized, but she struggled with her husband and his affairs with other women. At one point in early 1989 they reconciled and began spending time together. Sincere became pregnant but again, soon questioned her husband's faithfulness. She remained with us as we counseled her to somehow keep the baby. At the age of about 30, Sincere had already had two abortions. Just as Ruth and I were praying about what could be done, totally out of the blue we received a letter from a childless Christian couple in the United States. They told us about their deep desire to have children, but could not. Then they asked if we could help them adopt. At that point we had no idea if it was possible, but we couldn't help asking ourselves 'what if Sincere having a baby she didn't want could be their answer? What if Joann's vision was starting to be fulfilled? We didn't know, but it seemed to us to be the beginning of SOMETHING. God directed Sincere to us not only for her salvation, but for the emphasis in our lives to continue pursuing our calling in saving many Chinese orphan children.

Question: Have you ever had God do something or take you in a direction even though things absolutely didn't turn out the way you thought they would? It's happened to us a few times in our lives, and that's what happened at this time. We wrote back to the couple who sent us the mysterious letter telling them about Sincere, and that we would begin researching the process of adoptions from China. We were never to get a response from them and they never contacted us again. A short time later, without our knowledge and after walking in on her husband with another woman, Sincere angrily went to the hospital for a third trimester saline abortion. We were devastated! It felt like getting an unexpected gut punch from your best friend that leaves you doubled over in pain. In her anger, Sincere spitefully exclaimed to her husband "It was a boy!" which you may know is the preferred gender for a Chinese couple since they were only allowed one child at that time. Filled with deep regret, Sincere described the terrible ordeal of aborting her six and one half month old baby to us. She endured 30 hours of labor, much of which she felt her baby writhing in pain inside her. After a week in the hospital, Sincere remained in our home for another two weeks for her recovery. Ruth nursed her back to health both physically and spiritually. Her Christian sisters from our fellowship prayed for and counseled her as well. Years later we learned Sincere divorced and remarried a Christian man near her home town in northern China and they had a beautiful baby. Though the road be very difficult and filled with land mines, God is good!

DIVINE PIECE #5: God used the unexplained letter to begin a conversation about adoptions from China. One of our disciples we were close to by the name of Harry had two aunts in his southeastern China home town of Zhanjiang. One was the director of the orphanage there, and another who was a midwife in her community. The midwife often secretly performed "illegal" deliveries of second children, who if taken to a hospital would be forcibly terminated. Harry agreed to accompany me to Zhanjiang in July of 1989 to visit his two aunts, and take a tour of the orphanage. He also agreed to stop off in the large city of Guangzhou to visit with officials at the orphanage there to see what we could learn about the process. Travelling by bus in China is inexpensive, but quite arduous. We made our way to Guangzhou, found the orphanage and just walked in to see if someone could take the time to talk to us. A nice lady sat with us and freely allowed us to ask questions. She mentioned that in the last ten years, they had completed a total of ten adoptions. They were all done through attorneys in China and the USA and all of the couples were 35 years old or older, childless, proved they were unable to have children and each couple was of Chinese descent. To say the least, that was pretty disheartening. We still asked if she could provide us with a list of all the requirements and paperwork needed if a US citizen was to apply for an adoption, which she happily provided.

In the evening we began the long trip to Zhanjiang to meet with the two aunts. To break up all the details of the trip, I want to tell you of a funny incident I had while on the nearly all night bus trip to Zhanjiang. The bus we rode on was your typical school bus, with the same style of bench seat having an open space between the seat and the bottom of the seat back. At about 1:00AM I was startled awake by the guy behind me wiggling his toes against my rear-end. I sat there trying to figure out if I should do something or say something, but then he stopped. It wasn't long before he started again for several more minutes. This time I was hearing a chuckle between him and his buddy sitting with him. It went on like this for what seemed like an hour: tickle/pause, tickle/pause, and tickle/pause. During our time in China, we rode buses many hundreds of times, but I'd never had any problem. Our fellow passengers were usually students, professionals, etc. On this trip however I was going through a very rural area with what were mostly poorly uneducated farmers. "Guilow" (foreign devil) was what we often heard when we were among these people. I guess I endured it so long he finally got bored and stopped.

When we arrived in Zhanjiang in July 1989 we first met with the midwife. She was nice but nervous about doing anything risky with foreigners. I know now it would not have been possible to adopt any babies through her anyway. The aunt overseeing the orphanage was more accommodating. We discussed what we learned in Guangzhou and took a tour of her facility. I'm sure they were doing the very best they could with what they had, but they had so little. Their building, furniture, play area, and equipment to care for the children could have easily been available in 17th century Europe. One child was tied to its potty chair. The ones who couldn't walk because of disability had very rudimentary, homemade wheeled carts. It was eye-opening and difficult for me to keep from crying. The director set me up a meeting with the head official of the area's Civil Affairs Bureau, which I later learned was a primary local contact for any orphanage. If an adoption didn't meet their scrutiny, it went nowhere. This particular official believed it would be very possible for me to start doing adoptions there. I only needed to send them all the proper paperwork. We returned to Shekou with a more realistic picture of the challenges we would face moving forward.

DIVINE PIECE #6: Let me get back on track with the puzzle God was putting together. The painting He was creating included a middle aged couple living in Hong Kong who ministered full time with YWAM. I knew of them through my number one contact in Hong Kong Alvin Cobb. In fact, on a

The precious family I met on the train traveling to the Changsha orphanage

couple of occasions we stayed in their apartment while they were out of the country, but didn't really know them or what they had been doing with YWAM. I learned in mid 1989 that Mick Marshall had been communicating with an orphanage in Changsha, China for the purpose of doing adoptions. I became aware of this from a wonderful German man who was studying at Shenzhen University and living on campus with his wife. I met them when they began attending our Sunday morning bible meetings. This German couple began the process of adopting a Chinese orphan from Changsha through Mick, a process which they completed in late 1989. No doubt Mick and the YWAM organization went on to complete many adoptions in China, but I don't have direct knowledge of how many or where else they facilitated them. I do not want anyone to be misled by my book into thinking I was the only one God was using to save these babies.

So much was happening and further encouraging us to continue pursuing this ministry of facilitating adoptions, all the while I was teaching English three days a week at Shenzhen University and doing church and bible studies three times a week. After being asked to leave Shenzhen University in the fall 1989 due to my ministry activity, I went to two local area technical/trade schools to teach conversational English. These teaching positions provided me with a "reason to be there" and therefore a 6 month work visa for me and my family.

DIVINE PIECE #7: In June of 1989 Ruth's best friends Deby Taylor and Cindy Bogle brought several of their family members to visit us. Their coming was a great encouragement to our family, but especially Ruth. Deby gave me details about Karen and Chuck going through Open Arms for their Ecuador adoption. I later connected with Sharin Moznette of Open Arms adoption ministry and Sharin and I began discussing possibilities for adoptions from China. That same summer I continued communication with Sharin and we decided I should make direct contact with orphanages I knew to be doing adoptions, such as the one Mick Marshall was working with in Changsha. Changsha is famous as being very near the birthplace of Chairman Mao. Sharin graciously promised to pay my expenses, since I could not afford to finance the trip on my own. I booked a night train to Changsha, but this time I traveled alone to reduce expenses. I did not know any one there, but by faith I went.

THE GLORY - DIVINE PIECE #8: Soon after boarding the train I met a couple of young American children. After a short conversation I asked them to introduce me to their parents. We hit it off right away. They were from Tulsa, OK working as English teachers placed by an organization ran by Dwyatt Gantt. You might remember me talking about Dwyatt earlier in the book when Ruth and I made our first 10 day trip to China. Since they were from Tulsa, I asked them if they happened to know Mike and Jackie Farrell, whom I also mentioned earlier in this book in connection to our first trip. Yes! They exclaimed. "The Farrells are our good friends!" The way in which God works when you by faith put your life entirely in His hands is so wonderful to experience.

As you might imagine, we talked all evening about ministry in China, much like you would reminisce with a best friend you hadn't seen for many years. It turned out they were travelling back to Changsha where they had been teaching English. Of course I detailed to them the reason for my trip, to which they replied that one of their disciples worked at the orphanage in Changsha and that they would certainly introduce us. Upon my visit, I found this orphanage was well run and cared for more orphans than what I'd seen on my previous trip. I was to learn that adoptions would be a great benefit financially to the orphanages which did them. The connection I made with this orphanage was strong. In fact, over the next couple of years, very many of the orphans I facilitated adoptions for were from there. But that day after my tour and continued research of the process, they began telling me about a couple of other cities they knew of which were also working with foreigners. The ones they recommended were Wuxi and Changzhou a number of miles west of Shanghai. It was going to add many more hours to my trip on the train, but I strongly felt led to go. It was my first of several visits to the magnificent city of Shanghai. I found my disciple Jerry Zhang's family who welcomed me to stay the night with them before getting on a bus to Changzhou the next day. The day I arrived was a major holiday in China so I didn't even know if I'd be able to speak with anyone.

I wandered around the grounds of the orphanage for a while before I was approached by someone who worked there. They took me to an office where I spoke briefly to the co-director. There was no translator, so our communication was not great, but said he would set me up a meeting with their director. I found a cheap hotel to stay in and arrived back the next day at the appointed time. They had not done any foreign adoptions, but indicated they wanted to. The director then began speaking of us buying them a new vehicle in exchange for an adoption. He told us of such an orphanage up the road in Wuxi which had received one from an organization based in Montreal, Canada. To my knowledge, this organization was the very first one to facilitate adoptions from China, but again, I don't know how many or from where in China other than Wuxi they did them. Of course I was very intimidated by the Director's presumptuous demand. It was something like learning the house you thought you were going to buy for $40,000 was actually going to end up costing you $100,000. I tried to remain calm and not fall out of my chair. I cordially continued the conversation, ever so slowly steering him away from the vehicle he dreamed of, until we finally got down to discussing the nuts and bolts of the required paperwork needed to do our first adoption. By the time I left, we had begun a relationship which would lead to very many adoptions. Some months later, we did provide them a new Toyota minivan for them to use as medical emergency transport for their staff and children. When I got back home, I contacted Sharin. We were now getting quite excited, but a bit nervous. She had some families who were at varying stages with their adoption paperwork, so the ministry had already begun taking shape. So now I want to return to the events which took place in a more chronological sequence. I will return to the adoption ministry of Open Arms in chapter 11.

No struggle, No strength!

10

The Testing of Our Faith

Our January 1989 newsletter ended with these words: "Another semester of my Chinese study comes to a close and I'm seeking God for direction for studying next term. My speaking ability continues to improve, but it's a long hard road. Pray for all the new Christians. We are really seeking God for more to be baptized in the Holy Spirit (ten so far this month). Also pray for God to continue working through us and our disciples to witness and minister in boldness and power."

Ruth wrote in this same letter: "For Christmas I prayed that my helper Sincere would become a Christian. On Christmas day she and her husband joined us for Christmas dinner and later asked me if she could come back the next day to become a Christian. I said today is the day of salvation. I want to show you the way to Jesus today! So we went in to another room and she accepted Jesus as her Lord and Savior. She immediately said she felt like a changed woman. She had been having bad dreams, but the next day she said she slept soundly the previous night. Praise God!"

Following Chinese New Year in February, 1989 dear friends planned a four day retreat to a lovely lake and park in Zhaoqing with Chinese Christians who had not left the area to go back to their family homes. They invited us and any of our disciples who remained in the area to join them. It was a great time of rest, teaching the word and exploration of the beautiful area. Altogether, there were about 36 of us. We would travel by train from Shenzhen to Guangzhou, then transfer to the train to Zhaoqing. While waiting among the massive crowd of two thousand or more in the middle of the huge cement staging area in front of the train station, we had made a formation you could liken to what the American settlers did when they circled their covered wagons to protect themselves. In our group there were several children, and all our luggage in the middle. To say the least, we were a novelty! Within minutes we had a crowd around us in excess of 100 expressionless, Chinese who all had their eyes fixed on us and especially our playful children. Since none of them were trying to practice their English with us, we guessed they were mostly common folk from the countryside. By their attention, we guessed they had very rarely, if ever seen white kids. For us it was quite unnerving. After about 15 minutes, Ruth began to tire of our awkward situation and decided to have some fun. Without warning or reason, Ruth without saying a word quickly turned, looked up and pointed into the sky to her left as if something strange had just happened. Our group and all of the Chinese surrounding us suddenly turned and looked off to see what Ruth was pointing at, which of course was nothing at all. Realizing what she was doing, we all chuckled to ourselves. Fifteen seconds or so later, Ruth did it again, but in the opposite direction. Again, everyone looked but nothing was said. We chuckled even more, but still the Chinese surrounding us remained expressionless and refocused on us the entire time we were there. For the next 45 minutes or so we all just sat and stood out there like fish in a fish bowl, waiting for our time to board the train.

When we arrived in Zhaoqing (pronounced Jow ching) excited to see the beautifully clear finger-lakes with adjoining caves Zhaoqing was famous for. First of course we had to get checked into our hotel. One of the disciples had been put in charge of getting us rooms, but when we arrived, the deal fell through and our group of 36 was stranded without lodging. We were all tired and hungry, so several of our disciples got busy with the difficult task of searching for a place to stay which was affordable. One of them found a hotel which had enough empty rooms to accommodate all of us and it was definitely affordable; only ninety cents per night, per room! So in your mind's eye perhaps you can try to imagine the quality of a room that inexpensive. Whatever it is you imagine, it probably is better than the one we experienced. This seemingly ancient hotel appeared never to have been painted since it opened in the 1800s (just guessing). The ceilings were approximately 12 to 14 feet high. The open windows were very tall and unadorned. The walls and ceilings in every room were largely covered in green and black mold. Each floor had huge, very nasty men's and women's bathrooms with the traditional squatty potties and sloppy wet floors. All the bathrooms, halls and rooms were fully stocked with very large rats which enjoyed splashing through the standing water in the bathrooms even more than scurrying down the halls. They would then proceed to go under the doors to our rooms before disappearing into a gaping hole in the wall to munch on who knows what. As I recall it now, perhaps that's why there were seemingly no roaches crawling around; the rats kept them in check. Just a guess though.

In southeast China that time of year it is cool and very, very humid. While living in China we had witnessed the humidity this time of year to be 100% for several days without it ever raining and it was nearly that during our time in Zhaoqing. Therefore you might imagine the other grand feature of this hotel: hoards of mosquitoes. Thankfully each room came with mosquito nets. We also brought our "PifPaf" warmers which used a small paper insect repellent wafer to rid mosquitoes from a room. Ruth and I slept very well that night because at least the beds were clean and very comfortable. The room actually had feather beds and pillows. If you're familiar with adventurous children, you might imagine how absolutely wonderful all the kids thought this hotel was. It was more like a jungle safari than a hotel.

The next morning we found a restaurant which offered Chinese Dim Sum (Cantonese for small snacks) which was the very best Ruth and I have eaten ever. Next to that restaurant was a hotel we were fortunate to get rooms at for all of us; a huge improvement, but still only costing us eight dollars per night. Those four days of close fellowship were some of the most enjoyable days of all our lives in China or the United States. We were treated with boat rides into local caves, hiking through a lush forest, exotic trees and flora, as well as waterfalls with intimate, crystal clear pools. The excitement didn't end however until we headed home.

After returning by train to Guangzhou, again we found ourselves back at the Guangzhou train station, this time waiting on benches inside the train station for our train to depart for Shenzhen. As our departure grew close, the crowds grew exponentially to the point that all you could do was stand sandwiched among the masses. This rather sudden influx of people left us wondering exactly where all our four children were. We nervously called out the names of the ones who from boredom, ran off in search of further adventures. They dutifully began to push their way through the sea of legs and luggage to join us; all except our three year old Emily. Where was Emily? No one knew where she was. We all began calling her name just as the departure of our train was announced over the intercom. We found ourselves being pushed along with all our bags and other children by what seemed like thousands of Chinese; all wanting to board the train we were going to board. The closer we got to the train the more frantic we became. All 35 of us were shouting Emily's name trying to be heard above the chaotic noise of the immense crowd which filled the cavernous train station. Within two minutes of being pushed onto the train, we heard a loud voice calling out in Chinese- "she's here!" We looked to see a young Chinese PSB police officer holding Emily above his head shouting as loudly as he could, all the while pushing through the crowd to reach us before the train doors closed. What a relief! Anyone who has ever lost a child in a crowd for any length of time knows these indescribable feelings of horror. We learned later from our Chinese friends that the policeman had spotted Emily hiding behind a large post, willfully and playfully not responding to our frantic calls for her. That little stinker!!

Quote from our February 1989 newsletter: "We want to choose our words carefully so as to neither bore you nor exaggerate. Stories come so often from this intriguing mission field but occasionally we read the accounts other missionaries tell and understand these stories are actually events they only knew about, not ones they were actually a part of. Life as a missionary is often just ordinary life in another place." The third world circumstances are of course different and more difficult, but even the novel becomes mundane after awhile, but then the Fight or the Glory comes. I'm going to relate a couple of stories which were truly times of great difficulty. These were four of our most brutal sufferings and fights up to that time, followed by God showing up and bringing Glory to His name.

THE FIGHT - In chapter two I spoke of our friend Jimmy Gafford. He was our very first contact in going on our initial ten day trip to Hong Kong. As I mentioned before, he was an American Assembly of God missionary from Lubbock, Texas working for China Radio in Hong Kong. Ruth and I were committed to synergistic ministry relationships. Whenever possible we continued to work in any way we could with everyone God led us to. Jimmy was often smuggling bibles into China which were sent to believers in underground home fellowships all over China. Jimmy approached me to assist him with a very large number of bibles and Christian study books which needed to be boxed up and shipped out to the province of Henan from the Shenzhen train station. This operation had been tried from the somewhat easier location of Guangzhou, but never from the Shenzhen station, which was known for its tighter security. Besides this, Jimmy was not well familiarized with the details of the shipping process in Shenzhen. His need was for one or two of our Chinese disciples who was bold and smart enough to succeed in handling this shipment for him. My first choice was my disciple Mr. Y but I really did not want to put him in such a dangerous position. I was afraid he'd feel obligated to do it because of our relationship. If discovered, I could only imagine the suffering and jail time which could ensue. So I first approached another disciple who quickly declined, but Mr. Y enthusiastically said yes. Mr. Y realized the great physical demands of the operation, so he enlisted one other disciple of ours, Roland. Jimmy, Mr. Y, Roland and I gathered up over 1200 bibles and other materials from various locations in Shenzhen, went to a hotel room and packed them into 11 large boxes. I dropped Mr. Y off at the shipping area of the train station and waited at a distance to witness what was about to occur. They were nearly finished with all the forms which needed to be filled out in triplicate for each box when a customs officer came over to open and check one of the boxes. Mr. Y gave him a box he had specifically packed with legal materials on top. The officer looked through the entire box however and found the bibles and books which did not have the required stamp indicating they were printed in China, therefore illegal. But, instead of arresting Mr. Y or even going through the other boxes, he simply told Mr. Y he needed to move them out of the shipping area. After assisting Mr. Y with the move back to a hotel room, we made plans for the following day when I would not be needed but Mr. Y would prepare a different "sample box" containing all legal books and go to a different customs officer. I didn't hear from them for two days even though I told Mr. Y and Roland to contact me as soon as the bibles were shipped. I was deep in prayer and asked everyone I knew to pray. In our February 1989 newsletter I mentioned that if any of our supporters were feeling a need to pray January 24th through the 26th there was a reason, and I explained the whole ordeal. My mind was saying they're in serious trouble but my heart kept faith. I finally got word that because the same customs officer was on duty, Jimmy just helped Mr. Y load the boxes into a van they rented and took them up to Guangzhou leaving Roland behind. Jimmy was not able to assist Mr. Y at the train station there so it was all up to Mr. Y to wait in the rain outside with a peasant helper for four hours doing his best to keep all those boxes dry. His box strapping tool got stolen and the customs officer made mistakes on the forms so he ran back out to Jimmy for more money.

THE GLORY - It was 10:30pm before Mr. Y was finished, but the boxes were shipped and no arrests were made hallelujah! At one point Mr. Y told me he was so exhausted, he cried out to God, "Where are you God? I need you!" When Mr. Y finally emerged from the shipping area Jimmy was said to have 'danced for joy'. Mr. Y finally got back to me, and we were so glad to see each other. Then he exclaimed "let's do that again!" As I wrote in our newsletter, Mr. Y said "I learned not to be so self confident and more God confident. I myself learned to trust the peace in my heart more than the torment in my mind."

Erika and Emily were in Chinese Preschool/Kindergarten their first semester, but after seeing how much they were suffering there, we decided it wasn't healthy for them and put them back into home school with Stephanie. Later that year we pulled Adrianne out as well. The constant teasing, hair pulling and confusion with the language was taking its toll on her as well. We loved all the Chinese songs and dances she brought home to entertain our family with, but her emotional stability was far more important.

No storm, No peace!

11

The Battle Rages

THE FIGHT - We made a run to Hong Kong to pick up our support check to find once again that it hadn't come. So again we were somewhat stuck in Hong Kong with bills to pay and food to buy but no money. We called our friend Deby to inquire when the check was sent. "It should be there soon" she said, but she had more bad news than just that. Deby informed us the couple who rented our beautiful home at 301 Dover in Valley Center had taken off owing us two months' rent. Our friends went in to discover the place was a mess and the refrigerator had quit working and could not be fixed. Also, all the nice furniture we left in the house for them to use was gone: our sofa and love seat, coffee table, our formal dining room set, our breakfast dining set, an upright piano as well as the complete bedroom set I gave Ruth as a wedding gift. From the attic they even took our five gallon glass jug half full of pennies and a special hand-made quilt given to us as a wedding gift by Ruth's mom. When someone at the church reported it to the police, they gave them no assistance except to write a report. They thought the couple had moved out of state and there was nothing they could do. We got word that our church was so angry they wanted to hunt them down for a good old tar, feather and railing (joking). I won't lie- it was a terrible blow to our emotions. The Holy Spirit comforted us and reminded us *"We accept joyfully the seizure of our property, knowing that we have for ourselves a better possession and an abiding one." Hebrews 10:34* We continued to lose more and more of this world, but continued to gain more and more of Christ and His Kingdom. Our treasures on earth may quickly fade, but our treasure in heaven grows daily.

THE GLORY - Cindy Bogle and many from our church pitched in by doing a lot of cleaning and painting. They replaced the refrigerator and also found another renter within about a month. As we left the telephone office from where we made our international call, we were simply dumbstruck. But the church and discipleship ministry God gave us was bearing good fruit. The opportunity to begin facilitating adoptions was absolutely taking shape. Our family was thriving more than ever before. The stability of getting our six month Chinese work visas so that we could continue ministering in China was provided by a teaching contract at Shenzhen University. But as the title of this book states, along with basically every story in the bible illustrates, with glorious blessing and victory from God come times of suffering, testing and trial.

"God will make a way, where there seems to be no way" as the song so perfectly puts it. Returning back to where I left off, we needed money, our family was hungry and we had less than two dollars to our name. We dropped by our friends from Pittsburg, Scott and Tina Marcassi's home to rest a bit and to let our girls play together with theirs. They could tell we were hurting so we told them our circumstances. Even though they were running low on food and funds themselves, Tina began loading up a box of food for us and they gave us $40. We returned home with faith that our God would supply our needs. The next day with no expectation of it, some bible couriers left us about $70. The day after that one of our dear disciples, Karen gave us $25 and John and Carol from our American ex-pat bible study gave us another $70 and dropped off several bags and a full box of groceries. Ruth's parents sent us $100 and the church in Ark City Kansas sent us $45. My mentor in Hong Kong, Alvin Cobb, gave us $140. When our support check finally did come, it was the largest amount we'd gotten in the year we'd been there. It was a blessing so big we could not contain it as scripture puts it. It was only a few days before our friends in Kansas found a family with two children to rent our house. They attended a church there in Valley Center, so that was more encouragement.

Another joy I want to share is not in reference to the fight I previously described, but it is something wonderful I discovered in that same month. I'll simply share a quote from a letter I wrote to my parents on March 11, 1989. "I got a precious letter from a former AT&T co-worker by the name of Randy Schroeder. This was the only communication I'd ever received from him or anyone else I'd worked with at AT&T, but it was beautiful. He'd become a Christian! What a precious testimony he had. God used his mother, the 700 Club and others like me and my missionary journey, to bring him into salvation and obedience to Christ. To take this smart, prideful, selfish, foul mouthed, good looking young single man and turn him into a tender baby Christian with an 'overwhelming hunger for God's Word and Spirit filled books' as he put it, is a great miracle indeed."

There are others who watched us and our "crazy" obedience who to the glory of God, were impacted, including my brother Rick's amazing story which I told in chapter four of this book. The other story I want to mention at this time is the effect our mission call had on my dad. I was raised in the local Methodist Church. My dad's childhood and adulthood were extremely difficult but he went to a Salvation Army altar and received Christ when he was young. He suffered all of his life with grand mall seizures due to a brain injury he sustained when getting himself into in a drunken fight at the age of 18. In his 30's he was given powerful, new on the market drugs but told he'd still likely die by the age of 40. Since joining our local Methodist church in Ark City, Kansas, dad led a moral life and quite faithfully attended our church with his young family. He served the church as a Cub Scout leader and in other ways. He was a kind, patient man who was proud of and dearly loved his beautiful wife and two boys with all his heart. Later as an adult however he found it easy to skip church, but mom remained faithful; working tirelessly in church ministry in many ways throughout her life. Dad was never one to study the bible, but when God called me to the mission field; it rocked his world and challenged his faith. He began regularly reading the bible, praying, attending Sunday School, church and even attended an evening mid-week bible study. For the first time in his life he was hungry for the things of God. The point I want to drive home is this- your life and the way in which you obey God are a powerful part of your testimony. It is visible and real to everyone who witnesses it. So let your light shine by the way you obey and serve God.

THE FIGHT – I mentioned in the previous chapters a young disciple with the English name Roland. In the middle of March I was informed that Roland had been interrogated by agents of the Religious Affairs Bureau. The Religious Affairs Bureau is the national policing agency of the Communist Party which conducts investigations and makes arrests of those they find guilty of illegal religious activity. What I'm about to share was the first evidence that the Religious Affairs Bureau had begun what was to be a very long investigation of our ministry. Evidently these agents were tracking people who came and went from our meetings. Perhaps it was also the result of police "spies" in our meetings. The agents interrogated Roland because they tapped his parent's phone and recorded a call from a visiting brother in Christ, Hodge Hadley, a bible courier from Indiana who'd come with a group on their own to China. He first made contact with SC. He, along with us and our disciples were asked to join him at a Shenzhen hotel for a time of worship and ministry. Fifty-one from our number attended and it was a very sweet time of fellowship. Hodge was charismatic and bold, but naive of the negative impact his open communication

All our friends from Valley Center who visited us.

could have for those underground Christians he connected with. He discussed all the ministries he was involved in over a public phone also mentioning what Mr. Y had been doing. I blamed myself to an extent, since I allowed Hodge access to our meetings and therefore, to our disciples. Because of Hodge's zeal, he was able to draw in a few of my most zealous disciples to utilize them in his short term ministry. As they interrogated Roland, it was evident that Mr. Y, and the underground church in Shenzhen as well as Shekou, were the real targets. They did not arrest Roland, mainly due to the fact that his father was an important business man and fairly high member of the Communist Party. Mr. Y was not fearful, but we both felt it best that he travel back to his family home and just disappear for awhile. He mentioned that he'd heard about an underground church he wanted to visit to learn all God was doing there. Once he arrived in the village he found a very large underground church led by an 85 year old man. This small village pastor led a house fellowship which numbered over 1700 in this remote village and surrounding mountainous area. When Mr. Y arrived he quickly located many of their fellowship, and exchanged testimonies of God's goodness. When he finally made contact with the aged pastor he learned more about this pastor's successful ministry, and also his needs. This somewhat disabled pastor would be assisted by a couple of his helpers up into the mountains to different villages to minister the gospel every week. There were only about 80 bibles in their entire fellowship, which they shared by passing them from one Christian family to another. Because of their great poverty, they had need of clothing as well. When Mr. Y returned to us a couple of weeks later, he was more spiritually charged with zeal for the Lord than ever before. His testimony to our fellowship of what he'd experienced charged all of us as well. We later sat down with Mr. Y and worked out a plan to obtain the bibles and clothing we'd need to take them. We would later take them a great many bibles and articles of clothing collected by Ruth and her expat ladies group. We prepared and made the trip back to the countryside village. At about this same time Mr. Y was called upon to make another large shipment of 10 boxes and 45 small parcels of bibles and teaching materials into China for China Radio ministry.

In April we were informed of an article published by Shenzhen University (the school Ruth and I taught at) saying that all foreign teachers and students who were preaching the gospel at the university are being investigated and not to associate with them. At about the same time I was informed by the Foreign Affairs office at the university that by request of the students, my English class was being cancelled. When I asked why, I was told I was too hard on them because I required them to show up for class- at least most of the time. A couple of my other classes were cancelled for the same reason soon after. You may be as shocked as I was to learn that many of the students were carrying more than 30 hours of class per week. I even knew of one who had 50 scheduled hours a week. The unwritten rule was that teachers were not supposed to lower their grade simply for not being there or completing their assignments. How foolish of me to think otherwise? ☺ But after visiting with some of my students, I was told by them they all signed the review of my teaching and stated I was an excellent teacher. They all started a petition to get me reinstated but to no avail. So it seemed the office lied to me. I can only conclude they must have cancelled me due to my religious activity. By the way, perhaps you're wondering how much money I made teaching English as a second language for three hours an evening, three to four days a week? $100 - $140 a month. The real benefit of course was building personal relationships with the students, and obtaining six month work visas for my family.

In April of 1989 the Tiananmen student and teacher demonstrations began in large cities across the country. They were trying to get the government to allow freedom of the press. They'd grown weary of all the news being used as a propaganda arm of the Communist Party. Of course we now know the deadly retribution which soon came because of their effort. It makes me wonder if Americans as a whole will ever grow weary and angry of the propaganda and infringement of our first amendment rights we are faced with now in the USA. I will finish this chapter with a quote from Ruth in our April newsletter: "We've experienced problems with a few of our disciples who are single and being drawn into sexual sin. They want to continue "ministering" thinking it's between them and God. These people are setting bad examples for the new converts. Please pray for them to become truly repentant and turn from evil.

No discipline, No disciple!

12

Tiananmen Harvest

Trip to baptize at local duck pond.

THE FIGHT - When a missionary goes into a tremendous mission field where people you're ministering to are SO hungry for God and sharing the gospel is so exciting, that missionary needs to understand there will not be an unending flow of converts. Their ministry will go through cycles; seasonal changes. In one season miracles are happening nearly every week. Your meetings are overflowing with converts, but then perhaps persecution comes and the flow is interrupted. Persecution often itself produces a harvest such as it did with us in Beijing, June of 1989. But if not persecution, maybe it's just an unexplained interruption. Perhaps it may be one of testing the missionary's faith, such as an interruption of funding or some type of injury to their precious family. Maybe more often, the next season may be one of heavy feeding and watering, so deeper spiritual growth in the disciples and even in the life of the missionary and his disciples. The point I'm attempting to make is when seasons change from glory to what seems dull or difficult, do not be discouraged. The young missionary wants to believe that victory continues to follow victory after victory, but it does not. If you are doing what God called you to do, where He called you to do it- simply be strong and persevere. There's no need to question God's work in you or your ministry. Simply seek God in humility and rely on his grace.

Let me now insert a quote from my May 1989 newsletter when I was feeling relatively dry and unfruitful: "God lifted my spirit the other day by reminding me of all the mighty men of God, and how they also had dry, doubtful times, defeated times, weak times mixed in with their times of victory. Many of them had decades of waiting. God's word to my heart was that they all had one thing in common. They all remained faithful!"

THE GLORY – One way to be refreshed is to hear testimonies of those you're ministering to. One evening we asked who wanted to share their testimony. Our precious disciples went on for one and a half beautiful hours. Here are four of them: Dr. Wanda confirmed the healing of two cancerous lumps she had from which she felt she was healed of a couple of weeks earlier. Wanda also told us about a patient she bumped into in the hall of the hospital who had been hiccupping non-stop for six days. Another doctor had just told her there was nothing they could do to help her so she was on her way home. So Wanda asked if she would like her to pray for healing. She said yes, so Wanda prayed and immediately the hiccups stopped. She learned later that the hiccups hadn't returned in the two weeks since.

Twenty-two year old Karen told us about the chronic stomach pain she'd had for as long as she remembered, until she became a Christian. A spirit filled disciple of ours prayed for her healing and the pain immediately stopped and never returned.

Jane testified she was tasked with organizing and funding all her high school political science classes to go on a field trip to Guangzhou. She was very anxious for a while until she realized she should put her faith in God. Then at nearly the last minute Jane saw God provide a large bus and the $150 she needed for the trip.

Mr. Y talked about his second trip he took to a small community (which I mentioned earlier in the book) in a remote part of Guangdong province. Mr. Y took 120 full bibles, 125 New Testaments and several hundred tracts and study helps. During a bus transfer, he was stopped and questioned by a policeman about all the large bags. The policeman looked inside them and walked him to the police station where Mr. Y was given over to one of the police officials. After he looked through all of them, the man questioned him about it. God gave Mr. Y a supernatural peace and he simply told the officer the truth about taking them to poor peasant Christians in the countryside. Without hesitation, the officer released him without even writing down his name. When Mr. Y reached his destination to distribute the bibles, it still meant that there would only be one bible for every 20 Christians in their church. While there, Mr. Y had the opportunity to pray for some non-Christians who were sick. When he prayed for one boy who had a condition which caused him to drool and his legs to shake constantly, God touched him and the boy's symptoms stopped. A crowd started to gather as word quickly spread, but the symptoms returned later, so Mr. Y prayed again. Again, all the symptoms stopped, but then returned. The crowd had become quite substantial by that time. Mr. Y prayed a third time and the symptoms stopped and never returned. The entire crowd bowed to their knees worshipping Mr. Y. He was stunned and quickly had to call on them to stop, "It was the almighty God who did this, not me!"

THE SNARES – We were contacted by one of our friends from the Valley Center Kansas church who felt in her spirit that she needed to warn us about someone we would soon meet. Didn't know who she was referring to exactly, but took her warning seriously. Our ministry was now on the government's radar, so getting a work visa from Shenzhen University was becoming impossible. I began exploring other options that were coming to light. The first was a job was with a Canadian joint venture company called Tong Guang - aka "Nortel" a joint Chinese venture with Northern Telecom. Having worked in the telecom industry with Southwestern Bell, I was somewhat familiar with this company and their equipment. They were particularly well known for their central office digital switch, PBX systems and key phone business equipment. They needed someone to travel to various parts of China as needed and oversee installation of their equipment. After filling out their application, they did a background check and called me back in. They wanted me in a big way, but of course I was flagged for doing Christian ministry, which they said I would have to give up. They offered me a whopping $150 USD per month plus expenses. The small salary was because I could not be hired as a foreigner, but only as a common Chinese employee. As you might guess I gave them a hard pass.

The other company I actually signed a contract with was as a consultant with a Chinese international trade business. Charles introduced me to Louis Xiong, a charismatic Chinese man who was chairman of a "too good to be true" international trade company. I was pretty skeptical from the outset, but I liked that the company driver picked me up every morning and returned me home each afternoon. The impressive title on my business card read Vice Chairman, Chief Consultant and Director of Foreign Markets for

Hainan Success Ltd. I was told this was a multimillion dollar company located on Hainan Island with branches in Beijing, Wuhan and Shenzhen with an associate located in New York City. I was promised a small salary, 20% commission on any sale I was a part of, flexible 30 hour work week, paid travel, a work visa (to include all of my family), housing, food and other allowances. As the benefits mounted, I became increasingly more suspicious. After a short time, it was becoming clear to me that actually my main task was just to make them look good. I guess they thought having me around gave them some sort of clout. After a couple of weeks, I didn't see any point in continuing the ruse, so I quit. I may have gotten paid, but if so, I don't remember it. A couple of weeks later I was picked up by the PSB (police) and questioned regarding my affiliation with this company. It turned out they were under investigation for smuggling VCRs and cigarettes via a shipping container from Hong Kong. After my interrogation, the police realized I had no real knowledge of their operation and had since quit, so they released me. Louis Xiong was subsequently put in jail however. But low and behold a few days later he was out and wanted me to come back. Of course I declined. All of it was exciting! I must admit it felt kind of good to be treated like a VIP, even if it was a ruse. As it turned out though, this was not to be my last trip to a police station. As often occurs in a Christian's life, all the opportunities which float our way, though they seem to be good ideas in the beginning, they're only distractions and tempting snares in disguise. Independent missionary beware!

THE FIGHT – Things were heating up in Beijing and other cities with the protests in Tianenman Square. All that was happening filled the newspapers, TV and nearly every conversation the young Chinese had. They had hope for a China with some measure of freedom. The US Embassy was warning visitors to not come to China and those living in China to leave. This warning went out just as our friends from home were about to leave to visit us for about 10 days. After discussing it with us, they chose to come anyway.

It was so wonderful for our family to welcome more visitors from home. There were lots of hugs and conversations with our dear friends Deby, Cindy, Deby's parents, Harvey and Dorleen Martens and long time playmates of our children Tiffany, Janelle and Julia. After touring Hong Kong for a few days, we all sailed up the Pearl River to Guangzhou on the night boat out of Hong Kong and they experienced bible smuggling first hand. We also took them to popular places in Guangzhou where all the tourist attractions were.

One morning back at our home in Shekou, Deby got to share Jesus with a very precious young lady we named Penny, who Sincere had been witnessing to. Soon Penny prayed to become a Christian and there was much rejoicing. They instantly bonded with all our friends and disciples, and loved being part of our worship services. One planned event, I'll give more detail on which happened the evening of June 6th (night of the massacre) the day before they were to return home. We'd all been invited to join our friends from Inner Mongolia who had a large tourist shop located on the permanently docked cruise ship turned tourist destination called Sea World. These friends welcomed us into their yurt (a round, animal skin covered shelter supported with arched poles) for a very authentic Mongolian meal. At the end of the dinner, the owner of the shop who'd always loved talking to me when our family visited his shop wanted me to be joined to him as his Mongolian brother in a special (non-religious) ceremony where I shared a cup of warm Yack milk with him. Yes! It's as nasty as it sounds. Somehow I choked it down, we exchanged small gifts and the deed was done.

Our precious friend Deby with Penny and a few of our dear disciples

Next they took all of us to their Mongolian horse ranch and had snacks out under the stars with them on that beautiful June evening. At one point during the evening, one of the workers there wanted to take me on a tour of the stables to see their horses. Mongolian horse men are some of the most renowned in the world;

trick riding their rather small horses. Just as we got to the entrance of the completely dark stable entrance, a leashed guard monkey lunged at me from the darkness and screeched very loudly. Talk about being scared! It nearly ended my life! I was not happy with my Mongolian guide who could hardly stand up he was laughing so hard.

    We all awoke the next day in disbelief as the English Hong Kong TV news was reporting the horrors of the Beijing massacre. You may recall, this was a very tumultuous time in China. Beginning April 1989, a huge demonstration of students and others asking for freedom of the press 24/7 at Tiananmen Square in Beijing occurred day after day for several weeks. The Chinese Communist Party put an end to it in the infamous slaughter of over 10,000 in the Square and the surrounding streets of Beijing on June 6th and 7th. This large number of deaths was not reported on USA news networks, but by first-hand accounts of foreign journalists, civilians but also implied by Hong Kong news media.

    We accompanied our friends back to Hong Kong for a couple of days to get their last minute shopping done, then on to the airport to see them off. Afterward, we stopped by our friends the Marcassi's home to consider what we needed to do. The US Embassy was telling Americans to leave China. After praying with our friends about it and realizing we had nowhere else to go, we returned to our home in Shekou. For the next few weeks every bus on the road was stopped and searched for Chinese dissidents from Beijing. These dissidents were desperately trying to board container ships at the Shekou harbor to travel to Hong Kong. Many wealthy businessmen and organizations in Hong Kong were doing their best to smuggle these men and women out of China.

    THE GLORY – Our family never felt we were in any real danger, but many local disillusioned university students began seeking God for answers. So glad we were there to witness to them the hope and freedom we have in Christ. Our friends left to go back to Kansas June 7th if I recall correctly. The successful response to our ministry from that point on with students grew quickly. We were reaping a harvest in the months following June 6th when students were being persecuted. They started to be fearful of their government, feeling betrayed and disillusioned. More and more were seeking answers and came to us for hope.

In concluding this chapter I want to tell you a story of a couple of Chinese ladies who were brought to us by a disciple who visited our apartment a short time after the tragedy in Beijing. One of them worked at Shenzhen University that I'll refer to as Mary. The other was her friend who had traveled to Shekou a long distance with her newborn baby girl. I'll call her Susan. Mary was aware of our "Bible Parties" as the Chinese referred to them, and knew one of our disciples, so Mary wanted him to introduce her and Susan to me to perhaps get my help. With our friend translating, Susan began to open up to me her heartbreaking history. She began by telling me that when she was born, her family could not afford to keep her and no one in her village could take her. Her parents felt forced to bury her alive in a shallow grave one evening when she was only a couple of weeks old. The next day her family woke to hear her crying, so they dug her up and eventually found someone to raise her. She came to me because she heard that I might be able to facilitate adoptions from China to the USA. I had to explain to her that it was not possible because of all the US Embassy regulations, not to mention the Chinese regulations. She was so desperate she instantly began to tear up, as did we all.

Mary began relating her story that she used her summer to act as a "mule" to carry large sums of money from Hong Kong supporters of the demonstrations in Beijing to buy food and supplies for those who were demonstrating. On a bit of a side note, the wealthy in Hong Kong were motivated to try to bring about democratic changes to the authoritarian Chinese Communist government because in eight years, the British would hand ownership of Hong Kong back to the Chinese. Mary then explained what she knew anecdotally about what happened in Beijing the night of June 6th. What she heard was the Chinese government grew more and more frustrated because their local army based in the area seemed to be somewhat sympathetic to the demonstrators. As an example, when the famous photo of a young demonstrator standing against and stopping a Chinese army tank in the street made the front page of most every major newspaper in the world, they were embarrassed and therefore greatly motivated to put an end to it once and for all.

Mary went on to tell me how the Communist Party soon came up with "a plan", as she put it. The government brought in an army from the countryside which was to a large degree, poorly educated. The senior officers of this army began relaying news of a serious disease that was quickly spreading among the demonstrators in the large 53 acre square and the surrounding streets. In the early evening they began a mass "inoculation" of the soldiers. What the doctors were actually giving them she wasn't sure. But this drug created intense anxiety in the troops which then brought about the terrible impulsive massacre that ensued for most of the night. By morning, Mary told us the consensus estimate of deaths she'd heard from sources who were there, was near 10,000 plus the countless injured. As I said, I cannot confirm any of these details, so for now it's simply one more unproven conspiracy. Understandably, the young people of China were questioning a great deal of what their government was doing and how they were doing it. The irony was stark though- TianAnMen in Chinese translates as "Heaven's Peaceful Gate". Without the peace which comes from the Prince of Peace, there is no true peace.

The mood the morning of these two lady's visit was heartbreaking and somber. So with our friend's help in translating, I began sharing the gospel with them. They both made Jesus their

Savior. I never heard from either of them again, but they've often come to my mind and heart over the years for me to pray for them.

No fire, No purity!

13

Friends and Neighbors

We got new American neighbors! The Lewsetters moved in nearby us. Sharon had lived there previously with her husband, one daughter and two sons. You may recall from earlier in this book we bought a bit of their furniture from them when we moved in. They had bought an apartment, learned Chinese and lived there to do missions work in the couple of years before we arrived. They had some family problems and returned to the United States. Sharon came back with her beautiful children to win and disciple the Chinese. It was nice for our girls to have more playmates. Sharon took part in our meetings and passionately interacted with those who were coming to know God. As too often happens though, it just didn't work out for them. After several months they did return home. You may notice that so many stay less than six months even though their plan was to remain years. The reasons they leave are varied, but I believe each missionary left a mark of Jesus' love in the hearts of those they ministered to. They too were greatly impacted by the experiences they had and the people they interacted with.

At the end of June Ruth wrote to her parents: "It's very hot! It's been in the 100s F with 90% humidity. Sometimes we feel like we're melting, especially when the electricity powering our fans goes off, which it was doing from 6:30am to 9:00pm for three days a week. This has gone on for the past few weeks now." About that same time I suppose, I was startled awake by a large heavy bug (or something) landing on my sweaty bare chest. I quickly grabbed it and threw is across the room where it made a significant thud. I had to get up and see what it was. It was a roach like, flying water bug about three inches long. Ruth and I really had a hard time going back to sleep after that.

Ruth had a slumber party for the women who had been attending her weekly women's meeting. She had 25, ages 18 – 33 show up for their FIRST EVER slumber party. As if they were only 8 years old, they were so excited they couldn't stop giggling and wiggling. She showed them all how to make their own pizzas, something none of them had ever tasted. They played a couple of games, did a skit, sang songs and shared about their lives and testimonies. Then they all wanted to shower which took nearly three hours before they finally got to sleep. It was Sunday morning and Ruth fixed them all French toast which was the first time they'd ever eaten it. SC came over for a combined service of over 50 Chinese that morning. What a wonderful time of fellowship we had.

Since my relationship with Shenzhen University was going downhill quickly, and after all the efforts to connect with a business in order to obtain a work visa failed, I finally submitted to God in His wisdom to simply accept a short term English teaching position. In August 1989 I began teaching a class sponsored by a large company called Nanhai Oil Development and Investment Company for its Chinese employees to learn English. It's was very close to our apartment, which was a great plus.

On a lighter note, and as a reprise of the subject of interesting bus rides we experienced, Ruth once had an incident while riding a minibus one afternoon. She was sitting alone with a group of rowdy young men behind her. They were being generally obnoxious and laughing loudly. When Ruth turned around, she realized they were talking about her. By their mannerisms and hand gestures she gathered that they were "impressed" by her full figure so to speak. She sat there for a while ignoring them, but they just wouldn't stop. Finally Ruth rose from her seat, turned around to face them and with her finger pointed at them began scolding them in English like naughty little boys. Well, this group was completely dumbfounded by how sharply Ruth was talking to them. Though they didn't understand a word she said, they knew what she was saying. They shut their mouths tight and quickly exited the bus at the next stop. The bus ticket lady certainly thought it was funny. Yay Ruth! She was very proud of herself, and so was I.

Ruth has been so patient with her small, traditional Chinese kitchen. The short 25 inch concrete countertops with messy white ceramic tile had a very large concrete sink area, the bottom of which barely off the floor. Since we signed a new one year lease, we decided it was time to doing some westernizing. I bought some plywood and Formica to raise the countertop nine inches and installed a double steel sink. I then installed a couple of drawers next to the sink insert. Next I installed some wall cabinets for food storage. Ruth also found a small BBQ grill. She had missed grilling so much; she used it four days a week for a while after she bought it.

We whitewashed our dirty white living room, hall and dining room a pale mint green. Then I fixed the western toilet to flush better.

We started a Monday night "Inquirers" meeting to add to our Sunday morning home church service, Thursday night Women's meetings and Sunday evening expat bible study. All our brothers and sisters cherished taking communion. It was certainly among their most favorite services. Some of our baptisms were done in a bathtub, but most were in a duck pond a couple of miles down the road from us. All of which as I mentioned before, are illegal in the sight of the Chinese government. During our time living in Shekou I later calculated we had done approximately 200 baptisms, for which all the glory certainly goes to God for in ourselves we can do nothing.

Earlier I mentioned the number of people coming to our meetings had diminished due to most of the students returning to their home towns. Well, due to the hunger created by Tiananmen Square massacre, by the end of July our living room meetings were busting at the seams with 25-30 each Sunday morning. We were wondering where we were going to fit everyone when our regulars returned for class at the university.

Because discipleship and training are so important, over the next few months I began gathering up various Christian books in the Chinese language, but there were also many written in English. Several were actually Chinese bible college text books. I was able to put together well over 200 which I then correctly Dewey Decimalized, labeled and created individual index cards for. Calvary Chapel of Ark City, Kansas also sent us large number of cassette tape recordings of their pastor's sermons where he taught verse by verse through the bible.

In August we got together with friends and all went to Ocean Park in Hong Kong. This is an amusement park on Hong Kong Island. They had some wonderful rides! Their roller coaster had one side which stood on the edge of a 150 foot cliff overlooking the South China Sea. What a thrill it was to be hurled up to the very edge, then quickly be turned and skirt the precipice of that fabulous cliff. They also had a number of shows which featured dolphins, killer whales, sea lions, seals, high divers, etc. My favorite ride was the 200 foot long outdoor escalator which gave me the option of not needing to climb the several hundred steps.

In our August 1989 newsletter Ruth told the story of a young lady by the name of Trudy who came to one of our meetings. When Ruth sat down with her after a meeting to visit with her, she took Ruth's hand and began doing a palm reading to determine the length of her "life line". She exclaimed she herself had a very short life ahead of her, but that Ruth's was very long. Ruth responded yes, my life will be eternal, but without Jesus, hers would be rather short. She said she needed proof that God is real. Ruth and others witnessed to her and gave her a couple of tracts, and scriptures. "We plant, we water, but God gives the increase."

Our friend Hong was Ruth's Chinese language tutor early in our ministry. Ruth would often witness to Hong, but her mind struggled with many questions. One evening at a friend's bible meeting we accompanied her to, Hong was gloriously saved. A week or two later I accompanied our friend Kevin Cobb, Hong and Hong's mother to the Guangzhou US Consulate to reapply for a student visa so she could attend a university in the United States. Hong wanted to obtain her master's degree in business from Idaho State University. My secondary reason for tagging along was to inquire with the US Consulate about their requirements and process for completing foreign adoptions from China. After two days of waiting and waiting, Hong and I were both successful. She was so happy! We all danced and praised God for this wonderful open door. Hong later attended a bible school in Texas, married a fellow student there, and over the past few years has written several Christian books. She recently informed me she included Ruth's and my name in one of them. Hong has a great job now and continues to serve Jesus with all her heart. She and her husband have been leaders in a Korean church in the area for many years now. We had the pleasure a few months ago of having a meal with her in San Antonio. Her family is doing wonderfully and still faithfully serves their Lord Jesus.

Also that summer, Ruth found a helper named Linda who lived there in Shekou, but her family lived in the popular tourist city of Zhezhang, China. She and another girl recently became Christians at a women's bible study dinner party when Ruth fixed burritos and tacos. One of the ladies brought shrimp, so it was a great feast. Linda did an excellent job for us, so with her help and with the growth in her ministry to the Chinese ladies, Ruth began embracing her life and ministry here in China more and more. This is such an answer to prayer!

We wrote in our September 1989 newsletter the following regarding one of our special converts. "God has given us several converts this month. We give all praise to God! Joselynn was a lively English Professor from Guangdong University who was seeking a job in this area. Two of our disciples met her while she was filling out a job application and directed her to our meeting. She came very early Sunday morning and we had an interesting conversation before the meeting. She related her experience in seeking for God. She began with how four years ago she would hear a voice speak from time to time over the course of four days that she should seek for the true God in the Bible and spoke of Jesus. She found a bible and read it sometimes. She then located a Catholic church to go to, but she was still confused. She was trying to, as she put it, 'find a common link between Christianity and all the other religions'. I ministered to her about the uniqueness of Christianity and after the service; I went through the entire gospel story as simply as I could. She and another girl, Ellyana were gloriously saved. Pray especially for Joselynn, she didn't find a job, and all I could do for her was to refer her to a church in Guangzhou before she returned. Pray also for other very new Christians, Jarrod, Miss Li, Linda and Shirley."

For three weeks in September I fought off a serious infection making me weak, and giving me serious headaches along with 15 boils. Linda took me to a local clinic and they gave me some Sulfa which knocked it out in just three days. At about that same time, Emily's foot was bitten by dozens of fire ants leaving her in a lot of pain. It swelled badly and she had difficulty walking. She was good as new after a few days, so again- to God be the glory!

God brought Ruth and I, another precious couple from the United States by the name of Andy and Kathy Barnes. The Barnes' were believers who came from Texas. They were a young, vivacious couple who had a young son who had moved into our complex of apartments. A year earlier their young son and his grandfather were out for a nice walk in his neighborhood when out from behind one of the adjacent houses ran two aggressive adult Pit Bulls at full speed. There was nothing for them to do to escape or protect themselves except for papa to sacrifice himself by picking up the little the two year old as high as he could to protect him. The dogs viciously attacked both of them, but since they could only barely reach the boy, they completely ripped up the grandfather. And yet, papa somehow kept him held up. By the time someone came to assist, he and the grandson to a lesser extent were a bloody mess. Once at the hospital, it was clear the grandfather might not survive the attack, but praise God he did.

Our missions pastor Dave Cundiff with our family

This little boy required over 100 stitches while the grandfather needed well over 400. I don't recall all the reasons they happened to have come to China, but this life altering trauma could have had something to do with it. The Barnes showed up with enough money to nicely furnish their apartment and live there for a few months that year. We do know that their ministry to our family was a great blessing. On occasion Ruth or I will quote the young boy. This three year old didn't say this a lot, but when he did, it always made us laugh. One day he and his mom dropped by for a visit. Ruth had been cooking a delicious lunch using garlic and other spices which caused the boy to exclaim, "What's that smell like?" with his high pitched Texas drawl. We still use that line whenever we smell something odd, and remember how we were very thankful for this precious family who graced our lives and assisted us in ministry for a short time.

Kendall brought us more bags of bibles again. He's preparing a total of 28 large bags to be taken by a group of seven to Kunming. Later he was able to transport 34 bags there. I finished teaching for the Nanhai Oil Company on October 13th but I had another teaching position lined up at the Shekou Training Center. It's sort of a technical school which offers a number of different classes to assist employees working for foreign companies to improve various skills. I of course was asked to teach conversational

English. Since I often speak of getting various jobs teaching English, I might mention here something that was surprising about teaching English in China. I was not allowed to "preach" the gospel, but I could talk about it whenever it was somewhat appropriate- like various Christian holidays. I was free to tell my testimony without a problem; it just had to be in the context of American culture.

Ruth started up our home school again. We made due with some basic materials for the little ones in Pre-K and Kindergarten, but the two older girls simply did some work from last year to get back in the groove. Dave Cundiff, Missions Director from Valley Center A/G came in October and brought all our home school books. We were so very excited to see him and a young single girl named Rachel Straw from Valley Center A/G church. She came with Dave Cundiff to stay a while and assist Ruth with our home school. We were also excited to see her and catch up. She was such a great blessing.

For the next many days we gave them a tour of Hong Kong, a night on the slow boat to Guangdong China, tour of Guangzhou, then back to Shekou and the university to be part of and teach as many bible studies and services as possible. I had him teach my English class a lesson on the effect of Christianity on American culture. Before he began, I asked my class of 40 who were from many parts of China, how many had met a Christian before. Only four raised their hands. Dave was thrilled to have the opportunity to speak to them. I want to share here a few of the responses I received from the students who filled out a report of Dave's lecture. Kong from NW China wrote "I was unfamiliar about Christianity, although I wasn't to know it very much. I never had chance to touch it before. I have got regret for that. I sincerely hope Mr. Randy give me another chance to understand what Mr. Dave told about". Irene from Shanghai writes "Very long before, I wonder to be a Christian, but I don't know how to be. Nobody guide me. Since last Friday's class and your Sunday meeting I seem to be bright. You can guide me, but I feel another voice said round me believe in science, so I feel very confused now. Please help me." Miss Lu from central China wrote "I never believed any religion in the past. But now, maybe I will believe in Christianity because of Dave's lecture. How can I get a bible?" Xian from SE China wrote "I think this story is wonderful. I want to hear it again if have the chance." Yi from northern China wrote "I was so impressed I wanted to read a bible immediately. I want to know God's prophesy words and hear his sweet sound. I'll ask God what I will be in the future. Sir, how can I meet God? Dave said you could tell me." This class and all the classes I taught at the Shekou Technical School were the most delightful and profitable of any I would teach while in China. This was finally the place God had for me.

In mid October, we discovered that Religious Affairs Bureau and the local police (PSB) were once again increasing their investigations and crackdown on religious activity. We believed that the atrocity which took place in Beijing was the primary reason for them putting more emphasis on us. We also learned that soon after the massacre, all students at the university (perhaps all universities in China) were being required to take a Communist political studies class. In the two week class the teachers were singing the praises of the party belittling the rioters in Beijing. The students of course knew the truth, but considered it pointless and perhaps dangerous for them to object or raise questions. With added pressure came added response to the gospel. In the last week of October and first week in November we had twelve saved and five baptized. Praise God!!

Also, as a result of the heightened scrutiny, the postal services were being closely guarded and packages screened. This led to a backup in the small packages of bibles we were sending for China Radio into underground churches and people all over China. In October we'd received 50 names and addresses to package up and send. We had them all ready, but had to wait on the heat to die down. The November newsletter mentioned a recent Sunday service where, I ministered to a very large group from all over the world, twenty-five from all over China, two from Germany, one from Belgium, two from New Zealand, two from the Philippines, and one from Australia, two from Texas and one from Oregon plus our family of six. I preached on the "Beautiful Feet" who take the good news worldwide.

THE FIGHT – The good news was soon followed by some very bad news. Our new friends the Barnes who had recently moved here from Dallas, just received word that Andy's younger brother had just committed suicide, so they immediately flew home to be with their family. They had just gotten their apartment put together so beautifully. Later we learned they would not be returning to China, so our family was certainly broken hearted to lose such good neighbors and friends. But then we got word of a new family moving into the Barnes' apartment. This new family was very blessed by the Barnes' nicely furnished apartment.

THE GLORY – Now let me introduce the Hickmans! They were able to purchase all the furnishings from the Barnes family, take over the lease and move right in. Marshall and Linda had two daughters and a son. They became our family's very closest friends. They were there as missionaries, but officially Marshall had been formally trained in TESL (teaching English as a second language) so he was able to get a contract to teach at Shenzhen University. Marshall and Linda were a bit older than us. Marshall was a very good bible teacher with genuine humility, which made him very effective in his ministry to the Chinese. Linda was a laid back mom who became a dear friend and co-laborer with Ruth. We began integrating them into our many bible studies. I cannot express all the many ways this family blessed Ruth, me and our daughters. Christian fellowship is critical for missionaries on the mission field. Of course the work of the ministry to win the lost and train up disciples is the primary reason a missionary is sent. But with that as I reflect on our years there, I can say with some certainty that being on the mission field without the fellowship of those from your own culture would be extremely difficult for most Christians.

To close this short chapter, I want to share a couple of humorous stories from our days with the Hickmans. Our whole family dropped by their apartment for a visit just as their kids were finishing breakfast. When Linda offered our girls some breakfast cereal, a couple of them exclaimed "yes", even though all of them had already eaten. As they sat down Linda poured some cereal into their bowl and added some UHT milk. I noticed that the box appeared to be bran flakes but the bowl had many black chunks in it, which I assumed to be raisins. When I asked Linda about it, she gasped "Those aren't raisins!" On closer inspection it was pretty obvious they weren't raisins, but actually large roach eggs. Yikes! Linda explained when she looked in the back of her cabinet that morning, she found a box of cereal which had been opened, but only partially eaten. Evidently it had been there for a while and roaches had found a savory place to lay eggs. No doubt the kids all learned that morning there was a good reason to close up the wrapper tight on their cereal boxes.

On another occasion, Ruth was asked to color the Hickman's young teenage daughter's hair. Unbeknownst to Ruth, the girl had been given a perm not long before that. As Ruth was lathering up the color solution in her hair, she was aghast to realize the girl's hair was turning to mush and coming out in clumps. They immediately washed and gently combed out the hair, but the damage was done. Incidents like these only served to draw us closer in a strange way. They were a great blessing to us, and it seemed we were to them as well. Relationships like these are fairly rare here in America. The busyness, various stressors, and privacy of our western lifestyle too often preclude us from this level of dependence on friendships outside of our own families. To this day, we reminisce about what great blessings these people were in our lives, so we're driven to pursue every opportunity to have these types of relationships now.

No faith, No works!

14

Divine Appointment with Caleb

The number of people being added to the Kingdom continued to increase. The first Sunday of December we rejoiced as eight souls surrendered to their Lord Jesus! After lunch, we were visited by a large group of bible couriers who wanted to know more about our ministry and how the gospel was reaching China.

In the evening our family all attended a Christmas party we put on for my English class. Our children of course were the center of attention. All parties in China always include one particular activity. Everyone must give some type of performance. One man sang the John Denver song Country Roads. None of the Chinese spoke very good English, but they all knew every word of Country Roads perfectly. The other popular song for them was John's "500 Miles" which I think was the flip side of this 45 record. I inquired why those particular songs were so very popular and well known, but no one knew. It would be many years before my answer would come. While attending a John Denver tribute performance in Branson, MO the performer (who knew and performed with John) told the story of how a Chinese delegate visited America and heard two John Denver songs on the radio. To say he loved them would be an understatement. He obtained recordings of the songs "Country Roads" and "500 Miles" and began marketing them to radio stations all over China. Their popularity skyrocketed, and for a very long period of time they were played on the radio repeatedly there. Mystery solved!

On another evening, I was able to secure a large room at the training center where I work. SC joined our group of Chinese believers for a really great time of singing and fellowship. We had a total of 143, not including our children. And yet there were many of the regulars from each group who weren't able to come.

Later that month we happened to meet a large group from America who had begun their missions' excursion in Zimbabwe, then travelled to Kenya and India before coming to Hong Kong. They still planned to stop in Philippines as well. We learned they were leaders of two large ministries in the States so we invited them to come to our Sunday service and minister, which they did. There were two Chinese who surrendered their all to Jesus in the service. The group asked me if I'd be willing to give them a two day tour of Guangzhou the following week, which I was happy to do. We enjoyed making so many new friends from all over the world coming to do ministry in China. We loved playing a small role in their ministry experience as we sowed into each other's lives. Ruth noted in a letter dated January 15, 1990 that in addition to Americans from a great many states, we'd met up to that time believers from England, Hong Kong, China, Finland, Switzerland, Philippines, Thailand, Malaysia, Romania, Canada, New Zealand, India, Belgium, Singapore, South Africa, and Japan.

Quoting from our December 1989 newsletter "Let me share a few testimonies with you of God's grace. God has been bringing more to salvation this month. Salvation has come to Carine, Jimmy, Julie, Jay, Nadine, Yang, Fang and Pan Jing. Also, a rededication which Harry made. I particularly want to share Miss Yang's testimony with you to give you a feel of the thrills we enjoy here. As I was eating breakfast yesterday, my friend Harry brought two girls over that he'd witnessed to who wanted to hear more. Harry, with a twinkle in his eye introduced them as "lost lambs". I joined them in the living room and Miss Yang, a teacher at Shenzhen University, poured her heart out about her search for hope and truth. She began with their childhood in Shanghai when every day she sang and chanted praise to the greatest of all China's gods, Chairman Mao. The young people of those days were taught by their teachers, by radio, TV and movies and by their parents that Chairman Mao was god, even that he would never die. Mao's words were the only truth they knew. Their saying was that one of Mao Zi Dong's words was more valuable than a thousand from a common man. Miss Yang said that Mao's death brought shock and fear to all of China. After all, their god had died. Of course they discovered him to be much less than a god, and one who either by design or by simple mismanagement caused great suffering and death in China. Miss Yang later went on to graduate from the most famous Beijing University (the Harvard of China). But her study of Psychology brought her no hope or peace either. When the student movement in Tiananmen Square began she threw herself into it diligently. She had many friends in Tiananmen since she recently graduated from the university which was most active in the demonstrations. The names of the dissidents which are now infamous were some of her former classmates.

Of course her hopes were dashed to the ground by bullets and ascended in the smoke of her friend's burning bodies. After the massacre she sought out Buddhism, but found only superstition and meaningless, mindless faith. With that she looked at me and said 'my heart is empty, my mind is always in turmoil. I'm outcast by my country and rejected by my friends because of the dangerous association I have with enemies of the state'. With humility and heartbreak for the Chinese I opened my mouth and God filled it for the next two hours. Both girls were more than ready to confess their sin and make Jesus Lord. Even Harry was so moved, he began to confess sins of insincerity and of lying to me. We prayed together and then joyously sang together. We were all spiritually aglow! *"Blessed are the hungry, for they shall be filled." Matt 5:16"*

Caleb and his wife Rebecca

THE GLORY – I hope to do a good job of relating perhaps one of my favorite of all our salvation testimonies; that of Caleb and Rebecca. Caleb grew up in Shanghai. At the age of nine however, his father who had been pastoring a local church and his mother were abducted and sent to prison, then later to a labor camp. His older brother was also sent to off to an agricultural pioneering project (labor reeducation camp) in far northern China. Caleb was left alone in the house with an unrelated 80 year old Christian lady. They had lived in his family's large home which once house several Christian families, but now they were alone. The two helped each other the best they could. Caleb told us how he learned to cook standing on a stool during that time. After a year, his mom was released, but his brother died in an accident at the agricultural labor camp. His father spent the next 18 years in his labor camp, but was eventually released. His father once again began preaching in Shanghai at the age of 68. Caleb went on to receive a great education, a good job and a beautiful Christian wife, Rebecca. Of all the Chinese women I ever met, I had never seen one which radiated the brilliance, light and love of God as did Rebecca. She had been praying for Caleb for several years, but Caleb continually resisted making a complete commitment. He happily lived a Christian lifestyle, but would not humble himself and repent to make Jesus his Lord.

After a month of deliberation and conviction, Caleb was truly born again in one of our Sunday morning services. There's no way to describe the level of joy on Rebecca's face. To play a role in any part of this testimony is a priceless honor and treasure to my soul when I think not only of Caleb's loving wife, but also of his dear and faithful parents. They suffered so much for sake of the gospel, having been forced to leave one young boy at home and losing the other. In my mind, knowing their son chose to give his life to Jesus was so wonderful for me to be a part of. Caleb and Rebecca were eventually accepted to further their education at the University of Hawaii. As for all those we ministered to, we pray they remained faithful to their Lord and Savior Jesus.

We had a man visit us during this time who'd heard of our Christian meetings and he sought us out. After the meeting he asked our help to become a Christian. He began telling all of us his back story. His home town was the northeast Chinese city of Tangshan. Immediately, everyone who was listening drew back with stunned looks on their faces. I had no knowledge of this city, so I asked what was so alarming about Tangshan. Unknown to me was that twelve years earlier when this man was just a teenager, a 7.6 plus earthquake shook their city early in the morning while most were in their beds. According to Chinese government records, ninety percent of all the buildings in this industrial city of one million were completely leveled. Death toll estimates ranged from 242,000 to over 600,000. Serious injuries totaled nearly 165,000. This man sitting before me was one of only hundreds who survived without serious injury. Sadly, his grandmother was killed. Once they were finally able to dig her out and pull her broken body from the rubble of their home, they laid her out front in a clearing and covered her with a blanket. Government assistance was days in coming because all roads and trains were completely blocked. In their pride, China refused all foreign assistance to help. In the mean time, a lady they knew to be a Christian came by to check on them. She prayed for the injured as well as his long dead grandmother. Shortly after the lady left, he noticed the blanket began to move. When they went to her, they were of course shocked that she was alive; slightly injured with scrapes and bruises, but absolutely alive with no broken bones. She would go on to live many years afterward. Our visitor said he's been desiring to know this God who raises the dead ever since. Such awe and joy filled our living room when he prayed and began his own relationship with the God who died to save him, powerful enough to raise his grandmother from the dead and loved him enough to give him back his grandmother during a time when he needed her.

In February, Mr. Y and I took me, Marshall and some other foreigners to the house church (mentioned in Chapter 11) where Mr. Y had discovered their need for bibles. We took them enough bibles and other ministry materials to greatly reduce their need. The underground church had just purchased an old warehouse to hold services in. They weren't able to fit the whole congregation into one room and the building was filled to overflowing. I'm guessing about 600+. Their total congregation which spread throughout the area totaled over 1700 believers meeting multiple times in four locations.

Pastor D was their shepherd who in his youth was a disciple of Watchman Nee, a well known Chinese preacher whose books were much loved and appreciated worldwide in the 1960's and 70's. At the age of 61, Pastor D was imprisoned for eleven very hard years. He refused to read Marx or Chairman Mao's writings, so they punished him continually. At the age of 85, he was still preaching the gospel with all His heart. I was so full of joy from worshiping with all of them; I nearly blasted off the stage as I began sharing for ten minutes the love of God with this precious congregation. Others of our group were also honored to share a testimony and take communion (rice wine and bits of sandwich bread) with them.

Mr. Y was also working on a couple of other major projects to assist the four bible courier operations we'd been working with for the past year or more. The first was seeking out a couple of printing companies in China which we could pay to print "unauthorized" Christian books in China. This would circumvent the need to carry them across the border. Books illegally printed in China do not have the Communist Party authorization stamp in them, and if discovered in China, they would be confiscated. On February 13th I signed a contract with a printer Mr. Y found for printing 30,000 small books. We were told by other ministries other orders were coming our way also, one for 20,000 and one for 100,000. China Radio also brought me 50 more addresses to gather the books for, package, address and send by mail. The second was to locate and rent a house within walking distance from the main highway bus route where bible courier ministries could store bibles or other Christian materials. Once each ministry had enough for a large excursion into other areas of China, they would show up with a larger group, gather up the books needed, and then transport them to a specific city farther into China. Such a house would allow us to store books and tracts printed in China to wait for others to again, carry farther into China. Also, after many hours of my labor of love, the Chinese Christian library was finally finished.

Pastor Lam had spent 25 years in prison for his faith and was so well known and respected for many other reasons as well. So much so, Billy Graham once visited him. We

Pastor Samuel Lam

were also blessed to spend a little time with him. At the time we knew him he was 66 years old and in quite good health. He was taken in and questioned for eight hours. Pastor Lam was then taken in multiple times after that and was ultimately arrested February 22nd, 1990. It was all connected to the Religious Affairs crackdown following the aftermath of the Tiananmen Square demonstrations. The police accused the pastor of supporting the demonstrations, even though everyone familiar with Pastor Lam's ministry knew he very often spoke and preached against any and all support of the demonstrations. Approximately sixty police officers raided his church and confiscated a camera and two televisions used for closed circuit viewing of their services on two different floors of the building. They took $1665 from the church's treasury, the bibles they had in storage, as well as their storage of Christian teaching materials. They took his personal bibles, one given to him by President Reagan and another given to him by astronaut James

Irwin. They even took autographed photos he had with President Reagan and with Billy Graham. He was finally released several days later but the police posted notice at his church as being "Closed".

March 6th there was good news from our home church. They had finished raising enough money for our airfare which allowed us to come home on furlough. Hallelujah!! Of course we were all thrilled, but Ruth, the girls and our parents were especially excited. Our trip is planned for May, so our last few months here are going to be packed with making all the arrangements needed for us to be gone.

Interesting news! I just found out a student in my last class at the Shekou Training Center is the son of the Mayor of Shekou. I planted gospel seed in the classroom, but he has not come to any of our meetings yet. One of the Kingdom benefits to ministering in this area is that the students and administrators we are surrounded with, whether at the training center or the University, are often sons and daughters of very important fathers. Which is another way of saying; they are sons of Communist Party members with high standing. We also rejoiced that month with the news that Mr. Y's brother and sister were saved and baptized. Our sowing is not in vain, His Word will not return void.

Blasts from the past! An old friend of Ruth's, Beverly Lewis (before she became the author of her many best-selling books on Amish culture) had prompted a couple of her children to be pen pals with our girls not long after we arrived in Shekou. Beverly later encouraged her mom and dad, Jane and Herb to visit us while they were on their way to visit an area of China where Jane spent years of her childhood. Beverly's grandparents taught at a bible school in China before the communists ruled. Other friends who visited were Mike and Jackie Farrell (we've mentioned them in previous chapters) dropped by to visit us and stayed for our Sunday morning service. They were passing through the area after ministering in the jungles near Jakarta, Indonesia utilizing "The Jesus Film". We had four saved and six baptized in the Holy Spirit. And lastly, an old friend of ours, Darla and her husband Tim were only able to stay with us one afternoon. They'd spent the previous two weeks traveling through China doing a few concerts along the way. Darla went to high school and sang in choir with Ruth. Darla's father was the pastor of an Ark City church and was the one who married my brother Rick to his wife Cheryl. Tim and Darla at that time had a tremendous music ministry, traveling on tour, and had recorded a couple of very good albums. All these visits were very precious to us, and such a nice break to our "Chinese" life.

Chinese police continue their efforts all over the country to crack down on unauthorized religious activity. We learned that Shanghai had 80 underground churches shut down. One of our dear Chinese brothers in the area was taken in for questioning. Since we were returning to America for several months, we sought God as to what would happen with our apartment and all our furnishings, etc. In addition, we had all these disciples with no place to meet. But as I mentioned before, the Hickman family had been with us for a few months ministering alongside us, and they were much loved and respected. God provided! We then met a nice Swiss couple with three little boys. He was studying to get his doctorate degree in Chinese law at Shenzhen University and needed a place for his family to live. So we rented the apartment to him after getting permission from our landlord. The Hickman's were happy to take the reins of our ministry and there was no doubt in our minds they would do a fabulous job. Our church's secretary Deby informed us that our newsletter mailing list had reached 300. It was great news because we had only a handful on our list when we set out on this mission. God is so good!

No climb, No view!

15

Culture Shock In Reverse

April 16th, 1989 was our 12th wedding anniversary. We took an opportunity to take a hydra-foil from Shekou to Zhuhai, China and then crossed the border to Macao to spend the night in one of the nice hotels there. Macao was an historic, Portuguese controlled city from the spoils of one of the Opium Wars; then famous for its hotels and casinos. It will be a very nice break for us from the pressures and consuming work of the ministry, teaching and raising four daughters. While there, we stopped by an orphanage to gather information about their process for adoption.

In our April newsletter I wrote "we had a month of nines; nine baptized in water and nine baptized in the Holy Spirit". Also we are finally seeing progress with our burgeoning adoption ministry. Sharin Moznette of Open Arms in Redmond, Washington had been working diligently to prepare some parents to adopt from China. The first couple will be Peter and Pattie, from Seattle.

Quoting from Ruth's section of our monthly newsletter it said: "Yesterday as I was washing dishes and looking out my window I noticed a policeman walking by. That wasn't too unusual, but when our doorbell rang a minute later I answered to greet the policeman standing in my doorway with a stack of papers. I figured it was our last day in China! He talked to Randy for a while in Chinese asking all of our names, ages, etc. It seems he was taking a census of the area. Whew! Talk about relieved! I just knew he was here in relation to the crackdown on Christian activity." In retrospect, perhaps he was.

One of the challenges of living overseas in a place like China is dental care. Our family is not blessed with strong teeth, so it was always a challenge to find a dentist. Because Adrianne greatly needed some dental work, we asked around to see if there might be someone in China we could get an appointment with. We were referred to a dentist 26 miles away in the city of Shenzhen. Ruth traveled with her for the appointment to get a tooth filled. When the dentist came in after his "xiuxi" (afternoon nap) he was obviously drunk. We discovered that typically dentists in China don't use anything to dull the pain, so drilling out that tooth and prodding around with one of his instruments caused Adrianne to begin screaming. What a nightmare! He decided maybe he should give her a shot for the pain, however Adrianne and I had enough. We left and soon made an appointment with an Australia trained Chinese dentist in Hong Kong. It cost more, but well worth it because he was one of the best dentists our family has ever gone to.

In our "Puzzle Pieces" chapter, I related the story of my trip to Changsha and Changzhou China. The beginning of April, 1990 was when this trip occurred. As you know from reading what transpired in that chapter, this was a pivotal trip for the progress of forming an adoption ministry. In Changzhou we had an invitation to send a couple's orphanage paperwork. Sharin had Peter and Patti's paperwork nearly ready to submit. In that nearly two week trip I took, I learned the Changzhou orphanage, though fairly clean and well managed had a total government allocation of $4.00 per week for all the needs of each child. As we worked through the process with the Peter and Patti's paperwork, it was a great challenge to push their adoption through since they already had children. Perhaps you might recall that one of the Chinese rules for adoption was that the American couple must be childless. Peter and Patti had children, but were medically unable to have more. It helped that Peter was Chinese, even though Pattie was not. The orphanage was very motivated to get an influx of money and moved mountains (with God's assistance) to accomplish their adoption.

As May 17th grew closer, our family was more and more giddy. Ruth wrote to her mom and dad: "The girls are almost unbearable these days because they can't comprehend how long two weeks is. Poor Emily wakes up every morning and immediately asks if today was the day we are going to America. She cannot even imagine what America is like. I'm sure we'll be in complete culture shock. Please be patient with us when we seem to be confused about American things."

Ruth relayed the message to our friends that the large underground countryside church I'd been to see a couple of times were in need of clothing. May 12th and 13th Ruth, I and a few others went to visit them and took 1500 bibles and several bags of clothing. It was Ruth's first trip to such a church. She was very blessed by the experience. Our last Sunday service in China before leaving happened to be Easter. What a service we had! Forty-five were in attendance and the mood was electric.

As we got on a bus to leave our apartment for the Hong Kong airport, a sizable group of our friends and disciples came to see us off. It was a very emotional going away experience for sure. After a long journey to the Shenzhen-Hong Kong border with all our luggage, we then carried it through customs for both countries, boarded the train, then two taxis to the airport for a 21 hour plane ride back to Wichita, Kansas. There was a large group of our precious friends and family waiting for us with great anticipation. Such a joyous reunion it was! As we walked through the Wichita airport and out to a waiting car I exclaimed "where is everybody?" It was like Wichita had been evacuated. There was hardly anyone in sight and I simply could not believe it. Truly I was absolutely stunned! Then I realized it was normal for Kansas, but we were so used to being constantly surrounded by people and cars, to experience Kansas again was a total shock. The second thing was the extreme numbers of birds in the skies and trees. It was amazing! We didn't have birds in our area of China. That may surprise you, but at least at that time, it was true. The entire time we lived in China, the only bird I ever saw was one that was injured and being chased by a small group of Chinese boys. I was told that because birds were thought to be carriers of disease, the Chinese government sometime in the recent past decided to eradicate them, at least in the areas of China I frequented.

What a joy to be back in our home town of Ark City, Kansas with both sets of our parents. The first chance Ruth had, her and the girls were off to the grocery store. All that the girls were familiar with were small street shops and vendors or in Hong Kong; the largest of which were about the size of one of our nice convenience stores. Ruth had to constantly remind the girls they could drink water straight from the tap. They were so glad not to be forced to boil pot after pot after pot of water to fill a five gallon water jug we used to cool the water to later be able to drink it. Fresh milk with breakfast was so delicious compared to the UHT milk we had to buy in China. Ice cream was actually real, not the rather tasteless black bean "ice cream". Oh, and the Mexican food we loved so much was plentiful, but of course good Chinese food was not so plentiful. Barbequing hamburgers on the grill served with baked beans, potato salad, etc. was probably one of our biggest treats. To tell you the truth, I gained 30 pounds the first two months there, and have yet to lose it these many years later. The girls greatly enjoyed attending a couple of vacation bible schools and the Assembly of God church camps.

In the lead up to our impending furlough and the few months after we arrived back in America, we were contacting churches across the country seeking an opportunity to share what a great God was able to do with simple but willing souls like us. Because of the trips I took into China's countryside, I developed relationships with a couple of the underground pastors there. They had need of a building to meet in, therefore I established a plan to make a plea to various churches and individuals our ministry was in contact with to see if they'd like to raise funds for us to buy or construct a simple structure to be used as a church. I specified two cities, each with a fair number of believers. My goal was to raise $20,000 in order to buy or build two buildings for them to use as churches. By mail I marketed the project to about 50 specific pastors and key individuals. I waited, and waited and waited. I was surprised not to ever get even a single response from any of them. Though I was quite discouraged, I discovered an important lesson. Our great ideas don't always originate from God. Once we returned to America, it was full speed ahead to schedule as many meetings as possible. It appeared our family would be driving toward the east coast, but I would need to fly to the northwest so I could meet Sharin Moznette of Open Arms and some of the interested adoption couples.

Before we went to China, we'd given away our vehicles. Ruth's dad was on top of it though. He'd gotten a good deal on a very nice blue 1973 Cadilac DeVille and it was ready and waiting for us. However, since we were going on a long road trip, he soon realized it wasn't going to be adequate for our needs, so he traded it in on used, but nice Ford conversion van. It was quite comfortable, so our road trip out east was great and everywhere we went, we were given lodging in someone's home plus an offering! Our first stop was a small church in eastern Kansas, then on to Chicago where we connected with an old Salvation Army friend of Joe Voss, our home church pastor.

From Chicago, we made stops in Belle Vernon, PA where I preached at Pastor Derrico's large church and stayed with the Duncan family who had a wonderful property originally surveyed by George Washington. They had a large two story barn they had remodeled to include a beautiful suite on the top floor. Our girls were very thrilled and it was by far the best accommodation and hospitality we experienced on our trip.

We then preached at a small church in Newburg, PA and stayed with wonderful people who lived in a somewhat restored log cabin built in the 1700s with ceilings which had a mere six foot clearance. We passed through Gettysburg to tour the battle grounds and stopped in at the Hershey Factory in Hershey, PA for a delicious tour. Our next stop was Philadelphia. We loved going to all the places talked about in our American history books. So much rich history! After our touring, we traveled across the Delaware River to Moorestown, NJ to stay with our old friends, Stan and Beth Schroeder. From there we made a day trip to New York City. First we visited Ellis Island, and the Statue of Liberty. Next we drove into Manhattan to go up to the top floor of one of the World Trade Center buildings, then over to tour the United Nations building before returning to Moorsetown.

We went down into Maryland for a meeting in Rockville. The next day we spent in Washington DC touring the Lincoln Memorial, the Vietnam Memorial, the Jefferson Memorial, the Washington Monument, the Holocaust museum, the Capitol building and briefly at one of the Smithsonian buildings. The next day we were back on the road up to NE Pennsylvania to see a friend I worked with on my mission trip to Ecuador. Then we traveled up to visit Niagara Falls and drove across Canada, through Detroit and on to Saline, Michigan where we were invited to preach. After spending Sunday there, we rose early to make the long trip back to Ark City, KS. It was a wonderful vacation for our family, mixed with building stronger relationships with a few churches, and new relationships with other believers.

Once we got back for a week or two it was time for me to fly to Seattle to solidify our relationship with Sharin Moznette and have a nice get acquainted fellowship with some potential adoption couples. I actually stayed with Peter and Pattie, which was to be our first couple to adopt. They were so very gracious to me. Peter even took me to a University of Washington vs. University of Oregon football game and Pattie grilled some salmon. I felt so special. They also loaned me a car so that I could travel down into Oregon to Albany where I stayed with an incredibly hospitable couple by the name of Bob and Terrill Banks, who assisted Sharin with the Open

Arms ministry. After my night there I was off to preach and share at meetings near Eugene, Eagle Point and Medford. I stopped off at Crater Lake, which I'd always wanted to see, before returning to Seattle and later flew back to Kansas. Altogether I spent two and one-half wonderful weeks in the great northwest.

Not long before we returned to China, our family was asked to share our missions experiences in an evening service at First Evangelical Free Church our in nearby Winfield Kansas. The next day we were invited to dinner with a couple we met the night before to get to know us a little better. After dinner they gave us a high quality Panasonic digital video camera. I had been praying for a way to buy one since arriving in China. We felt so very blessed! This would allow us to capture on video the amazing life we had there and to send videos back home to our family and friends.

After a much appreciated time of rest with our families and a fabulous vacation, we were excited to return to China on November 1st, 1990 but the 28 hour trip was very exhausting. Once arriving in Hong Kong, we all got a rush of peace. It was like returning home after a long trip away! Yes, it was clear- Hong Kong/China was our home and we truly loved being back. It was soon clear however, religious persecution had not subsided in the least in our absence. All our friends and disciples had continued having trouble with police. Just after our Swiss renters in China moved out of our apartment, but before we arrived, we learned our apartment had been broken into. We never found out by whom, but nothing seemed to be missing as far as we could tell. Could it have been the police?

No struggle, No strength!

16

The Orphans

After a couple of days of rest and jet lag, I contacted the Shekou Training Center and got my old job back beginning November 19th. We had a little extra money which we used to make some improvements to our bathroom. A couple of workers installed a bathtub, new toilet and replaced the nasty tile in the bathroom and kitchen. We also split up the four girls so they only had to share their bedroom with one sister, perhaps the best present ever in their minds.

Since this chapter will contain the first wave of our Chinese adoptions, I thought I should give you more background information about the impact international adoptions had on the babies affected. First let me disclose a hidden truth regarding the one child policy which existed in China from 1980 to 2015- the policy was first begun due to pressure from the International Red Cross. I'm betting you probably have never heard this before, because I never had. I found it to be true according to an International Red Cross official I spoke with. I was in Chengdu, Sichuan province of China working on adoptions from the orphanage there. In the lobby of the China Hotel there I happened to meet an official from the International Red Cross. She was visiting Chengdu to monitor the progress of their one child policy. She asked what brought me to Chengdu. I explained my efforts to facilitate international adoptions. She then startled me by saying "I'm here basically doing the opposite." I of course asked her to explain. She related that in an effort to curb the population growth in China, the International Red Cross (part of the United Nations) had asked China to make this their policy in order to reduce its population.

There is another piece to this sadness as well, which perhaps led to more forced abortions than did the one child policy. Their family control quota system worked as follows. Each year government run companies, schools, hospitals and other organizations were given a maximum quota for marriages and births for each of their employees. For example, if they had 1000 employees, perhaps they might allow 50 marriages and 30 births. As a result, even if you became pregnant with your first child, you were forced to have an abortion if yours was birth number 31 or higher. In this way they could also limit the population.

As additional examples, I want to share with you some real life experiences shared by the students at the training center where I taught. One evening I was alarmed by a very somber mood among the students. One of my very brightest students, about 32 years old had been talking to several of his fellow students before the start of class, and whatever message he was relating seem to be spreading all across the room to the other 25 in the class. When it was time to start class, I asked what it was that had everyone upset. The young man spoke up and talked about the terrible predicament he was in. His wife was pregnant with twins. His only choice was to pick which one would die after they were born OR, pay a fine equaling two years wages. I've read since then that twins were supposed to be allowed since they were in actuality just one birth, but the local government was not allowing it in this case. There was nothing which could be said to advise him, it was simply one of the sad realities of living in China at that time. I and everyone there expressed how much we were hurting for him and his wife. After a minute or so, another young woman in the class spoke up and said "I'm very sad also". So I asked her why, to which she replied "I hate my job". When I asked what her job was, she replied she was a nurse in a large, nearby hospital. I was confused and simply stated it seemed to me you have a very good job. She continued, "My job is to drown babies; babies which were not supposed to be born because they were in violation of the one child policy". As a nurse, she said that this was her one and only duty. I pressed on to teach as best I could, but there was no recovering from these kinds of revelations.

During our first visit to Hong Kong in October of 1987, Mike Farrell told us about a report coming out of China from a major news reporter he knew. It was about an entire village in the countryside which had been completely bulldozed in the middle of the night because of their widespread abuse of the one child policy. Everyone there was forced to flee for their lives and somehow, somewhere find a new place to live. It was common knowledge that for many years the one child policy in China was such that if the family of a newborn could not find a family member or friend who could take their child, the child had to be destroyed. The most common was to bury the child. Other options were to throw them in a river, leave them out in a field for the animals, or just put them in trash cans. Of course there were a fair number who would bravely leave their child at a train station, a bus stop, a police station or an orphanage gate. Why do I say 'bravely' you might ask? It is because, to destroy your "illegally" born baby was not a crime, but to leave it to the care of "the State" was.

The ministry of international adoption we were engaged in, increasingly caused more and more mothers to leave their children where they could be found. Even though to do so put the mom at serious risk of being arrested, they were taking that risk. We began to see this ministry as one which was actually saving children's lives, so our determination to continue was intensified. All this we soon discovered presented a secondary issue however. The Chinese government did not have a policy of having more than one orphanage in each city. For instance, when I was in Shanghai for the first time, I inquired at their orphanage if there was perhaps another one in Shanghai, since the city was about 15 million people at that time. I was told no, there was just the one. In addition, although I'd been to many orphanages in six of China's provinces, I never encountered one with more than 50-65 children in it. The very ugly reality was that if a child coming into an orphanage happened to be unhealthy or deformed in any way, they were starved or left in a place where they would freeze to death from exposure. The Chinese at that time, had no interest in adding on to or building new orphanages to allow them to house more children, even if there was a great need for them. I have with me a Hong Kong newspaper article from 1992 which revealed this practice at an orphanage in south China (one I had not been to or personally worked with) which I knew from other sources to absolutely be true. Another atrocious reality is that in at least one unnamed orphanage which I did work with, the police were given access to orphans as young as three for sexual entertainment. Given today's revealed atrocities of pedophilia and sex trafficking, I can't help but think this practice is likely still taking place in shocking numbers all over the world. In my opinion, God could not be more angry or upset over any sin and injustice than sex trafficking children.

You may be familiar with the number of abortions done in the United States over the years. In addition to the countless living children which were destroyed by infanticide in China, I gathered the statistics and discovered 379 million abortions were registered in

China from 1971 to 1985. I'm just guessing, but perhaps the number of unregistered abortions could easily be over 100 million. While I was in China working with orphanages, I was often being asked for sonogram equipment which would give the Chinese the ability to gender-select their abortions. Of course I always refused.

Since 2015, a two child policy which later became a three child limit in 2021. This policy exists to the present time. Hopefully this social policy may completely disappear soon, at least in China. But the consequences are now the growing problem that approximately 30-35 million more boys than girls were born during those 35 years. With more than 30 million bachelors wanting to marry, availability of girls to marry them has become a very real social problem for China today unless you're very good looking and have a measure of wealth. A few years ago Ruth and I went to China with a tour group. Our cute young female tour guide explained with a grin that desirable Chinese girls expected their wedding gift to be a BMW vehicle. It was commonly known to be short for Be My Wife.

The Hickmans reported that in our absence 21 people came to know Christ as Savior. Praise the Lord! The water to our apartment is getting turned off every day at 9:00am and not turned back on till the evening. Thankfully the electricity is now reliable. Since the Swiss couple who stayed in our apartment got for themselves a telephone, we decided it could be helpful to our adoption ministry, perhaps for a fax machine as well. The Changzhou orphanage informed us they would promise us 15 children for adoption, if we could provide them a new Toyota High Ace minivan. After talking to Sharin Moznette she suggested a plan to have 15 of the adopting couples each pay a proportionate special fee specifically for purchasing the van. I made contact with friends in Hong Kong and was able to arrange a sweet deal on the new van. God is so good! We also heard from the orphanage that our first adoption at Changzhou was approved, so Peter and Pattie were invited to come there to complete the process to adopt three month old "Annalise" on December 1, 1990. My friend Charles was to be their translator and guide throughout their stay.

Some new friends we met while preaching at a small church in Pond Creek, Oklahoma wanted to come visit, so they came to see our ministry first hand a couple of weeks after we returned. Their names were Bill and Sheri Shaw. They asked if we could put them to work as Bible couriers, so we did. They brought in a large number of them and were pretty excited about it. They provided funds for me to purchase a DOS 4.0 operating system desktop computer. Later we would be able to get a printer to setup an adequate office and help with correspondence. I was also able to purchase a Makita skill saw in order to do some woodworking to make our lives easier. We had brought with us a water bed mattress, but I had to build a bed frame for it and installed six drawers into its base. In addition, I was also able to construct a suitable free standing closet for our clothes, instead of the foot lockers we'd been using since first coming to China. Our apartment was finally at a point that was quite useable and comfortable. We all had a great time with this special couple, even though we were a bit overwhelmed with so much to do upon our return.

As I mentioned earlier, the Shekou Training Center had a class of 35 lined up for me to teach, so I quickly got back in the groove. One of my students, his wife and friend had already attended our church. Paul was the Vice General Manager of a well respected silk garment factory which provided high quality silk garments for major brands, including Jones New York- kind of a big deal at that time. The flow of Jesus seekers to our home continued to increase. One gentleman from northern China who was the head of a local trade union representing 150 factories showed up at our door asking to know God. Some days later he contacted me to find peace and encouragement. He had just given an embarrassing performance for the Shenzhen 10th anniversary celebration. The Chinese Communist Party Secretary Zhang Zhi Ming was there. Paul was part of a small group of talented dancers but he made a mistake during his performance. Afterword his boss humiliated him about it in front of a group of his important peers. I encouraged him and did my best to direct him to Jesus but he was really struggling. When we sow, we pray it is on fertile soil but we often must give them to God for follow-up. The response has been very strong for those wanting to know God, so Marshall and I decided to conduct a Sunday morning meeting at each of our homes. I even made the move to open our home on Sunday night as well, to accommodate the many who were coming.

We learned that another couple, Robert and Dianna, had been approved to adopt three month old "Kirsten" from Changzhou orphanage. Of course for our girls, these new babies being adopted were a big thrill, but I'm not sure it was as big a thrill to them as our disciple Jerry Zhang bringing them a six week old puppy. They named their pudgy black and white mongrel "Pippy", after their favorite show "Pippy Long Stockings". Poor Pippy came to us very lethargic and very soon we discovered she had what seemed like hundreds of ticks. After picking a large number off of her, we couldn't find actual flea and tick shampoo so we improvised with a can of OFF mosquito spray, then a bath in lice shampoo. Surprisingly she didn't die from poisoning. You'll be entertained I'm sure with a few more mentions of our precious Pippy in later chapters of the book.

THE FIGHT – Taken from a personal letter to my mom and dad. "We are quite under supported right now. Our support given over the summer and during November for our December funding was one-third to one- half what we need to pay our expenses, which was about $1100. I guess it will take a couple of months of communication to bring it back to where it was before we left. . . Please don't worry, it just another opportunity for God to show Himself great. A testimony will surely emerge."

For Christmas and New Year's 1990 we were blessed with friends coming to visit us. An American couple who were studying Chinese in Taiwan stayed with us through the holidays; the Swiss couple joined us for dinner as did the Ward family from Australia. It certainly helped having them all over during this time. It would have been nice to stay in America with family for Christmas, but there was just so much to do. And, we'd have missed our midnight Christmas visitor, which is a story we've loved telling every Christmas since.

THE GLORY – According to a letter home, I had over 30 letters to write to all who had sent us cards and letters during the holidays. We had a tremendous Christmas celebration with a ton of homemade goodies, Christmas songs, some preaching and powerful testimonies from our disciples. Our apartment was totally packed wall to wall with people. The most exciting part of Christmas Eve however, was our "midnight Christmas visitor". Once all our guests had left for the evening and the girls were in their beds, we had a knock on our door at about 11:00pm. With great curiosity, we opened the door to a completely exhausted young Chinese girl. "Is this the place with the bible party?" she asked in broken English. After inviting her in to rest, we got her some tea and a snack; we explained the party had ended before she arrived. As a bright glow returned to her beautiful, smiling face, we began listening to her precious story. Her name was Barbara, and she had been wandering all over our extremely large apartment complex since 7:00PM in search of the "bible party" she'd heard about. Barbara had been searching for Jesus for 15 years since at the age of eight when she lay under the stars one evening in awe of creation. She was new to the area having recently arrived from Fujian Province. Barbara talked for awhile about a hurtful upbringing. Recently a bright light had appeared to her and put slight pressure on her chest which puzzled her, but then was followed be a hunger for peace with God. We shared the gospel with her and guided her in prayer for salvation. Just as we raised our eyes, the clock struck midnight and Barbara's face was absolutely radiant.

In addition to Barbara, many came to Christ in the days after our return as well as God healing a Chinese girl's severe back pain which the doctors had given up on. Another memorable testimony that month was a young woman who had only come once or twice to our meeting, showed up late. She was disheveled, dirty, and scraped up. She also had a badly bruised and swollen hand. Everyone was asking her what happened to her. We learned she had ridden her bicycle from Shenzhen (more than twenty miles) but on the way she was hit hard by a minibus. The bus knocked her from the bike, and she landing her underneath the bus when it stopped. She was telling the group how thankful she was that she was not killed. Personally, Ruth and I have witnessed two such deaths. One in which our minibus hit a motorcycle and killed the rider and the other one where a bike and rider had been crushed by a dump truck. She had not yet even become a Christian, but being at church meant so much to her that riding the 12 miles from where she was hit was more important than returning home or seeking medical attention. To me this story and the previous story of Barbara on Christmas Eve epitomize what spiritual hunger looks and acts like. Her act of faith and testimony gave rise to another one of our disciples to retell his testimony. Ernie had recently been hit by a taxi going full speed (about 40 mph) and was thrown off his bicycle. The two believers who were riding beside him ran to him and after praying, told him to "rise and walk". Ernie got off the pavement with absolutely no injuries.

As you've read throughout this book, Mr. Y was involved in a great many things, many of them illegal in the sight of the Chinese government. As I've mentioned, Christians were being monitored closely. Also I mentioned Mr. Y had begun relationship with a couple of directors who ran printing companies. He was able to financially induce them with money from Hong Kong organizations, to begin printing books and tracts for ministries in Hong Kong who had grown tired of always having to smuggle their publications into China. Well, due to a fluke printing truck accident, the police who were investigating found a load of illegally printed Christian books which were being transported to our storage house. When the director of the printing company was questioned, it led the police to Mr. Y who was then arrested and put in jail. All of a sudden Mr. Y was nowhere to be found for the next several days. We were sick with concern, but did our best in prayer to let God take care of him. Finally after about a week, Mr. Y emerged and called us. I don't really recall, but I think Mr. Y just acted as if he was ignorant of the whole situation and they let him go after a couple of days. Our storage house and agreement with the other printers Mr. Y worked with remained intact.

On the home front, Ruth wrote home about our diet goals and plans, the girls' home school progress where she mentioned Erika was a bit lazy about her learning to read and how Emily had started attending an English speaking pre-school. Getting back in the swing of home school was quite a challenge for Ruth and the girls, but after a week or so, all was back to a normal rhythm. As much as our December support was half of what we needed, our January financial support approached twice what we needed. True to His word, God supplied all our needs once again. A week before Christmas, Ruth began talking to the girls about the needs of the children who lived near us. These kids basically had no toys or nice clothes, but our girls had so much they couldn't store it all. Well that was all that needed to be said. Our girls started dragging out and bagging up dozens and dozens of toys and stuffed animals; so much so, we began worrying they would have nothing left to play with. Ruth went out with the girls that afternoon and distributed all of it to the great many needy children who lived near us. The Chinese children were quite dumbfounded at first, but soon became very excited! When the girls returned home, they had truly learned the great joy of giving.

In January we were disheartened to learn that our great friends the Hickmans were returning to Idaho due to needs of their family. It's very lonely for all of us since they left. I suppose we are just so thankful for the time we had with them and they certainly were there in our great need to have our disciples taken good care of during our absence. To cheer us up a bit, shortly thereafter a delightful group of 14 from the YWAM base in Wyoming stayed with us and a couple other houses nearby and joined in our meetings. They ministered in music and in the Word powerfully. They were from various parts of the United States and we loved having them stay a few days with us. The last two and a half weeks of January we had eight find Jesus and make Him their Lord and Savior.

In February, the older girls were invited to attend the Shekou International School, for a free computer class. They and Ruth also became friends with others of the expat community, played some soccer and got involved in some of the other activities among their children. The last thing was that our electric, on-demand water heater went out, so we replaced it with a propane one. We were able to feed hot water into the kitchen as well as the bathroom so Ruth didn't have to carry hot water from the bathroom all the time. It was a pretty big improvement for her and she was very happy about it.

One of our newcomers, Jansen, came to us asking our help. He was having horrific dreams every night. He didn't want to be a Christian at first but he couldn't deny that when we prayed for him, he would sleep peacefully for a night or two. One Sunday evening he stayed late to speak with some of our disciples. We began praying and taking authority over the demonic spirits afflicting his mind. A peace came over him and he asked to become a Christian. After leading him in a sinner's prayer that night, he was never afflicted with those dreams again.

Update regarding our storage house rental, in January the pieces of literature we had on hand reached 150,000, so out of security concerns we were contacting and encouraging our ministry partners who had them printed, to move them out of storage and into China as soon as possible.

The Changsha orphanage I visited contacted us that they would like us to send them paperwork for two adopting couples and they would welcome them both together. We finished putting together the paperwork for Jerry and Susan from Georgia and Frank and Colleen from Washington. The adoption ministry was beginning to really put pressure on the time I needed for ministry and teaching

English. Each time couples arrived from America and while they were in China, I and Charles was with them each step of the way. Phone and fax communication inside China was very expensive. I began needing to rely more on Mr. Y to take the lead on the adoptions once I brought the couples in from Hong Kong.

Chinese New Year was a thrilling experience. It was like World War III in our apartment complex. The firework of choice seemed to be bottle rockets. The Chinese had a great time shooting them from their balconies on to others standing on opposite balconies. At one point, a couch on one of the balconies caught fire. No one was at home at the time, so we were pretty concerned, but it eventually stopped burning on its own.

No race, No medal!

17

Witness to the Miraculous

In March of 1991, our dear friend and co-worker Marshall Hickman returned from Idaho with some friends of his who wanted to see and experience the ministry we had in China. The man's name was Dr. Bob Heil and he was accompanied by three of his ministry co-workers. Dr. Heil in St Louis had led a ministry called "Praise the Lord Fellowship" as well as a small seminary there in Missouri. For the previous 10 years he had been developing an international correspondence course called "International Leadership Training Institute". Its mission was to train up Christian pastors and teachers in countries which had no formal bible training available. It would require the students to study two hours a day for three years in order to graduate. He was there to see if it would be a viable option for ministry in China. I was very impressed with Dr. Heil's humility and heart for international ministry education.

Dr. Heil had been in high demand for speaking at Christian conferences, but left the circuit to focus on his new project. He wanted to appoint me and five others in the area to act as a steering committee to oversee printing, distribution, and then to develop a plan for distributing his bible course throughout China. I was greatly honored and humbly accepted the challenge. It wasn't long after that Dr. Heil was diagnosed with late stage prostate cancer and subsequently passed away. Though nothing became of his vision in China or elsewhere that I'm aware of, I was deeply impacted by Bob's passion and love for raising up indigenous Christian leaders all over the world for the building of

Pastor Derrico and wife from Belle Vernon, PA

God's Kingdom. There were a number of people, opportunities and initiatives which came our way while on the mission field. If they were in line with what God was doing with our ministry, I endeavored to keep my heart open to each one till God revealed His will to me.

In late March a group of 16 from Pastor John Derrico's church we had visited in Belle Vernon, Pennsylvania stayed in the area participating in the ministry, performing skits and songs for our church and English class. Ruth also rented a local hotel conference room and put together my 36th birthday party for over 100 of our disciples. It was a grand time for sure. In the three weeks previous we'd had an explosion of new believers. That month, twenty-three saved and forty baptized in the Holy Spirit with the evidence of speaking in tongues. Also in March, we had a great Sunday morning service, one of our love feasts (after church lunch) for 60 and water baptized 16, including our daughters Adrianne, Stephanie and Erika. Hotel meetings are forbidden since they are done in a public place. Our birthday party we thought would not be considered a Christian service since no one preached. But it turned out that the police would indeed hold it against us a short time later.

THE FIGHT – Last night Ruth cried and cried until she finally fell asleep. Ever-so often she couldn't take the pressures of teaching the girls, and her loneliness or theirs. There was also the constant pressure of police presence, monitoring our every move. Following nearly every service we held, plain clothes officers would interrogate our disciples as they left our apartment. For the previous couple of months, they had been living in the apartment directly above ours in order to closely watch us. Although the hammer was poised to take us out, I can honestly say we did not live in constant fear even though the pressure was always present. We were determined to be busy doing all we could with the time God was giving us, and just leave the rest to Him. The Hong Kong newspaper ran an article on March 28th, 1991 reporting a total of 76 foreigners were picked up by the police for questioning as part of a nationwide effort to crackdown on abuses of their religious policies.

THE GLORY – On March 12th we were greatly blessed to meet and host a spry young 73 year old named Lois from Tulsa. She came to Hong Kong to minister inside China and was seeking God to lead her where to go. We hit it off so well, we invited her to stay with us, assist with the ministry, and teach our two youngest. We

Lois with Karen

only had Lois for a month or two, but she was a powerful, spiritual force in our fellowship. When God is in it, you don't need a great amount of time to have a great impact. This was the case for Lois Meyer. I want to relate one of our favorite testimonies. It's about one of our older disciples- Jane. Jane was about 50 years old and had been coming to our meetings for at least a year at this time. In all the time my family knew her, we had never heard her speak English more than "hello", "goodbye" "yes" or "no". She was always very embarrassed and self conscience to speak English, although her Chinese language skill was very profound. She was from the Beijing area, therefore her Mandarin Chinese was spoken perfectly, especially compared to the geographical mix of most of our disciples. When Jane spoke, she commanded everyone's attention. Unlike all the younger Chinese, she was not taught English in school. English grammar was very widely taught in elementary and secondary schools in China, but it was never "spoken" English. This is why native speakers like me were in such great demand. We were told early on that there are more people learning English in China than speak it in the rest of the world. Well, precious Jane had never learned it in any fashion at all, although she was very well educated. As a Political Science teacher at our local high school, she taught Communism. She was a joy filled, totally committed Christian and a powerful witness in our meetings; often witnessing and leading seekers to Christ.

Ruth learned early that our new friend Lois was a powerhouse when it came to praying for the ladies. She began giving Lois a greater role at her Thursday women's meeting. At one meeting, Jane asked to be prayed for to have boldness and to receive the baptism in the Holy Spirit. Well, all heaven broke loose and what followed blew the minds of everyone in the room. As Lois and Ruth prayed for her to receive the Holy Spirit, Jane began praising God; loudly declaring the greatness of her Lord- IN PERFECTLY SPOKEN ENGLISH with no detectable Chinese accent. She went on and on for more than ten minutes until she became exhausted. Those in the room were completely flabbergasted. Everyone there knew this was a miracle and they themselves could not contain their fully abandoned worship to God. But that's not even the end of Jane's testimony; now for the rest of the story, as the beloved radio host Paul Harvey used to say.

A week or two later, Jane was called into the high school office for a private meeting. As she walked, fear wanted to overtake her, but the Holy Spirit brought to her remembrance a scripture she'd learned. *"When you are arrested, don't worry about how to respond or what to say. God will give you the right words at the right time. For it is not you who will be speaking- it will be the Spirit of your Father speaking through you."* Matt 10:19-20 NLT. Jane arrived at the office in peace, but found the principle and the communist party secretary for the school looking very stern. They began by saying that it had come to their attention from the Police that she was attending Christian meetings held by foreigners. They told her that she was looking at dismissal; after all, she was supposed to be teaching Communism which is atheist. Jane told us later what happened. As she opened her mouth to respond to this dire accusation, God filled it just as He did the English which sprang from her lips little more than a week earlier. Jane couldn't really tell us what it was she said to them, except she remembered telling them she was now a better teacher because of her attendance at those Christian meetings. After she finished, their attitude completely changed and they were openly praising her saying what a great teacher she was. She walked out of there shaking her head in astonishment. Not only did she keep her job, she was praised by her superiors. Only God!! Her boldness reminded me of the testimonies of the apostles when they were brought before the Greek, Roman and Jewish leaders.

This and many other countless testimonies abounded from the newly saved believers in our fellowship. It was such a joyful time; I can't even begin to tell the half of it. Believers like Zhi, Yi, Linda, Ping and Song to name a few. Mr. Y at this time was traveling back and forth to his home town ministering to his family as well as the home church located there. As we understood it, there was dissention and God used him to counsel them and bring peace to their fellowship.

Many of our church during the Chinese New Year took bibles and teaching materials to distribute to those who were seeking them back in their hometowns. Our dear brother Jerry had gone home over the holiday and brought back a testimony about his elderly mother who lived in Shanghai. Weeks earlier a lady who had been caring for his mom's daily needs stole many of his mother's valuable possessions and ran away. Our fellowship had been praying God would provide Jerry's mom with a Christian girl to care for her. God answered! Jerry met the new care giver when he went home for this visit. They shared with each other all God was doing in their lives. She told Jerry about her 20 year old neighbor who had died, but was later raised from the dead and is now traveling widely throughout the poor countryside. She's followed continually by crowds of people everywhere she goes preaching the gospel, showing signs and wonders of healing, deliverance and salvation. We'd come to understand during our years there that this was not an uncommon occurrence. Evangelists, most of them girls in their early twenties were often traveling the hinter lands of China to preach the gospel "with signs following", to then establish small home churches. Testimonies of peace, healed bodies, healed relationships, financial miracles and the list goes on. Locally, SC prayed for and saw a deaf lady whose ears were completely unstopped by the power of God. I'll share one more with you which also occurred in March. Song had been searching for a job for two years and not able to find one. She started coming to our meetings and after a couple of weeks she gave her all to Jesus. At that time we again prayed for God to provide her a job. That week she had to choose just one of the five offers she received. God knows our every need!

    In mid March, I and my friend Charles who helped me with adoption couples, escorted Kim and Carolyn from Hawaii and John and Denise from Minnesota to adopt their babies Sarah and Leah from the Changzhou orphanage. I came home early to get back for Erika's seventh birthday, but got held up at the Changzhou airport. The planes were grounded due to snow. The large airport had no source of heat so I was forced to stay in one of their chairs nearly frozen for a total of 26 hours.

    Three more adopting couples are coming very soon. April was a continuation of adding to the Kingdom of God by leading 25 to Jesus in the previous three weeks. We were bursting at the seams. Around Easter, in addition to everything else going on, we had 33 people arriving in five groups over a period of two weeks. Most of them were from America wanting to experience ministry in China. They heard about and visited our ministry making us busier than "one handed wallpaper hangers". Even our daughter Adrianne was thrust into service as a "tour guide", leading groups of Americans around our general area on minibuses. I was also just given a new English class at the Training Center. As a time to get to know each other better, I invited my new English class over to watch the movie "Honey, I Shrunk the Kids". It was a great time. Adrianne and Stephanie were invited to what was called "Good News Camp" in Hong Kong and was there for one week. We did our very best to not only keep up with their schooling but also their need to develop social skills.

Our 14th wedding anniversary was coming up and God gave us an older couple from Hong Kong to watch our girls for a couple of days so that we could take a little trip to Guilin. Guilin is a very well known tourist destination in southwest China. It's famous for its amazing foliage covered, tall, thin mountains, which are occasionally engulfed in fog along the idyllic Pearl River. You may have seen a picture of them at some point in your life because they are the second most famous subject for Chinese paintings next to the Great Wall of China. We were able to fly there and back fairly cheaply and took an amazing cruise up the mysterious Pearl River with all those exotic mountains all around us. In late April Ruth put together a group of five expat lady friends to buy 16 bags of disposable diapers, 12 bags of cloth diapers, baby toys, clothing and other baby items to take up to the Changzhou orphanage. They got to tour the facility there and Ruth even got to pick out the little girl our next adopting couple was going to adopt. They also stopped off in Suzhou (the silk capital of China) and Shanghai for a bit of "retail therapy".

I close with one last miracle; one that without God interceding would have ended with serious injury and perhaps death to one or more of my family. Ruth and our 73 year old friend Lois Meyer were coming back with our four girls from Hong Kong on the busiest, most crowded border crossings Ruth had ever experienced. To set the scene, imagine getting on a jam packed commuter train bound for the China border from Hong Kong which was so full, not a single person could get on it for the previous two stops. Once arriving at the border platform which in total size (but not the shape of) a football field which was so backed up and full, no one from the packed train could even step off the train to get onto the platform. So the train had to return to the previous stop, only to return to the border platform hoping that enough people had been processed through the border to make room for passengers to exit the train. We are talking about a few thousand people; all hot, all loaded with packages, all in a big hurry and most of them getting angrier by the minute.

The day my family and Lois crossed the border with their two wheeled trolleys full of groceries, packages and backpacks was just such a day as I just described. Extremely large crowds of border crossers were not unusual, particularly on Chinese holidays. Our family of course was smart enough to avoid those kinds of days. But this just happened to be a day in which massive crowds were NOT expected by the Hong Kong or Chinese border authority and they were both severely understaffed. Security on the Hong Kong side utilized six foot tall steel barred barriers used for crowd control.

Now picture these hoards of very impatient, overheated Chinese losing control and climbing anything and anyone between them and the next section of border crossers, only to wait another 20 minutes to proceed from there. No one wanted to be stuck and left to wait again for an extra 20 minutes for the barriers to open. Therefore, when the barriers did open up, there was a fevered mass rush of approximately 300 people to get as far forward as they possibly could. At one point, my precious family happened to be stopped quite close to the front of this mass of angry Chinese, just in front of the steel barriers. Once the barriers started to be moved out of the way, the mass of people began to surge and run through them. They were doing everything they could to remain on their feet, but were forced to abandon everything they were trying to carry. Suddenly Ruth realized she couldn't see any of the girls. It was just her and Lois. Ruth began screaming at the top of her lungs, calling out their names. After all, they were only four, six, seven and nine at that time. Then as she felt herself begin to fall, she cried out the name above every name- "JESUS!" At that moment she felt a firm hand help her back on her feet. She looked to see who it was that was helping her, but there was only the mass of Chinese angrily pushing their way through; cussing at her because she was in their way. Suddenly Ruth and Lois found themselves being crushed against the six foot steel barrier, when out of nowhere a man and his son dressed in boy scout uniforms who saw the girls in danger, fought their way through to reach the girls and began lifting them one by one over the barrier where a few very frantic Hong Kong security officers were waiting to receive on the other side. Then by the hand of God, all of five foot three inches of Ruth by herself climbed over that six foot barrier. Lois had been spotted by security and taken inside the restricted area. Ruth looked for the scout leader and his son to thank them immediately after the crowd dispersed, but they were nowhere in sight. Once the crowd cleared Ruth and the girls were reunited with Lois and began gathering the great many groceries and other items which had been broken, torn out of their bags and strewn all over the floor. As Ruth tells it, she had never before, nor ever since been so terrified.

Early in May, Ruth and Stephanie went back to Hong Kong to meet Andrew and Lauren from New York City and drop them off at a Hong Kong hotel. I met them the next day and took them to Guangzhou on the night boat to meet Charles, where he took them on to Changzhou to adopt their little girl Rhiannon.

THE FIGHT – Photo shown below is of me baptizing who I later discovered was a local police officer. In late May some of our believers were stopped by a group of five investigators and our apartment manager. They were asked in-depth questions about what was going on in those meetings. To which one our bold disciples Dan-Dan replied "you should come to our meeting Sunday and find out for yourself." So our apartment manager came! Our apartment was very crowded and he got to see and hear firsthand what we did. DanDan, the girl who had been so bold on Thursday night was on Monday questioned by investigators at her workplace. She remained strong and faithful and suffered no real consequences. Another young man who had in the past come to our meetings and made a commitment to the Lord, heard there was an investigation against us, and voluntarily went to the city of Shekou's Communist Party Secretary to report all the activities he knew we were involved in. We were glad at that point we didn't discuss in our bible meetings everything we were involved with.

It was time to initiate splitting our fellowship into small Chinese cell groups. We'd been considering it for some time, but we kept delaying it. Now the anti-religious investigations reached an all time high. We realized our phone was being tapped, we were occasionally being followed and our apartment manager is telling us he is being pressured by them regarding our activities. In May 1991, it was clearly the time to split up the meetings. I met with a group of our most mature Christians and asked them to pray about leading bible studies. I ended up with twelve leaders heading up six groups and got them started. I met with the leaders once a week and even went to a couple of their meetings, when we felt it was safe. Let me quote some lyrics to a Maranatha Christian song I included in our May, 1991 newsletter. *"We're marching on with hearts courageous; we'll follow anywhere You want us to. And if You lead us where the battle rages, we're marching on with hearts courageous after You!"* I saw a brother in the Lord on the street while in Hong Kong during this period of time. He said "I hear you are under a lot of heat!" I replied "No, I'm not! I'm in Jesus and He's taking all the heat for me." In May, Lois who taught elementary school most of her life and teaching Erika and Emily, was joined by a charming 24 year old New Zealander by the name of Julie Bell, who taught Adrianne and Stephanie. Ruth was again, so excited to be freed up to just be a wife, mom and missionary.

Our friends the Cobbs had for some time been manufacturing hand crank tape recorders in China which they would distribute in rural and minority areas in the country along with bible audio tapes for those who could not read. Alvin called me to say that the police had come and taken the passports of the workers there, and was demanding a large sum of money in order to return them. Since the factory contained a great deal of equipment, raw materials and finished cassette players. Therefore, all of this was now in jeopardy of being confiscated. He asked me if I could possibly round up a couple of large trucks and a place to store everything NOW! I contacted one of my disciples and he was able to rent the trucks and we were off on a three hour journey to their factory. Perhaps you remember early in this book where the Cobbs came to my aid when

I had a dire emergency. When we got there, my disciple and I high tailed it out of there so as not to get caught up in the investigation. After sending my friend back to Shenzhen, I returned to see if I could help. The police were still there, but I was never questioned. Only by God's help, the Cobbs were able to retain their many thousands of dollars worth of equipment and goods. They also located a different factory in which to manufacture the players more conveniently, being closer to Hong Kong where they lived.

Back on our home front, perhaps you remember me talking about our mixed breed dog Pippy. Because a neighbor of ours pressed the issue, the area Health Department informed us we couldn't have a "common" dog as a pet. We had to get rid of him or pay a hefty fine. We asked around and found an expat home for him temporarily till we could come up with a better home. It was not to be our last contact with our sweet Pippy however, as you'll soon read.

No chain, No freedom!

18

You Need to Come With Us

THE FIGHT INTENSIFIES - On the morning of May 24th, 1991 I was at my desk working when I heard an unexpected, loud knocking at the door. Ruth was in dining room reading scripture with the girls. Later she told me which one, but I'll share it with you toward the end of this story. Ruth answered the door to find four men. One of them she recognized to be our apartment manager. They wanted to talk with me, so Ruth came back with a very worried look on her face to get me. I emerged with my dark blue "Jesus wants your heart" (picture of a heart) t-shirt and told them my name. They asked me to get my passport; that I needed to come with them. After retrieving my passport, I quickly kissed Ruth goodbye and went to the car they had waiting.

In the beginning, there was very little conversation during our 45 minute trip to the Shenzhen central police station. As you can guess, I was focused on praying to God for His will to be done and confirming my trust in Him. The officers I rode with were grim and threatening, but I was able to get them to loosen up when I began conversing with them in Chinese. When we arrived, they escorted me to a conference room upstairs, asked me to sit, poured me some Jasmine tea and offered me a snack to eat. About 9:00am everyone gathered and sat down with me. I was a bit uncomfortable because I found myself in a circle of about seven officials with me as their guest of honor. Most of them didn't appear all that scary, but there was one older gentleman who was very serious. It seemed he couldn't wait for the opportunity to eat me. From this point on I'll just refer to him as the Big Dog. It was obvious the Big Dog and perhaps a couple of the others were from the Beijing Religious Affairs Bureau. In America we might refer to them as "the Feds". It was to be about one and a half hours before the Big Dog would speak. He just sat there staring at me with an intimidating look. His brief interactions with others made it pretty clear; he truly was the Big Dog. Seated to my right was a nice translator, I'll call him Joe. Also in the room was a professional young lady who was there to take notes. After a brief introduction of themselves, we were "off to the races" so to speak. There was one middle aged man who conducted the interrogation. He was quite calm and professional and began asking me all about my life in America and why I brought my entire family to China to live. He asked about my education and my prior employment. A couple of them grilled me on my purpose in China, what I'd been doing, and how I could afford to raise my big family there with the small amount of money I made. To which I responded "my family" were my primary support; of course meaning the "family of God". It occurred to me, had I been part of an actual missions organization like the Assemblies of God, it would have been bad not just for me, but for them as well. They then revealed they had their "top spy" (their words, not mine) in the United States investigate me. They confessed to what I'd thought for some time, that the four men who had been living in the apartment above our family for the previous three months were from the Religious Affairs Bureau to spy on all our activities. Well I couldn't help but be a bit flattered. All that trouble and expense over little ole me. I guess my story jived with their background check on me, because they didn't get upset with anything I told them. Most of the important questions were repetitious, but all were focused on two accusations. First, that I'd been conducting many illegal baptisms by immersion in a local duck pond, so they inquired how many I'd done. And second, which seemed to be my greatest offence, that I recently had a Christian meeting in a public place. Because of all the detail they knew about our crowded hotel birthday party, it was obvious one of their spies had slipped it to the party to gather evidence on us. All this questioning was somewhat cordial to that point. The niceties ended however when the Big Dog finally directed his intense anger toward me. There seemed to be confusion about my name. This may sound strange; after all they had my passport. But as surprising as it may sound, it's not as uncommon as you might think.

  What I'm relating next is completely screwy, but I'm going to attempt to help you understand how English names, when transliterated to Chinese pronunciations and then back to English names can be very misleading. I can only assume that the Chinese I was dealing with were ill informed about the details of what I'm going to try to explain to you.

In Chinese, the family surname is always positioned at the beginning. What we call the given name, or name they commonly go by is always shown in the second position. Finally, what we call the middle name, in Chinese will always be placed at the end. For example, the current President of the Communist Party of China is Xi Jin Ping. Xi is his family name. Jin is his given name and Ping is what we'd refer to as his middle name. Therefore, when these Chinese officials looked at my name Randall David Ryel, in their minds they saw my first name Randall, was surely my surname. Then as they looked at my middle name David, they perceived it to be my given name. And lastly, when they looked at my last name Ryel, they thought of it as only an unimportant middle name.

The T-shirt I had on when I was arrested and taken in for questioning

So at that point I can only assume they had been looking through their dictionary of how to transliterate English names into Chinese word pronunciations. When they looked up Randall, the English to Chinese transliteration became "Lambert". Therefore to them, through a transliteration comedy of errors, Randall became Lambert. Next there was the issue of my middle name David, which to them was my given name. Transliterating this common name was much easier, whether English to Chinese or Chinese to English, David doesn't change. David is Dawei and Dawei is David. So after giving no importance to my actual surname Ryel, to them my name magically became David Lambert.

Now back to the Big Dog. I have just spent nearly a whole page trying to explain this transliteration nightmare to you. Maybe after reading it three times, you still find it hard to follow. What chance do you think I'd have had trying to explain all that to the Big Dog? None at all! So all that said, when he began referring to me as David Lambert, I was confused. I told him my name was Randall David Ryel, not David Lambert. That's when 'all hell broke loose' as they say. It was like an old sleeping dog which had suddenly been poked awake with a sharp stick. The Big Dog started furiously "barking" loudly in Chinese. He went on and on! As I waited for him to finish and the English translation to begin, I was thinking I sure wouldn't want to be Joe trying to translate all of that. He did the best he could I'm sure, but when Joe's translation was about one tenth as long as the Big Dog's Chinese version, Joe became the recipient of all the vicious barking. When the barking and chewing finally stopped, Joe sheepishly looked over at me and amended his translation to include more of what the Big Dog had actually said. After all that, I resigned myself to having the name David Lambert, which if transliterated from English back to the common use of those Chinese names, David became Dawei and Lambert became Rambo. Therefore my name became David Rambo, or as it means in Chinese, the great conqueror Rambo (Dawei is a deliberate reference to the great King David). From that point on in the interrogation I couldn't help but have half a smile on my face. I kind of liked my new name!

    The Big Dog had finally settled himself back into his seat and remained pretty sedate for the remainder of the interrogation. They finished with me at 12:15pm and asked if I wanted something to eat. After finishing my meal, they handed me a pen and paper to write out my confession. I admitted to all the crimes they'd brought up in the interview and laboriously stretched my story out to be an impressive six pages. I of course never gave them anyone else's name, and I was thankful they never really pressed me for any. Neither did I relate any of the other ministry endeavors I was involved with.

    When I'd finished, a couple of them came back in to look over my signed confession. My crime as they read it to me was that "I interfered with the religious affairs of China, and had engaged in activities not in keeping with me teaching English." When I was finally released, they handed back my passport with a cancelled work visa. They had given me a new one which expired May 30th. I only had five days to find a place to live, find a moving van, load up our all our belongings and move the family out of China to Hong Kong. I was not barred from re-entering China, but if I came back and was caught breaking any law, they would red flag my passport and I'd not be allowed to enter China again for an extended period of time. I finished up with them and walked out at 3:00pm after six hours of interrogation.

However, this was not to be the end of my "fun" day. As I left the police station, I realized I had no wallet; therefore, I had no money because I'd left it in my other pants. Also I was nowhere near the bus route I normally used. In fact, I really didn't know where I was for sure. I began asking directions as I walked in the direction I thought was correct. When I asked for help I had to follow the Chinese three person rule for getting directions. I learned shortly after arriving in China if you're going to ask for directions there, it was imperative you ask at least three people. Yes, it's actually a widely known unwritten rule. I confirmed it with a great many of my Chinese students; they all knew it. The first person you ask is absolutely going to be wrong. The second one is more likely than not to be right, but the third one if it agrees with the second one is going to be correct. If all three are different, you'll need to ask a fourth person. So after adhering to the rule, I got a clear idea of where to go, but it was going to take me nearly an hour to get back to the main bus route.

When I finally arrived back to the main road, I still had the problem of having no money. It was a very well travelled road for everyone I knew, so I decided that if I waited by the bus stop long enough, surely someone I knew would happen to be on one of the buses and would loan me the money I needed. So I waited; scanning each bus for someone to help me. Bus after bus after bus came by with no luck. After waiting in the hot sun for nearly an hour, I gave up and just got on the next bus. So let me describe how these minibuses operate. Each one has a sign above its front window showing its destination. As you get on the bus you tell the door monitor/cashier where you're going. They either wave you on, or if it's the wrong bus, they'll wave you off. While in town, the bus just goes along stopping and starting. With each stop they take on passengers until they're full. If they're not full by the time they leave the city, they'll stop and take on more passengers along the way. In the event someone yells to get off, they'll quickly pull over to let them off.

Once I had gotten on, many of my young educated co-passengers began talking to me, wanting to practice their English. We were all laughing and having a good time. I of course especially wanted to engage in friendly conversation with them since at some point I was going to need some financial help. Well, at one point the monitor began asking for the appropriate fare. So picture this, I'm

Our main modes of transportation

literally seated right under her nose on this trip, but she is asking all the other 25 people on the bus for their money. To me however, she shyly avoided eye contact. Normally I'd just hand the monitor the money to save the poor girl from having to ask me for it. But, since I didn't have any I couldn't do that. Finally she worked up the nerve to ask me in Cantonese for the amount she needed.

To help you understand the dynamic everyone on the bus found ourselves in that day, let me explain. With regard to foreigners, there were three things for you to know. First, foreigners very rarely rode minibuses. Second, I was considered to be rich compared to everyone else the bus cashiers encounter. And third, a country girl working on a minibus is very intimidated talking to a westerner. When she finally worked up the courage to ask me for my money, I smiled and told her in Mandarin Chinese "Sorry, I don't have the money. I don't even have a little money!" She was so stunned she would have fallen off the bus had her door been open. She didn't know what to say. After a very brief pause of disbelief the entire bus erupted in uncontrolled laughter. Suddenly I had five of my new friends waving their money at the cashier to pay my fare for me. But to everyone's surprise, the door monitor emphatically and very uncharacteristically refused. As she slapped her chest she said with authority, "I'll pay for him myself." There was non-stop chuckling for the rest of the long bus ride. Later, as I was getting off, the entire bus load of people, including the driver enthusiastically cheered for me. As they pulled away, I heard a couple of them in Chinese and English reciting my words "I don't even have a little money" and then laughing. All of them had a great story to tell their friends and family about the poor American on the minibus. It certainly lifted my spirit after the difficult day I had.

When I walked through the door, my family had never been so happy to see me but they were more than a little curious as to why I was smiling, until I told them about my bus ride. Ruth and the girls had a story for me as well. Just before the police came to our door, Ruth had read to the girls the following scripture, which for a long time has been one of my very favorites. *"The Lord is my Light and my Salvation, whom shall I fear? The Lord is the stronghold of my life, of whom shall I be afraid? When evil men advance against me to devour my flesh; when my enemies and my foes attack me, they will stumble and fall. Though an army besieges me, my heart will not fear. Though a war breaks out against me, even then I will be confident."* Psalms 27:1-3. After I left with these intimidating men that morning, Ruth, Lois, Julie and all four girls began to deeply intercede on my behalf. After some time, Ruth got on the phone with our church in Valley Center to put me on the prayer chain. Then she called to spread her prayer request to our friends in Hong Kong and China. Ruth told me that for the entire time I was gone, she had an unexplainable peace. At the exact hour I was released from the Police station, Ruth felt God telling her not to be bitter about the outcome. After all our story telling, Ruth and I began planning and packing for our move. Two days later our twelve cell group leaders met at our house for our last bit of last minute training and encouragement. We had communion together, I anointed them with oil, prayed for God to bless their ministry and to protect them from persecution. And now looking back, we know that He did. I wish I could tell you that all of our disciples kept the faith, but just as Judas was tempted, their testing and persecution sifted some of them from their total trust in God. Ruth and I pray for them often.

THE GLORY - Another move for the Ryels! Through our friends the Cobbs, we were able to set up a moving van from Hong Kong to come and get our stuff. An Australian friend James Ward from Hong Kong and a couple of friends from Shekou helped us load up.

By divine appointment our helper Julie Bell met a man on a train in China a couple of weeks before I was even arrested. This Baptist missionary couple with the last name Kline had an apartment in Hong Kong. They were going to be leaving their Hong Kong for a month and needed someone to house sit for them. Julie didn't know of anyone at the time, but she got his phone number just in case she came across someone who was interested. Julie gave us his phone number, and when I called it was still available. It was small, but very nice two bedroom apartment and we felt very blessed. We had many sad goodbyes, hugs and tears with many of our disciples as we were leaving, but it seemed to be time for a new chapter in our lives as missionaries.

We showed up at our new apartment completely exhausted. The Cobbs and other Hong Kong friends had already met the moving van and dropped the majority of our clothes at the new apartment. Then they took and unloaded all our of our furniture and belongings into the huge living room of our precious Assembly of God missionary friends Joe and Gloria Thorne. For a month, their gorgeous and extremely well kept apartment was completely cluttered with all our furniture and boxes of miscellaneous stuff. But let me joyfully relate to you how it came to be that Gloria was so willing to make such a great sacrifice for us. Three years earlier, which was before we were ever called to China, Gloria had a dream and saw her living room full of someone else's furniture and belongings. At the time she had no idea how it would play out, but when she heard about our need, she was absolutely thrilled to do it. Ruth, I and our girls were so wonderfully blessed with such wonderful friends. Probably it's one of the greatest parts of serving God on the mission field. We all become family in the most amazing ways. I believe this is the correct understanding of the scripture which says *"And everyone who has given up houses or brothers or sisters or father or mother or children or property, for my sake, will receive a hundred times as much in return and will inherit eternal life. Matt 19:29*

Life in our little two bedroom apartment in the community of Sheungshui had many benefits. Ruth was so glad not to be forced to go so far to buy the groceries she wanted because it had a nice sized Park-N-Shop. Although our new home was very far from the majority of all Hong Kong had to offer being next to the border of China, we were much closer to our friends with all their children who lived in Hong Kong. There were major down sides as well though. We now had no ministry or connection to our beloved Chinese church. Also, it was going to be very challenging to live in one of the more expensive cities in the world.

Soon our girls were begging to go back to China to see our pet dog Pippy, among other things. They had visited her couple of times before, but this time we learned that the woman we had left her with was very upset. Ruth had told her we would make other plans for Pippy if she would temporarily watch her. With everything that happened in our lives, we'd lost track of how long it had been. Four days before Ruth and the girls arrived; this lady had lost patience and tied Pippy up to a tree near her villa just to get her out of her house. She then told Ruth that as far as she was concerned, it was up to other people to feed and water her. Pippy was looking very weak and starved out in the hot outdoors. Upon seeing the girls, she mustered all the energy she had left to then lunge forward and break the rope. I was told their joyful reunion was priceless! When they rejoined me, I was faced with a family of crying eyes desperately pleading with me to take Pippy back to Hong Kong with us. I explained it simply wasn't possible. The apartment we were going to be staying in did not allow pets. But more importantly, border customs on both sides would not let us pass through with an animal, especially not a simple mutt like Pippy. At least they wouldn't without paying a fee we couldn't afford to have her put in quarantine. The more I tried to reason with them, the more they all cried. It became clear I was not getting out of China without that dog. I reasoned Pippy indeed had been checked out by a vet and had her shots. We just couldn't prove it because it was the police who had to produce the legal paperwork for us. Since Pippy was just a mixed breed, they wouldn't license her. All in all I trusted Pippy was in good health and I wouldn't truly be taking a totally reckless risk in taking her to Hong Kong.

Ruth came up with one of her famously "bold plans" thinking we could just put Pippy in a "rice bag" and smuggle her across the Chinese/Hong Kong border. Rice bags were very commonly used in Asia. They were strong, plastic fibered, light weight bags with handles and a zipper; able to carry heavy amounts of rice, but used to carry nearly everything you can imagine in Asia. Ruth reasoned it would be simple to carry Pippy in there all zipped up for the 30 minutes or so that it would take us to get through the border that very hot quiet evening. In my mind, there was simply no way Pippy would stay quiet and still for the entire time it took to get through Chinese and Hong Kong customs. "It would take a miracle!" I said. "Well I believe in miracles" Ruth said. Of course all the girls believed in miracles too. They were going to pray for a miracle and that was all there was to it. I'm thinking shut up Randy and get with the program. This is a battle which you have no chance of winning.

That evening we finished getting everything together and left for the border. Just before walking up the ramp to the building where we would be going through Chinese customs, I put Pippy into the bag on top of piece of cardboard and a folded towel. I zipped up the bag and made our way to what was sure to be an interesting trip across the border. She was hopping around in it for a while, but the whimpering only lasted until we got to the building. I reached into the bag to pet her and asked her to quiet down. Zipping the bag up, I encouraged the girls to be extra playful and charming around the customs agents so that if Pippy did happen to stir, the agents would be distracted and not see it. At that point I can't say that I really had the faith to believe that young, squirmy 30 pound pup would be completely quiet and still for so long a time, but my daughters and wife sure did. Once through China customs but before going through Hong Kong customs, I inquired about the process of quarantining an animal. The person told me I need to stop in on the other side of Hong Kong customs to quarantine an animal. After going through Hong Kong customs I got to the bag scanner, but they just waved me on through. I never saw the quarantine desk so I just went on through and got on the train to Hong Kong. Since we'd gotten Pippy that far, what was the point of searching for, or asking about quarantine?

God is still a God of miracles, even small ones! Our playful not so little dog was absolutely motionless the entire time. We didn't even need the girls to distract the passport agents and security guards. That dog didn't move or whimper at all until we were completely finished with both the Chinese customs, the Hong Kong customs and were back on the train into Hong Kong. Now if you've been around untrained puppies, you might agree with me, this was a miracle. All it took was a loving God and the faith of four little girls and their mom.

We were now in our apartment, and thought we had 25 days to find a new one because the owners were soon coming back from furlough. Also we had Pippy, the pet we weren't supposed to have in this cute little apartment. It was a good thing he wasn't a dog which did a lot of barking but we were constantly sneaking her in and out of the apartment to go to the bathroom.

We put out feelers with all our friends and before long, we had a great prospect. Joe and Gloria Thorne was the couple who was storing nearly everything we owned in their living room. They and another missionary couple who were also friends of ours, John and Pam McGovern, told us about the availability of a great place they all felt was a very good deal. One problem though, the apartment they were recommending rented for $1000 per month. Our monthly support averaged $1200 per month and we had been paying $265 per month to rent our apartment in China. By Hong Kong standards it was a steal, but to us it was a fortune. In addition, the overall cost of living in Hong Kong was at least, three times more than living in China. We prayed about it for a couple of days and sought the counsel of our home church. We also contacted Sharin Moznette of Open Arms about what we were facing. She reminded us we had not charged adopting couples any money for any of our first six adoptions; we were simply reimbursed for our travel, hotel and meal expenses. Sharin encouraged us to start adding a facilitation charge. We both could see how our family moving to Hong Kong was going to be a big benefit to our ability to communicate and take care of incoming adopting couples. In the end, we settled on what we thought was a modest, but adequate fee of $500 for each adoption. We still had to rely on God for our provision, but this opened a secondary avenue for funding our ministry. Then surprise! We were informed the Klines who owned the apartment we were in, were returning early and needed us to move out pronto.

Since we felt God was in this and had no other options, we quickly moved ahead with leasing the nice apartment. Once again many of our friends jumped in to help with the move. Please let me brag on God a bit and tell you about the apartment because for us at the time, moving to this location was like winning the lottery. It was on the top of a mountain called "Mount Pleasure" near the community of Taiwai, New Territories. Another benefit of this location was that our family's most favorite places to go in all of Hong Kong were either in Taiwai or just one short train stop away from Taiwai in Shatin. This apartment was quite grand in several respects, but still rather dated and a bit rough. It had 16 feet of folding glass balcony doors which completely opened up our large living room to the balcony. This balcony had an astounding view. As you looked to the left, there in the distance was a beautiful view of majestic Amah Rock and Lion Rock Mountain, both popular natural landmarks in Hong Kong. We could see the profile of the lions head perfectly. Directly in front of the balcony was the descending mountain side jungle which was inhabited by wild monkeys from time to time. To the right was a mountain trail (they always called it the "snake path") which the girls loved to walk down to the shore of one of the main reservoirs for the country. Since we lived on the top floor, we had near exclusive access to the spacious flat roof with all its great views of the cities of ShaTin and Taiwai, as well as the jungle and the rock formations I described previously. The girls were giddy when they realized they could go up there and play at their leisure.

Our new home featured mahogany wood parquet floors, a very large living/dining room combination adjoining the magnificent balcony, two large bedrooms, a hall bath and a maid's quarters which we used for a bedroom which had its own bathroom/laundry area. The kitchen was fairly spacious as well. The icing on the cake was that we now had air conditioning. We had been through a great number of battles, and although it would not be our last battle, we joyfully received this blessing from God with overwhelming gratitude. It was now a divine time of rest from battles for us; a prolonged period of peace and blessing for our family. Adoptions were now in full swing. In addition to working with Open Arms, I began working with a total of eleven other adoption agencies across the United States.

No suffering, No Humility!

19

Comin' 'Round the Mountain

In my last chapter I talked about some of the great benefits of our new home. There was one major downside to it however, and that was the lack of transportation down our big beautiful mountain. Only a couple times a day would a minibus arrive at the top and taxis were too expensive to use regularly, so we were faced with the fact that we needed a vehicle. Once again, we turned to our friends to help us locate something we could afford. As it turned out, our dear friends the Kimbrels were selling their old Toyota Lite Ace minivan, and they offered it to us for just $600. We couldn't afford it, but God used precious friends in California who felt led to supply this need. They quickly sent us the money to buy it. Since the Kimbrils were moving back to the States, they also sold us several appliances and pieces of furniture at a great price. The insurance and licensing were nearly as expensive as the van, but God used others to supply that need as well. As for our new van, it desperately needed attention. I taught myself by trial and error how to use "Bondo" to patch up all the rusted out places, sand it down smooth and use a can of white spray paint (not exactly the right shade or sheen of white as the van) to cover up the ugly. Of course I soon had to locate an auto mechanic shop which could keep it running, but the Ryels had a vehicle and Ruth was elated. There was no stopping her from taking to the road. Surprising to us was how easy it was to transition to driving on the left side of the road. I think we actually had more difficulty adjusting to driving on the right side once we returned to America.

Our winding mountain road only had one lane with the occasional turn out to let someone else by. Occasionally we'd have just passed the turn out when another vehicle would be coming from the other direction. One or the other vehicle would be forced to back up to the turn out and let the other one pass. Backing down a steep, narrow, winding road was not easy. The girls would sometimes sing "She'll Be Comin' 'Round the Mountain", of course referring to their mom in her ugly minivan.

We now had neighbors who spoke English. One was a missionary family from Texas named Terry and Lynn Chestbrough who had three handsome, active boys about our girl's age. You can imagine how excited they were to have four cute blondes to play with, and vice-versa. There was also a newly divorced, quite stuffy British business man who owned a factory making denim jeans called "Get Used Jeans". His mischievous 9 year old son was one of the girls' playmates and his lovely elderly grandmother enjoyed having tea with Ruth and watching the kids play. They had an older Jaguar and a brand new one. He had a Chinese maid which dutifully dusted off his cars every morning. There was an Australian radio DJ and his Chinese wife. Lastly there was a British Hong Kong official with a Chinese wife who stayed to themselves. These were just the neighbors living in our building. There were a few buildings around us which had quite a mixture of cultures as well. Looking back, our building and the general neighborhood might have made a very successful, internationally flavored television reality show if there'd have been such a thing at that time.

All those girls and boys were often scolded for playing too close to the new Jaguar. We sensed "Mr. Jaguar" had a somewhat condescending attitude toward our family, especially our ugly old minivan which we weren't allowed to park in the vicinity of his. This leads me to tell you about a funny incident I had with him one evening. I was just turning off the highway to enter the road leading up the mountain to our apartment and noticed a familiar new Jaguar parked on the side of the road. I pulled over and discovered Mr. Jaguar had car trouble with his new car. I'm sorry, I couldn't help but smile. Strike that, actually I chuckled out loud. He got out and I asked him if I could help. He said yes, so I took him on what was a very quiet ride up to our building. It was obvious he was very embarrassed about having his fabulous Jaguar break down and needing to ride in my ugly minivan so I gracefully kept my mouth shut about it.

Ruth quickly picked up driving a manual shifter on the column with her left hand. In no time at all she was driving all over Hong Kong, including Hong Kong Island, like a pro. She was honking and weaving through traffic with the best of all the Rolls Royces, Bentleys, Jaguars, and Mercedes which were such a common sight on the roads of Hong Kong.

Our second daughter Stephanie had a birthday July 6th of that year. Twenty-one of her good friends gathered at the park for a grand party. It was so much easier to get all the friends together after moving to Hong Kong. We all had such a great time. Ruth and I began updating our apartment with paint and wallpaper, Rhoda Cobb helped Ruth measure and order some colorful curtains for our new place. We got plugged in to a local Taiwai church which the Kendall Cobb family attended called Elim Full Gospel church. The pastor was a Welch man by the name of Paul Sachett-Waller. At the time, he was an internationally known author and speaker who travelled 100,000 miles a year in ministry. He asked me to assist him with some printing projects for his books which he wanted to distribute in China. I quickly arranged one of the books to be printed in China for him. Later Pastor Sachett-Waller asked if I'd be interested in filling in as pastor of our church while he traveled, and on occasion, travel with him. He even spoke of advancing our adoption ministry to other Southeast Asian countries. As I was praying about it, he discovered I had not been to bible school, licensed or ordained by any church denomination and dropped me like a hot potato. I won't lie, that was discouraging, mostly because after that happened he barely ever spoke to me. It took me a few days, but I decided no matter; I had enough other things to do anyway. I did finish the one printing job we had in the works which I was handling for him though for which I never even received a thank you for. Eventually we began attending a charismatic Filipino church on Hong Kong Island.

Me with some of my buddies: John McGovern, James Ward and Joe Thorne

Once a week I was meeting with my cell group leaders in China. Our family was adjusting fairly well to our new home, but not all the girls. Emily wanted to go home. She wanted to go home in China because she missed all her little Chinese friends she played with everyday. They were so cute together as they played. Emily would try to mimic them in talking Chinese, at least in her mind. It was mostly gibberish probably, but not being able to communicate well didn't stop them from having a good time. She was actually crying because she missed them so much! Come to think of it, of everyone in our family, Emily has always had the most trouble moving to a new home, and we were always uprooting her. So now looking back over all our moves, it is something I certainly have regrets about. Parents seeking to follow God wherever he leads should count the cost that each uprooting will have on your family.

When we left China I gave my computer to a friend for ministry use, but kept my printer. Now in Hong Kong as the adoption ministry was making great progress, a new computer and a fax machine was greatly needed. I had given my old computer to a missionary friend in Shenzhen. Sharin with Open Arms agreed, and sent the money needed to buy a new HP 386 desktop computer running Windows 3 operating system. It not only had a five and a quarter inch floppy drive but also the three and a half inch disk drive. And if I remember correctly, it also had a "huge" 40 megabyte hard drive. I was also able to get a fax machine. With help from Kendall, I picked out some programs I needed for my new computer. Now I had no clue about installing programs properly or operating a computer so I had quite a learning curve to be able to do anything with it. If I got in deep trouble I would usually just reformat the hard drive and start over. So I want to introduce you now to some of our very best Hong Kong friends on Mount Pleasant, the Hedleys. Jeff and Judy Hedley were missionaries with a great organization called "Asian Outreach". They headed up their Hong Kong office to write and produce the organization's monthly magazine was distributed internationally and was called "The Asia Report". It was a very important voice communicating the growth and needs of ministries all over Asia. The Hedley's had recently moved from their home in Adelaide, Australia. Jeff was originally from Glendale, California and was to me at least, an absolute whiz with computers, whether an Apple or an IBM compatible. He would often come to my aid when I screwed things up and patiently get me back on the right track. Judy was Australian and had met Jeff in California where he and she worked for Zondervan Books. Judy was a prominent Christian book editor. At the time, she was the book editor for Paul Kauffman, the president of Asian Outreach ministry. This very talented couple had four children, three girls and a boy, two of which were close in age to our three youngest girls. Our families grew quite close.

Jeff asked me one day if I could assist him in his office. Since taking over the Asian Outreach ministry office and working as a one man team, he was overwhelmed by the tens of thousands of printed photos which had been randomly boxed away by previous managers. His primary duty was to produce the monthly magazine as I said, but impactful and accurate photos were an important part of creating the issues of the magazine. Photos streamed into his office on a continual basis from all over Asia. Since nothing was categorized according to date or geographical location, Jeff was spending too much of his time digging through boxes of photos every month to illustrate with. He was desperate for help and called on me. For several weeks, I loved spending my days sifting though photos. I was told to throw them away if they were blurry, simply not very good or which could not be identified as to its location or time period; which was at least three fourths of them as I recall. Those which were good enough for publication, I would organize and store them properly. If Jeff needed a couple of recent photos from Inner Mongolia or some other location, he could access them quickly.

Jeff used an Apple computer, not an IBM compatible for desktop publishing, but as I watched him work, I gleaned much basic knowledge as he explained and created great looking newsletters and magazines. I would later use his training not only while I was a missionary, but also later in life doing the same type of thing for three different local magazines and newspapers I wrote, designed ads, edited and published here in the United States. Please let me share an interesting excerpt I pulled from one of the Hedley's personal newsletters which they had copied from a publication in Guangzhou and sent to their supporters back home. It's entitled "Why Not Start a Rat Restaurant". "A Guangzhou restaurant owner Zhang Guoxun, opened an establishment and is doing a roaring business selling rat dishes. The menu includes brazed rat, sautéed rat, rat casserole with mushrooms, black-pepper rat, rat with oyster sauce, fried rat with raccoon as well as a clear rat broth." So I ask you, which one tickles your fancy?

In all seriousness though, I often had the pleasure to enjoy many different exotic dishes while in various Chinese cities. The orphanages, to impress me or celebrate an occasion such as an adoption, would take us out to one of their prime local restaurants. If your stomach can handle it, let me tell you about some of the dishes I enjoyed. If you're starting to feel a bit queasy, just skip the rest of this paragraph so as not to get sick all over my book. ☺ From memory I can recall eating whole goose hearts, chicken feet, chicken heads, Peking duck, yellow eel, various fish served whole complete with its eyes, silver fish head, silver fish head soup, drunken (live) shrimp, six inch deep fried pork fat spears, Alaskan King crab (yum), varieties of snake, turtle, some type of large fried black bug, dog (my most unfavorite - too tough, strong and bitter), and of course sweet and sour rat. I never had the opportunity to eat cat, monkey brain, tiger, or bean curd with leaches or anything with snake bile. Oh well, maybe some other time (not). Surprisingly, the sweet and sour rat and Alaskan King crab were my most favorite dishes while enjoying the adoption celebration dinners. I've got another very special story about one of our adoption banquet meals which deserves to be told in its own context, so I'll "keep it simmering on the back burner" till later.

As you have probably figured out by now, playing it safe was never my strong suit. I'd just been arrested for "illegal" activities in China and told I would have to behave myself, but I just couldn't. We were determined to do ALL we could for as long as we could. Our connection to the ministries in Hong Kong doing bible courier work became easier since I now lived in Hong Kong. I was asked if I could assist two other brothers to take nineteen large bags of bibles along with 30,000 tracts to Chinese believers in Chengdu, Sichuan Province. Chengdu was somewhat close to most all of the ethnic minority groups such as the Zhuang, Hui, Manchu, Uyghur, and the Miao. Also there were a great many Tibetans. All the bibles and tracks had been stored in our rental house and desperately needed to be moved inland. I was pretty excited since I'd never been to central China before. While there I wanted to see if I could speak with orphanage officials about foreign adoptions. Our delivery was very successful, as was my visit with the orphanage. We now had done adoptions in Changzhou and Changsha, but a door was now open in Zhangjiang and Chengdu. At the same time, my initial connection for working with American couples to adopt from China,

Open Arms, was going through changes. Sharin was facing some personal and professional challenges and not able to continue. I was then contacted by a lady named Judi Whittaker from Tigard, Oregon who took Sharin's place.

One lesson I learned is what might seem as chaos to the secular on-looker is more like a God maze. Some doors shut, some doors open, some doors open for a season, and then unexpectedly shut. Some doors never open no matter how much you think they're going to or think they should. Maybe this stems from something I learned as a young Christian, that God can't steer a boat that isn't moving. In the great Kingdom of God, it is the Lord Jesus who commands His troops and we are to trust Him in all ways. Also I've found there are closed doors in ministry that God undoubtedly tells you to go through. These doors you must break down in faith. You might say these are the "gates of hell" which will not stand against the advancement of the Kingdom of God, in loose reference to Matthew 16:18.

THE FIGHT – There was trouble in China. The leaders and members of our cell groups were being tested by persecution and rumors of more police investigations. I wish I could say they all stood strong. Many did stand, but sadly some stumbled. They were being tested and all Ruth and I could do was to reach out to them when possible and pray continually.

I wrote in a letter to my parents on July 29th, 1991: "If Mr. Y is able to stay out of jail it will truly be a miracle. He is under full investigation. I've advised him to get out of Shenzhen, but he's not done it yet. Our storage house appears to now be under police watch, so we've been doing our best to get everything out of it. Our friend SC is also under full investigation.

After a few months, Judi Whittaker, the new director of Open Arms ministry notified us her work load was more than she could do, so she would no longer be working with us. Although I'd begun reaching out and responding to a number of other international adoption agencies in the United States, it was now even more important. I also began communicating with individual couples who heard about our ministry. Some of them were simply referred directly to us by Open Arms. I had already established my business name as Open Arms International, so I continued to be known by that name. As more and more agencies and individuals contacted me, I was becoming overwhelmed. It was clear I'd have not been able to do a fraction of this work had I remained in China. God moved us to Hong Kong for a reason. Let me quote from another letter to my parents. "Yesterday I worked non-stop from 6:30am to 9:00pm on a number of parent's adoption paperwork, but due to all the new inquiries which were coming in, I was farther behind when I finished than when I started."

July brought Jack and Joyce to us for their baby Rachel. Our friend and former school teaching assistant Julie Bell happened to have been a nurse in New Zealand. She also had experience as a medical volunteer in a Thai orphanage, so I approached her about accompanying Charles, Jack and Joyce to Changzhou. We thought it would be great for her to tour this facility and get a first hand sense of what they needed. Perhaps they were falling short of excellence in their care for the orphans which we could assist them with. She brought back some ideas, but sadly they could not get onboard for any of our ideas and we had to reject their main request for sonogram equipment. After a smooth transition with the adoption in Changzhou, Jack and Joyce's last step was going to the American Consulate. They needed to process a few legal aspects for their adoption and get a United States visa for taking baby Rachel back to America. The previous seven adopting parents had no issue at all, but this particular consulate official had a different opinion of what the Consulate needed from the Chinese. Their paperwork showing that Rachel was in fact verified as an orphan was inadequate in his opinion. Meaning, Rachel's paperwork in his view did not prove she had no family member in China to later lay claim on their baby. Jack and Joyce were forced to remain in China five additional days while Charles returned to Changzhou 800 miles away to work out the problem there. Jiangsu Province officials were also being stubborn saying there was nothing at all wrong with any of their paperwork. We had a real problem! Jack and Joyce absolutely could not take their baby out of China without the Consulate paperwork and visa. The window of opportunity for Jack and Joyce to get a return flight was closing in fast. Although they remained as calm as they possibly could, Jack and Joyce were under a great deal of pressure. Not only for getting a flight back, but they had a job and responsibilities awaiting them. After checking with the airline, they were told the soonest date they could reschedule a return flight that time of year was a month out because every flight was booked solid till then.

While Charles was in Changzhou, I hurried to Guangzhou to be with Jack and Joyce and maybe help them see the sights of that historic city, but also to help confront the US Consulate officials about their delay. While I was in Guangzhou with Jack and Joyce, I received the terrible news that a friend of ours was taken in by the Religious Affairs Bureau. It was proceeded by an 18 officer raid, complete with a video camera on one of their bible studies with 45 Chinese believers and seekers in attendance. He was interrogated and ordered to leave China. Later my friend told me the story about his interrogation. Remember my own story about the Big Dog and the confusion about my name? Well it came up again when they questioned my friend. The Big Dog accused him of knowing that dastardly (my words, not his) Christian, David Lambert. When he told me that, my friend and I both nearly fell out of our chairs laughing. At first, he had no idea who the Big Dog was talking about. My friend said the Big Dog exploded on him and accused him of lying. It wasn't long before he realized he was talking about me, and then confessed that yes, he did know David Lambert. Like me, he did not attempt to correct the Big Dog. I had to apologize to my friend for not telling him my David Lambert story. It took quite awhile before we could stop laughing, even though his life had just been turned upside down, just as ours had been. At this point two others of my most precious friends, Alvin Cobb and one other, each of whom I'd idolized for their bold, productive faith, had been arrested with more serious charges than I. They were both ordered out of the country, their passports red flagged, and were prohibited from returning to China for three years. Did that stop their ministry you may ask? Not in your life! Although one passed away some time back while still in ministry, Alvin Cobb still burns with missionary fervor at age 92.

THE GLORY – After such a long wait, with great expense and trouble, the obstinate consulate official we had been dealing with was told by colleagues located in China as well as Hong Kong, that not only was Jack and Joyce's paperwork adequate, it was exceptional. They were able to get all they needed and quickly made it to Hong Kong to get on their flight at the last possible opportunity, but not without one last potential snafu. A typhoon was imminent, and threatening to shut down the Hong Kong airport. Miraculously, the storm turned away just before their morning departure.

Charles was my partner in taking care of the couples. After those first several adoptions, he became comfortable handling them alone. He now knew the process better than I, and the families could not have had a better translator and friend to take them through the somewhat scary process.

After the intimidating raid on my friend I mentioned earlier, one of their key disciples accompanied by three other sisters went to the place where the Christian library I'd assembled months earlier. They successfully moved all the books and materials to a safer location. As for my friends, they left China quietly and even though I can't give you details, their ministry and Kingdom growth still continue to this day. As for me, I wrote in a few of my letters how much I missed my flock. I missed preaching to the lost, leading hungry souls to Jesus and seeing all the "signs and wonders" which followed the message of the Gospel of the Kingdom. I looked for opportunities to preach, but there were none, so I settled in to doing what God had given me to do, to the very best of my limited abilities and opportunities.

At this point I want to reflect and share something that is so dear to me, it would be unthinkable not to include it in this book. These are two precious poems written by Susan Linhares for her adopted daughter Lindsay Suling.

THE BABY IN THE BASKET

On a cold Day in November
At the dawning of the morn
In the city of Changsha
A little babe was born

In that far and distant land
One damp and dreary day
A baby in a basket
Was placed along the way.

A humble basket woven
By a peasant woman's hands
To be carried on her back
As she worked upon the land.

A basket crude and simple
For gathering in the field
Would have a higher purpose
Yet to be revealed

A basket routinely fashioned
To carry rice and grain
Became a godly vessel
Precious content it contained

For somewhere in its future
Its destiny ordained
A protection and a shelter
For the life it would sustain

On a remote yet chosen corner
Along a city street
A baby only five days old
Was found there sound asleep.

How did it possibly happen?
How could it come to be?
That this baby in a basket
Could find her way to me?

A mother had to be involved
With a Father's plan
It was her heart that placed her there
But it was guided by His hand.

TO THE BIRTH MOTHER

When you found that you were with child
Instead of joy and celebration
Did you cast about within your mind
In fear and trepidation?

What was in your mother's heart
That finally brought her there?

Was it panic? Was it deep concern?
Or was it because of prayer?

A prayer prayed to a god
Made of wood or stone
A prayer that passed unhearing ears
Until it reached a throne.

A throne beset by many prayers
From halfway cross the world,
Prayers of a Christian couple
For an Asian little girl.

As you placed that basket on the street
Bending down so low
Could it be that you were serving
A God you did not know?

What were your thoughts and feelings?
Did you worry? Did you fret?
Why didn't you follow the example
That so many others set?

Knowing you couldn't care for her,
Couldn't keep her as your own,
Did you feel helpless, hopeless
And very much alone?

Perhaps you even found your way
To a clinic and stood in line,
But as you were waiting for your turn
Something made you change your mind.

So you chose to carry this babe
For nine months beneath your heart.
You must have often contemplated
The way that you would part.

Nine long months of cradling
This little life inside

I wonder how you coped;
I know you must have cried.

And after you gave birth
How did you spend those days,
Five days before she was taken,
To the orphanage to raise?

Did you take the child into the field
And place her on the ground
But as you tried to leave her there,
Something made you turn around?

You went back for just one more glance
At the place where the baby layed,
And looked at her lying helplessly
On the altar you had made.

Once again you tried to leave in haste,
But the baby made a sound.
You bent your knee and kneeling there,
Lifted this baby from the ground.

Did you walk beside the rivers edge
With a baby in your arm?
Did you hear a voice speak inside,
Saying, "Do this child no harm."?

And as you were standing there,
Where the water meets the land,
Extending the baby forward
What was it that stayed your hand?

Did you realize that she was meant
For more than you could give?
Was it at this very moment
That you decided she must live?

Though the odds were stacked against her
It seemed her fate was sealed

Did you have a distinct impression?
This child must not be killed?

But a female child meant bad fortune,
Born in the Chinese year of the horse.
Yet you couldn't perform an act
That would fill you with remorse.

And so you chose the only option
Opened in your plight
You slipped into the city
In the middle of the night.

And when all was quiet in the marketplace
And the China eve was still
You placed the baby in the basket there
According to His will.

Amidst Asian smells and Asian sounds
Amidst the dirt and grime,
You set your baby down
For the very last time.

And did you find a hiding place?
Where are you could spend the night,
Watching and waiting 'til the morn
Your baby still in sight?

There's no way you could have known
As the basket touched the earth
That it became hallowed ground
The place of her rebirth.

For this child was being prayed for
Before she was conceived
And every day for months and months,
Many would intercede.

A street corner in Changsha
Made holy by the One

Who heard every prayer
Lifted through his son.

This child that you thought doomed for death
In a land that is not free
Was really made for life
To live for all eternity.

What can I give to you
For all you've given me?
I'll keep you ever before our God,
That He will set you free.

I'll pray that you'll come to know Him,
That He will reveal Himself to you,
And one day in our eternal home,
You'll meet the daughter you never knew.

Because of the choice you have made,
I've become a mother
A priceless gift you've given me
One unlike any other

Do you think that a woman
Who lives a thousand miles away,
One who's face I may never see
Could touch my life this way.

Could be an instrument of God
To bring such a joy to me,
To play such an important role,
In my future and destiny.

The only words I know to say
Are simple and are short
" God bless you, my Nameless friend,
And thank you from my heart."

    Charles and I recently spoke fondly and recalled a very special, endearing couple - **Kim and Carolyn** from Hawaii who adopted Sarah from Changzhou I believe. As I went through our letters to home to write the correct chronology of this book, I was greatly disappointed to not find a number of precious couples such as Kim and Carolyn. In some cases, I'm hard pressed to remember the couples and the details of their journey, which truly vexes me. I do believe however that the list of couples and their babies you'll find at the very end of this book is fairly accurate, although it doesn't include adoptions I worked on but was not able to complete.

Regarding the following magazine cover, I truly don't recall how this happened. It was my one and only photo on the cover of a magazine, shown with one of the beautiful Chinese girls we were privileged to facilitate the adoption of.

No weeping, No joy!

200

20

Christmas in Kansas

As we tried to become more settled in to life in Hong Kong and heal from the trauma we'd just experienced, we realized that the level of missionary fervor we had become accustomed to in China was difficult to find in Hong Kong. This may confuse you as much as it did us. I do not wish to disparage anyone else's ministry or calling, but Hong Kong during all the years before it was returned to China was the primary hub for missionary organizations reaching all of Southeast Asia. We had several missionary friends there who were actually laboring diligently to advance the Kingdom of God in Asia. But we couldn't help but be disappointed by such a great number of missionary families whose materialist lives were really no different than if they were living in America. I myself was also distracted by the greater number of alluring material temptations we experienced in Hong Kong. As one example, Ruth enrolled the girls in an event called Bible Discovery Week. It was similar to what we refer to as vacation bible school. Our girls very much enjoyed making new friends, learning the bible and singing new songs. Each day that week, the mothers were invited to stay for coffee and discuss different subjects, crafts, and have good fellowship. Ruth was so thankful to be able to enjoy making new friends. It seemed to Ruth however, that most of the women were in Hong Kong as denominational missionaries. They seemed to have very little interest in being there, reaching the Chinese with the gospel or ever even going in to China. To Ruth, these ladies were looking for purpose in their lives. Ruth commented in our newsletter: "I was quite baffled as to why so many are out on the front lines with no apparent calling to engage the enemy; no armor or weapons for spiritual warfare." So writing this leads me to ask myself now, am I or the church in general on the American front line with no apparent calling to engage the enemy; no armor or weapons for spiritual warfare? God wake us up. Shake us to action! Are our weapons and spiritual armor lying dusty and rusty at the back of our closet? We are the Kingdom of God. We belong to the King. We are commissioned by Him. We are His ambassadors. We've been chosen by the King, taught, trained and guided by God's Word and the Holy Spirit. Our obedience has been tested by the things we have suffered. We've been given the fruits of the Spirit to show and communicate the loving, merciful character of God. The King has given us ministry gifts by the Holy Spirit to advance the Kingdom of God. We've been given a direct line of communication with God called prayer. Shall we march forward or sit down in our Lazy Boy? Shall we fight or watch a reality show? Shall we live righteous, generous lives of humble Christian service in love, grace and mercy toward one another, or stew with bitterness and unforgiveness? Are we going to be the Lord's "salt and light" or tasteless, useless and full of shifting shadows? These are all valid questions each of us should search and ask ourselves.

As I visited with a Christian brother one day in September there in Hong Kong he raised the question why the Chinese were taking such a hard line against foreign Christians. We talked about the atheism of communists and Satan's influence over them, but he had another idea as well. I didn't mention it when I talked about my arrest and interrogation, but it was well known that the Chinese government was always looking for foreign spies. One of my friends pondered the idea that the Chinese thought many Christian missionaries must be spies with the CIA because we seemed to be so well coordinated and multifaceted. We must all be sent by the United States government to infiltrate the Chinese government. In their opinion perhaps there is someone at the head of such a massive operation to bring the gospel to the Chinese. They were right! We do have a Captain at the head of all the great many efforts of a great many people to take His gospel to the world. We utilize covert secret code to communicate called the Holy Spirit and prayer. We absolutely are an invading Army here to advance our Lord's worldwide Kingdom. *We use God's mighty weapons, not worldly weapons, to knock down the strongholds of human reasoning and to destroy false arguments. We destroy every proud obstacle that keeps people from knowing God. We capture their rebellious thoughts and teach them to obey Christ. 2 Corinthians 10:4-5. NLT*

THE FIGHT – After much opining about the Kingdom of God, let me get back to the reality of our family's life at this particular time in early September. Frustration and depression was starting to affect my family. The girls needed to be starting school, but we'd lost focus for making a plan for their education with all that we were dealing with from May through August, Ruth and I didn't really have a plan for their schooling. Lois and Julie were no longer available. We had no valid curriculum; we had little money to be able to afford new curriculum, nor a way to get the materials without it costing a fortune in shipping. Ruth always battled with thoughts of inadequacy to teach our four girls effectively, but especially the older two. Thoughts like these weighed heavily on Ruth. We had established a "One Week Deal" for our family early on in our ministry as a kind of safety valve. It was as follows: if any member of our family for a solid week was desperate to leave Asia

Those at our house warming party for our move to Mount Pleasure are seated front left Alvin and Rhoda Cobb, from left standing are two of our girls, Gina and Kendall Cobb as well as neighbor Terry Chestbrough

and return to America, we were all going to pack up and return home. Typically those feelings lasted only a day or two at a time and with only one family member, but those feelings started to last longer and was affecting more members of our family.

THE GLORY – Ruth and I quickly came to the conclusion that we had to at least try to get the older girls into a Hong Kong school. This would take a miracle. First of all, Hong Kong had no public schools. They were all privately run mostly by Christian organizations which were all expensive. The school closest to us and the one our friends had their children in was $3200 for Stephanie and $5200 for Adrianne, excluding books, uniforms and transportation. We were told there was a long waiting list to be able to get in, but were also told if we were able to get a "sponsor", get Hong Kong ID cards and make application, we could apply for financial assistance to receive as much as an 80% discount. We went for it! A couple of days before school started, we visited the school office where the girls were tested and interviewed according to the rules of this high caliber British, English speaking only school. It was a miracle, but the next day Adrianne was accepted into grade 7 (American 6th grade) and Stephanie into grade 5 (American 4th grade) according to the British school system of class grading. One of their class requirements was to learn French. Ruth over the years along with her assistants did a good job teaching and preparing the girls for this stage of their life.

They had no problem fitting in academically with all the other children there. What it was going to cost us still remained an unknown, but we were confident of God's provision. While we waited on that news, we went ahead and ordered curriculum for our two little ones Erika and Emily. Lo and behold, a friend we mentioned earlier in the book, Herb Jones, happened to be coming back to China and brought us our young daughter's school curriculum. Until he arrived, we made due with a few store bought books we were able to get our hands on for second grade and kindergarten. Our ministry in China was still under pressure to the point it was simply too dangerous to meet with any of our disciples or leaders. From that point on and for the foreseeable future, we had to be very careful with any contact whatsoever with them. We completed the printing of 5000 copies of Pastor Sachet-Waller's discipleship book. These became part of the bible distribution I was going to be part of operating. In late September I joined a team of brothers to distribute a large number of bibles, teaching books such as Pastor Sachet-Waller's, as well as gospel tracts. We were going to the city of Changchun in Jilin Province which is in far northern China, not far from North Korea. While in Changchun I visited the orphanage and came to a verbal agreement with the officials there to begin doing adoptions. Later we were also able to help SC move into a new apartment and enjoyed sweet fellowship and support. SC had done a fabulous work of ministry. Adoption couples continued to contact us, as did contact with American international adoption organizations. At the time I was testing an additional ministry expansion opportunity that I mentioned in our September 1991 newsletter. To begin with, it was to set up an advisory board and begin to expand into the Philippines and other Asian countries in establishing orphanages and funding them through adoptions all over Asia. This effort might also open opportunities for pulpit evangelism ministry in other areas outside of Hong Kong. As time passed however, it became clear the ministry expansion idea I just spoke of was not God's will, so we focused our efforts all on what we absolutely knew God was leading us in.

The minivan for the orphanage in Changzhou finally cleared customs. A few of the officials came down to Shenzhen so Ruth and I took them around for a little tour of the area. One tourist spot we visited was called "Splendid China". This park was laid out like the country of China with scaled down replicas of all its geographically placed wonders such as the Great Wall, Terra Cotta Soldiers and the Imperial Palace in Beijing. They seemed pleased with our tour efforts, and especially when they took possession of their brand new Toyota Hi Ace 12 passenger minivan. We took them out for a very nice dinner the day before they left to celebrate our strong relationship. They thanked us over and over and promised to do everything they could to work faithfully to assist us in Chinese orphan adoptions.

Adrianne and Stephanie were happy and doing very well in their new school. Ruth and I got a kick out of their new-found British accents, and stories about their interesting international classmates. They looked so cute in their school uniforms. Ruth enrolled Adrianne, Stephanie and Erika into a local Girl Scout program and Ruth volunteered to be a co-leader.

Earlier in the book I talked about the Chinese requirements to allow American couples to adopt. As various couples applied, we continued to receive letters from couples who were under 35 years of age as well as ones who already had children, but for medical reasons could not have more. So whenever the opportunity was given me I pressured officials I met with to work with those above them in rank to bend the rules. You may recall our first adoption did not comply with the "no child" rule. Bit by bit, what they would allow began to change in our favor. In October we learned the official age for adoption was changed to 30 years old. We had three couples waiting on this law change and had additional couple named Larry and Susan who adopted five month old Mollee.

The older girls are truly finding their place at the International British Academy. Adrianne loves the great variety of classes; 14 different subjects in all. Her favorites are French, Science and Drama. Stephanie loves being in the school newspaper club, submitting jokes, stories and even took some pictures for them. She is exceptional at making friends. More social interaction was especially great for Adrianne. For her eleventh birthday she had some of her friends from school and some from our missionary friends come over for a great party. They all put on clown makeup, split into two groups and went out on the streets of Taiwai taking Polaroid pictures of themselves doing different things with different sorts of people. The group who collected all the assigned photos and got back first won the game. They had a bunch of fun stories to tell to go along with the crazy pictures. Later we received news that their tuitions were cut in half by the school when we finally did get tuition assistance. Praise God!

In our November 1991 newsletter I addressed one of the primary messages which I'm endeavoring to get across with this book- the battle! Had I followed this God thought later, it would have surely saved me from a boat load of pain. Therefore let me just quote from that letter and opine in detail to give you its full impact and hopefully save you pain similar to what I and most Christians needlessly suffer. "Are you in the midst of a battle today? Are you suffering or feeling crushed?" Do you seem to be in the middle of a raging fury? Like you, we all often feel this. It seems that you are helpless. It seems you are losing. Scripture says to wait. No one knows what to do in such battles. Whatever you try seems to be wasted effort. If you struggle, it is for nothing. If you worry, you dangerously weaken yourself. Wait on the Lord for *"He who calls you is faithful, who also will do it."* *I Thessalonians 5:24 NKJV*. Trust in Him because He loves you and His faithfulness knows no end. If you are caught in indecision, why should you struggle for a decision? Just wait! If you're anxiously looking and planning ahead thinking you need to prepare for something that God hasn't even taken you to yet, you need to wait. If everything looks very bad, just wait. If your world falls in around you just wait, because that's what we are told to do in scripture. The worst battles can often be the very best time to rest. His grace truly is sufficient for you and your family. God gives us work to do and we need to do it with zeal, but we can't if we are exhausted from the battle. The fight of faith is so often just the battle against our fleshly nature of wanting to fight. A true fight of faith is accomplished because we trust the One who fights for us; the One who has already won the victory. Scripture says that the *"battle is the Lord's" 1 Samuel 17:47*. Stay out of it and you won't get hurt. Get in it and you as well as your family may become cut and bruised both emotionally and mentally. This is not to say that there isn't a time for prayer because it most certainly is. But I've often experienced and witnessed in others great anxiety take over in times of prayer, and that is not spiritual warfare but just telling God how worried and doubtful we are. This is not the character of the waiting I'm talking about at all. It's not that which scripture calls us to engage in. The devil who brings the test would love to fight with you, and I know many who look for and love to fight with him. I've come to understand that if I fight with the devil, it will only serve to multiply his evil deeds. The warfare of the spirit I've learned about, has much more to do with faith than fighting. To trust, wait and rest in the middle of a battle is the faith that brings victory without injury. Will God desert you if you stand back and trust him to the very end of the matter? No! It is more likely that God will only stay out of the fight if you fight with your own strength. *2 Chronicles 20:15, 17, 21* Pray and hear from God! Wait! Trust! Worship! In so doing, FIGHT the good fight of faith and see the GLORY of the Lord.

    In the beginning of November, Jim Woodward the director of Christian Adoption Services (C.A.S.) of Charlotte, North Carolina came to Asia to meet me. Jim had a long history of doing international adoptions which he and his wife began in 1979. We had already started receiving couples from his agency for Chinese adoptions, but he wanted to witness for himself what the process looked like. We really hit it off and became quite good friends. I took him up to Changzhou to give him the step by step process look at what each couple would experience. Jim wanted to be able to give his interested couples the benefit of his first hand knowledge, and I respected him all the more for this approach. Since Changzhou was still overwhelmed with gratitude they indeed "rolled out the red carpet" for us. Three different departments involved with the adoptions celebrated our being there with five banquets in two and one-half days. Each banquet was 25 courses plus with all the exotic and delicious foods you can imagine. My mom used to call me a picky eater when I was young, but God and these exotic Chinese dinners must have cured me.

Also in November I took our first two adopting couples to Chengdu. David and Cathy came from Florida for baby Angie and Don and Diane brought their three other children with them to adopt baby Elizabeth. Later Ken and Brenda came from Texas to adopt baby Joy from Changsha. Brenda was quite a challenge for us since she was only 27 at the time. The official age requirement was just lowered from 35 to 30, but now we were asking for a 27 year old to adopt. Also, this family had already adopted two children from India. This was just one more adoption miracle we were able to get approved. They were such a wonderful and talented couple like so many of our couples. If you would like additional biographical reading material on the subject of international adoptions, Ken wrote a great book recently which is available on Amazon called "Coming Home – The Journey to Becoming Family". The adopting families and their babies were such a great blessing to our family. By the middle of November we'd completed fifteen adoptions, seven of which were in the previous 30 days.

The end of November and all of December brought us several couples. Jack and Nancy adopted baby Leah, but when they got home Leah's heart rate was too high and blood pressure was too low. Jack and Nancy immediately got her into see a Doctor and then to the hospital. The doctor's reaction was that she should have died twice. They couldn't understand how baby Leah could recuperate so quickly from the medicine they gave her. After two weeks of medicine and extensive testing the doctors concluded it was a virus which attacked her heart, but there was no way to be absolutely sure. By a miracle from God's hand, Leah got through it rather quickly and in no time at all was in good health. But what a scare and fight of faith they went through. Alan and Denelle adopted baby Merideth successfully, Steve and Kim adopted three year old Stephanie which was a miracle since in a couple of respects they didn't qualify as a couple to be adopting, Del and Laura adopted baby Catherine, as well as Michael and Penny adopted one and one half year old May Ann. I had all their large packages of paperwork done before we left for America. All of these adoptions went smoothly.

Therefore, in addition to Charles in China we called on our precious missionary friends Ross and Karen Barcham from

Melbourne, Australia. Ross was a dentist who had brought his lovely wife and daughter. They were missionaries working in Hong Kong and China. Others who lived there in Hong Kong also helped us with these adoptions.

One of the requirements incumbent upon the Chinese and American governments was that the children had to pass health examinations. Of the many adoptions we facilitated, I knew of three children whose physical or emotional health was not as it should have been. But of course these wonderful couples were totally committed to caring for every need their precious children required no matter the time or the cost.

Our family is about to bust with delight. A former neighbor of ours had a relationship with a man who wanted to help us be with our family during the Christmas season, but primarily to be in Ruth's sister Susan's wedding on December 6th. Bill Meredith from Wellington, Kansas, whom we had never met, very generously paid for all our round trip tickets. We arrived back in Kansas near the end of November. So much had happened in the short time since we left there just a little over a year earlier. The grandparents were elated with having their sweet granddaughters back home for the holidays. This was going to be a short break, but one we greatly needed. We didn't pursue any church presentations but we did go see some friends. Ken and Brenda invited us to the Dallas area for a visit. While we were in the area, we also dropped in to see our former neighbors and friends Andy and Kathy Barnes. On the way home we swung by and spent time with Bill and Sherry Shaw in Pond Creek, Oklahoma. It was wonderful to catch up with all of them.

To end this chapter I'm going to take another excerpt from our newsletter released in December 1991. "Recently we've been helping more and more couples adopt from China. One of the greatest battles facing couples is their lack of control over their adoption process, which tends to give many of the couples a great bit of anxiety. They find themselves having to trust someone halfway around the world they don't know with such a crucial endeavor. The temptation was to fear whether the organization is honest or not. Our telephone and fax machine buzz often with many of our couples wanting information on their adoption, and at times desiring some control. But the reality is soon to be realized that they must trust me and more importantly, trust God with the smooth and successful fruition of their dreams. Many who read this letter, are at present, preparing to adopt through us. Though I'm confident in my knowledge and ability to give them a fabulous adoption experience start to finish, there will be details which cause anguish. We as Americans are more apt to want to control rather than trust. During some of the trips in China there are points where the couple or group loses control to the very hands of God. Even the best planning, which we try to achieve, will not be enough in these times to prepare for every possible situation when dealing with the realities of a third world country. There are just no guarantees here in China. Jesus put it another way in *Luke 12:16-21*, the parable of a man who built bigger barns to hold his great increase of grain. But God said this night your soul will be required of you. Nearly every couple who travels to adopt tells us how they are challenged to walk their faith rather than just talk it. Personally, I feel that this aspect of the couples' trip to adopt in China is really a blessing if it causes the couple to see that God will lead them in peace if they don't anxiously try to hang onto control." Then later in that same letter: "Much grief we've brought on ourselves simply because we want to control people and situations, only to become disappointed or angry when we couldn't. I would say to you in regards to any of your personal difficulties, that even though you do not have control, God does! If you happen to be preparing to adopt through us, I pray that God will give you the grace to be stretched in your faith. Ruth and I pledge our deep dedication to your family. Though you may not understand all that happens, we ask you to trust we are doing all that we physically can to make sure that your adoption is as close to your dream as we can make it." This little lesson on "control" will be pushed to the extreme in a later chapter. In fact, it is the final and most personal Fight and Glory of the entire book. So perhaps when you later read the story, you might remember this exhortation. Had I held fast to it, perhaps it would have saved me thirty years of destructive personal torment. Presently, as I write this now, the Holy Spirit is reprimanding me and reminding me of how often I've been guilty of making plans for what I think is going to happen in my life, only to find I've wasted time and money on something which was not God's plan. Wait to act only on the plans God makes for you; don't get ahead of Him!

No hurt, No healing!

21

How Do You Say it in English?

While we were in America our Hong Kong apartment building owner decided unexpectedly to move ahead with remodeling he'd been planning. His workers began taking sledge hammers to bust out the original iron window frames and just left empty holes in the walls for several days. Our plan while we were gone was to allow two of the adopting couples to stay in our home in our absence. Therefore all the demolition sadly occurred while they were there. Hong Kong in December typically is somewhat mild, but not that year. That year was the coldest on record in 16 years when temperatures dipped down to freezing every night. Not only did these amazing couples survive, they covered up our furniture, watched over our possessions, swept up all of the dust and rubble from our floors, and cleaned up our apartment the best they could.

Stephanie with some of her classmates at the British School

Once we returned to Hong Kong from such a great holiday reprieve, we had a great deal of adoption work to catch up on. As you can imagine we returned to a huge stack of faxes and mail as well dealing with the mess of our windows being torn out and replaced. Ruth and I had our hands full. We were kept busy non-stop for a couple of weeks. Looking over the number of adoptions on my docket was alarming. Six couples would be coming soon. Charles and I needed to work out the schedule for so many going to various orphanages. The last thing I wanted to do was delay any of the adoptions just to make our scheduling easier, though I found myself being forced to do so. Once we had all the paperwork, it had to be proofread in English and Chinese; then put in correct order. It was simply a lot to arrange with the couples' schedules and each orphanage's schedule. Then all the Hong Kong and China travel and hotel plans had to be made. Since Charles was in China and I was in Hong Kong, communication between us also made for delays and difficulties.

Shortly after getting settled back in Hong Kong, two friends, Associate Pastor Bobby Massey and Jon Grady came from our home church to visit us. I gave them a bit of a tour of Macao and stopped in to introduce them to our old friends Pat and Windy Caspary who were mentioned much earlier in the book. Pat and Windy had begun a good ministry in Macao. We later met up with an adopting couple in Hong Kong from Maine, Paul and Louise. We would all be traveling together to the very first orphanage I visited in the Southeast Chinese city of Zhanjiang which I talked about in earlier chapters.

Paul and Louise, accompanied by their first daughter Deborah, were just like every other adopting couple; they were very special to me. I don't mean to single them out in my next story; I could truly write something interesting for nearly all of our couples. However, I had a couple of very unique experiences with Paul and Louise, and by extension, Bobby and Grady, which I must tell you about. One miracle story I'll share first is the seven of us one night on buses. After being on our first Guangzhou bus for a while, we needed to transfer to another one. Within a minute of getting on the second bus, Paul realized he didn't have his bag with him. It was a very important bag! Passports, money, travelers checks, camera, etc. He panicked as did we all. We screamed for the bus to stop! Paul got off and started running back with all his might back to where the other bus had been, nearly 200 yards down the fairly dark street. Of course there was no guarantee the bus would still be there. Since it was at night we couldn't tell bus from another at that distance. So here is the miracle. When Paul was perhaps a 100 yards from us, we noticed a man running from the other direction holding up something in his hand. They met in the middle and Paul returned but completely out of breath. A Chinese young man had noticed that Paul had left his bag and immediately stopped his bus. He then ran for all he was worth to return it. Yes, everything was still in the bag. Oh my, we could all finally breathe again. Praise God! Those of you who've traveled internationally can understand what a miracle this was, especially at night.

When the seven of us arrived at the office of the Zhanjiang orphanage, we were seated in a waiting area for quite awhile as I remember it. When an official finally emerged, it was to happily tell us that Paul and Louise would "get to choose" the baby they wanted from among the two they had available. Well that was truly a shock. It was a bit similar to being surprisingly told your surrogate mother's pregnancy produced twins, but you could only pick one. For months they had prepared documents and prayed for that one special baby God was giving them, and they were not at all prepared to make this decision. They simply could not wrap their head around the idea of them having to choose one. So it took a few minutes for them to decide exactly how to handle this. Finally they chose to receive the first one brought out as their own and not even meet the second one. Of course they and their daughter Deborah instantly fell in love with baby Sarah with little to no thought at the time of the other baby. As it turned out though, they did end up going back a year or so later to that same orphanage for a second child.

So then it was time to celebrate their adoption and time for the never to be forgotten, adoption banquet. Everyone was very excited and gathered around the eight foot round table as we awaited our grand meal. The officials from the orphanage had their own translator who I'll refer to as Kevin, and we had Charles. There were probably six officials from the orphanage and the local Civil Affairs Bureau. It was a very "auspicious" occasion, as the Chinese often put it, held at the most prestigious restaurant in the city. As we awaited our food, the conversation was very light and friendly. Since meeting Charles, Kevin was very excited to talk to him because he realized Charles' English ability was exceptional. Kevin could hardly stop talking, both in Chinese and in English. Our food began coming out and there were several wonderful looking dishes. One that caught our American eyes was what appeared to be chicken and noodles. Let me pause for a minute and say Pastor Bobby was out of his element. Bobby was long known to be a very picky eater. He'd been having trouble eating since he first arrived in China. Grady was somewhat the same. They were both "meat and potatoes" kind of guys, so now I'll proceed.

When the first dish which caught our eyes came out, we began commenting on it. Kevin with great joy jumped at the opportunity to tell us what it was. But first, he turned to Charles to tell him in Chinese exactly what it was. Upon this revelation,

Charles began telling us that this was a local signature seafood dish from Zhanjiang. Our response again was, "but what is it?" because it didn't look like any seafood we'd ever seen. Kevin couldn't restrain himself and was frantically trying to work out the English pronunciation so that he could be the one to tell us. Charles on the other hand was saying "it doesn't matter, just eat and enjoy it." Of course from looking at Charles it was obvious that something about this dish was not going to be so "special" to our American guests. But would Kevin give up? Not in your life! The more Charles tried to change the subject, the more determined Kevin became. At first Kevin was trying to pronounce the word that was in his head, but what came out was "sand wood". Of course we were completely puzzled and began guessing "is it a type of fish or crab?" "No," Kevin said. Though Charles tried very hard, he was still not able to get Kevin to give it up. While all the Chinese officials were observing all this, being a bit puzzled themselves, Kevin blurted out "so how do you say W-O-R-M? Oh yes, what we'd already begun eating was revealed to be a pile of large sand worms which had been dug out of the sand near the sea shore. They were adorned with tender chicken and bathed in a delicious, creamy sauce. Immediately those pretty linen napkins were quickly snatched up and held to American faces. I had rather liked the dish so you're probably not surprised I was the only American who cleaned his plate. As I ate however, I couldn't help but curiously examine my interesting, long, once circular morsels and found the expected wrinkled, pointy tail on all those "noodles". Yep! They were ten-twelve inch long worms alright. In Kansas we call them "night crawlers. "Let's go fishing" I said.

    From this point on, their meal and the adoption was more or less normal: appointments with local and provincial officials and the final trip to the United States consulate in Guangzhou before returning to Hong Kong. So now you understand why I referred to it as the "never to be forgotten" adoption banquet. Traumas at this level have a way of burning their memory into your American brain.

    When we got back to Hong Kong from Christmas in America I learned the girls were very glad to be back in school. Their friends were also very glad to see them, especially when Adrianne and Stephanie started pulling out American candy to give them. Oh yeah! For a day or two they were the most popular kids in school. One last surprise, upon our return we discovered Pippy was pregnant. The girls were ecstatic. Ruth commented that watching the pups be born would be great for their sex education. On February 29th we welcomed two puppies the girls named Sebastian and Ariel which we would later need to facilitate adoptions for.

From our January 1992 newsletter, let me take a quote. "Amidst all the joy of being home these past six weeks, I sensed a burden in my heart for Jesus' precious Church. In my own humble way I'd like to raise an issue common to all of us and that is the age old church sign of our spiritual pride. I've discovered this sin in spades here in Hong Kong; perhaps the largest of all melting pots of Christian denominationalism. What amazing things could be done if all those ministries worked together even to just win Hong Kong for Kingdom of God? Instead it seems the way to pull people into your church was criticizing how other churches and Christians do it wrong, and how you were doing it right. We as Gods people seem to thrive on judging another person's ministry. Couldn't we just teach the Gospel according to what God has given us and leave out the backbiting? Some might say to me 'Randy, I can't compromise the word of God'. Well, there are two things that I would say. First, you don't have to compromise anything of God's word to love someone. And second, you yourselves are compromising God's Word by not loving your brother. Church discipline is important but scripturally it is to be done within a single fellowship or denomination among people who know the facts. *"You my brothers were called to be free but do not use your freedom to indulge your sinful nature, rather serve one another in love. The entire law is summed up in a single command, "love your neighbor as yourself". If you keep on biting and devouring each other, watch out or you will be destroyed by each other."* Galatians 5:13-15 Scripture likened backbiting to indulging in our "sinful nature", and that's exactly what it is. Whether it's in your own community or on the mission field, love one another no matter the name on the door. Surely you can find a common interest and you might even find a way to bless what God has given them to do, with what God has given you."

The number of adoptions continues to build. Two were scheduled to arrive March 13th. Twenty more are nearly ready. I became aware of orphanage directors from all over China were to be having a conference in Shenzhen and I was invited to attend. One of the directors was from the orphanage in Wuxi. Wuxi is located between Shanghai and Changzhou where I'd done the bulk of our adoptions. It is also the orphanage which handled the first foreign I'm aware of in China by an agency in Montreal. I believe I mentioned them earlier in the book. The Wuxi director and I became fast friends. We were somewhat familiar with each other because of our common friends from Changzhou. He invited me to forward him paperwork for an adoption anytime in the future. This now gave us six open doors from which to adopt: Changzhou, Changsha, Chengdu, Zhanjiang, Changchun and now Wuxi. Meanwhile, we received three wonderful couples who were on their way to to adopt from Chengdu: Richard and Donna adopted Lianne, Frank and Pattie adopted Elizabeth and Frank and Ruth adopted Mariah.

April brought us John and Amy who adopted Lucy, David and Cathy who adopted Amanda, and Sylvester and Deborah who adopted Sarah. All were amazing couples full of anticipation and love to give their precious babies. I do have another humorous story to tell regarding this group going to Changsha. Syl and Deb was a joyful pair and everyone loved their enthusiasm. Syl had bright red hair, was an impressively tall man with a very muscular build. After all, he was a mechanic for a steel mining operation in Uniontown Pennsylvania as well as a ski instructor. To further set up the story, Sylvester and Deborah had a great deal of luggage, as did most of our couples. They were ready for anything. Included in their luggage was a large beautiful stainless steel video camera case. Commercial airplanes in China are made for rather small Chinese, not big steel workers. The seats are small and the airlines are able to fit five across where we would normally see four. The aisles we had to navigate were so narrow they all had to walk sideways to get to get to their seat. So let's proceed with the story Charles later told me about.

Charles was leading them all sideways down the tiny aisle carefully. Nearly all the Chinese had already gotten seated. Syl and Deb followed Charles. Syl's camera case was on one shoulder and a carryon bag over the other. He was being as careful as he possibly could, but fate took over. Deb said something to Syl which caused him to pivot to see what she needed. So as you can imagine, that heavy steel video camera case swung around fast to smack a rather small, dignified Chinese businessman in the back of the head. Well that middle aged man was quickly enraged. He rose and turned to face big red headed Sylvester. Quickly the man shriveled with intimidation. Being the tender hearted, gentle giant that he was, Syl of course wanted to sincerely apologize. The only Chinese word he knew however was Xiexie. You might know this means 'thank you' not I'm sorry. Syl, feeling so badly for what he'd done, just kept saying Xiexie over and over. The businessman's countenance turned from intimidation to utter confusion. Meanwhile Charles can hardly stand it. He wanted to laugh, but did not want to embarrass Syl more. We absolutely loved this couple so much we made it a point to reconnect with them years later at their home to see how they were doing. Of course I had to bring up the story. I think this precious man was still a bit embarrassed by the incident and I felt at the time it wasn't a welcomed memory.

Not long after I returned home, we were informed of changes which were to be made in how adoptions were to be done in China. There was nothing said that indicated it would affect us much, except perhaps to delay adoptions which were in process and maybe raise cost for the couples. We also received word that about 70 Christians in Shenzhen China were in a meeting that was raided by the police. Although our friend Mr. Y wasn't there, he was still in danger of being put in prison due to an irresponsible person who recklessly said too much about much of what he was doing in ministry.

To end this chapter in case you haven't noticed, I wanted to reiterate one thing which was a great challenge for missionary families and something I've made reference to many times in this book; the planning and execution to school their children. Missionaries, especially those working independently, often find themselves spending a great deal of time, effort and expense on their children's education. In our short time there we had developed relationships with many families dealing the same challenge we were dealing with, so we began putting our heads together to find a better solution. We settled on creating a home school cooperative which we named Emmaus Learning Center. This cooperative would consist of pooling all the member moms and dads together to teach subjects they were most competent in. Ruth would teach and I would act as their secretary/treasurer. We had a building donated to us and by the end of May, 15 students were enrolled. I set up the logo, newsletter and checking account and was responsible for various related tasks. This was for our two older children to attend. God brought us a teacher who we already knew and loved, She had been a teacher for our friends the Kimbrills. Erika and Emily loved

Heather and it seemed to be an amazing answer to prayer. Heather was a great help assisting me with adoption paperwork and communication, and was also a close friend to Ruth. God is so good!

No rejection, No exaltation!

22

More Than the Mind Can Bear

THE FIGHT – Whatever the country, I suppose the ramifications of new national laws can be tricky and full of consequences you don't expect. Looking back, I guess I shouldn't have been so naïve regarding China's new adoption law. I only thought Beijing would seek money and bring uniformity to the rules of the adoption process throughout the country. Before the law was passed, Beijing played no role at all in foreign adoptions. It was all handled at the local and provincial levels. The government had for some time been fighting against and prosecuting illegal adoptions. There were corrupt individuals going through back channels to buy children and arranging adoptions in other parts of China. I just didn't fully realize how the new law would affect what we were doing to the extent it did.

From the beginning we realized the new law was creating delays. We had invitations for Bill and Jane, Bob and Patrice and Robert and Patti to come in mid-April but then all of a sudden, the orphanage in Chengdu indefinitely postponed those invitations. Several other couples were put on hold as well: Mike and Joyce, Robert and Melinda, Gordon and Colleen, Richard and Cynthia, Richard and Nikki, Joe and Sandra, Mike and Patricia, Joe and Deann, A.J. and Kelly, John and Wendy and Jerry and Leslie.

With all Ruth and I had been through, and to an extent, was still going through, it was well past time to focus on our marriage. Although we had taken part in a very valuable Marriage Encounter in Kansas, years later we at that time had the opportunity to attend one in Hong Kong as well and it was very helpful in preparing us for what was to come.

Previously I mentioned one of our adopting couples, Robert and Patti. In the weeks following the completion of all their paperwork while waiting on the orphanage for the go-ahead, they became very frustrated. Perhaps I did not communicate with them as well as I should have, the reason for the delay in their adoption. I certainly don't blame them. They simply lost faith in me and chose to retain a local attorney who could assist them by picking up where we left off. This new lawyer had contacts in China and was able to secure an invitation himself to go to the Chengdu orphanage. I was quite broken hearted about it because I felt I had failed them. They arrived in Chengdu a few days before I got the invitation from Chengdu to bring Bill and Jane, and Bob and Patrice. When Charles arrived in Chengdu with these two couples it was very awkward. Robert and Patti were stuck and even though we'd been given the invitation for them to come to adopt, our two couples were stuck as well. Charles knew that Robert and Patti were originally working with us, but even though they had jumped ship so to speak, Charles still included them in everything he was trying to do to get the process going for his two couples. That pesky new law seemed to have bottlenecked every adoption in China, including the adoption for Mike and Joyce.

Although Joyce eagerly shared with me the highlights of her testimony when I first met them, I had never learned all the marvelous details of their testimony. Getting back to my difficult reality at that time; I had four adopting couples all struggling desperately to finish their adoptions and take the babies home which they'd already been given and become bonded with. There was a huge weight on everyone's heart and mind, including mine and Charles'. What if after all these couples had dreamt of, paid for, and gone through, resulted in abject failure? After they had held and bonded with their babies, would they be forced to leave China without them? Most confusing of all, the orphanage could not give them any explanation for why they couldn't do the adoptions. Beijing said no, and that was all they could tell us. It didn't matter that the Chengdu orphanage had received from us $11,000 for the purpose of building an already half constructed new orphanage and staff dormitories, we were shown no favor. Charles and the attorney representing Robert and Patty were dumbfounded and struggling to find any path forward.

In Changzhou where we had done so many adoptions and had recently given them their new van, they too were stuck and completely out of ideas. Even before we arrived, they realized the level of trouble this adoption was in. They sent a few representatives from their local and provincial offices all the way to Beijing with many gifts, as well as cash to "grease the wheels of government" to get this adoption unstuck. Their valiant and generous efforts failed however. When the envoy returned with no resolution, they sat down with Mike, Joyce and I to give us the very bad news. So, what was the big problem with their paperwork which warranted such a fiasco? The Changzhou officials had actually secured an answer from Beijing, but it was a ridiculous one. They wanted Mike and Joyce to have the United States government certify the authenticity of Mike and Joyce's state of Ohio marriage certificate. Not only had this never been requested before, it was completely impossible. No office of the US government can certify a state issued document. The states themselves certify it to be authentic with their own seal. As I sat in the room listening to this I was completely stunned. Then a very real sense of dread set in.

My friends, the Changzhou orphanage director and co-director were really feeling the weight of the situation. They were not wanting to "lose face" for any of it, so the director declared to Mike and Joyce that "if Randy had only brought them earlier when they'd first invited them, there would not have been any problems". To that accusation I really didn't have a defense. I truly had delayed their adoption by a couple of weeks. To be honest I can't to this day remember the exact reason I delayed it. I do recall I'd been trying to coordinate the number of adoptions I had in the works and most likely made the decision to delay their adoption based on that coordination effort. What I tell you next should no way cast any blame on either the orphanage or this precious couple for their reaction to this news, but Mike and Joyce were absolutely devastated. They felt betrayed and who could blame them! The thought of what I did and the very real possibility of them having to leave China without their adorable baby girl Maggie Mei was unbearable.

The responsibility of this fiasco was simply too much for my heart and mind to bear. When the meeting finished with an impossible path on which to move forward, the couple and I walked out into the court yard. They stopped and as I turned around to face them, Mike said "I could just punch you in the face right now". I certainly felt I deserved it. The hurt in their faces was so great, and so terrible; I truly never will forget it as long as I live. Looking at them, the shame and pain I felt was more than I could endure. It totally broke me and although I didn't know it at the time, something deep inside me would remain broken for next 30 years.

The next ten days or so I remained isolated in my hotel room from them and everyone else. One time I bumped in to the Mike and Joyce on the elevator, but nothing much was said and it was very uncomfortable. Unable to eat more than a few meals from the hotel restaurant during a several day period, I laid on my bed for days on end sleeping, praying and crying out to God. I later determined I must have had an emotional breakdown. Those days of my life would forever be only a blur in my memory. I called Ruth and the girls begging them to pray and often crying. We racked up a monthly phone bill of well over $1000. Ruth and the girls were going through a great deal of agony as well; worrying about me and not knowing how it was all going to play out. One evening before I called, Ruth, Heather and the girls watched a movie called "The Trip to Bountiful" about an elderly woman who desperately wanted to return to her childhood home. It was a touching movie but when the theme music played "Softly and tenderly Jesus is calling" then the chorus of this familiar hymn- "come home, come home. You who are weary come home", they all lost it. They all cried out together how much they wanted to go home; home to "bountiful" Kansas. They didn't want to live in China anymore.

I was also in communication with Charles, trying to figure out a plan. I was basically waiting to see if Mike and Joyce could obtain the help of their US Congressman or Senator. Could they find a way around this catastrophe? After much desperate effort however, it was deemed impossible by everyone they talked to. Charles had even greater challenges. He had three devastated couples who didn't know what was wrong; officials who didn't know what was wrong and no one who could figure out how to keep the couples from being forced to leave China without their babies. They were just told to wait, and wait, and wait. Charles and I at nearly the same time decided to take our cases to the top and depend on God for miracles. Charles planned to travel by train all the way to Beijing 2000 miles away to have an impossible to get meeting with the head of the Public Affairs Bureau for the country of China. For me it was only to take Mike and Joyce by train to Shanghai and visit the United States Consulate. We needed to get an unscheduled meeting there and appeal to the Consulate General.

THE FINAL ROUNDS - Our 100 mile train ride to Shanghai was very quiet. After all Mike, Joyce and I had been through, there was little to say. This was a "Hail Mary" which was now in God's hands. From the Shanghai train station I believe we took a taxi to the U.S. Consulate. We didn't have an appointment and I don't recall knowing for sure whether or not the Consulate General was even going to be in the China, let alone in his office. We went into the Consulate General's waiting area. His secretary asked us what it was we needed. We introduced ourselves and began telling her the shortest version possible of what we were facing and that we were there to ask for the Consulate General's help. She took the entire adoption dossier and said she'd pass it on to him with the background story. In complete abandoned and broken humility we all prayed silently as we waited for what seemed forever for the Consulate General to see us. When he finally emerged we could tell from his contrite countenance he did not have good news. He began explaining to us that even though he was absolutely sympathetic to our dilemma, he could not legally put his US Consulate authentication seal on their state certified marriage certificate. After expressing his deepest sympathy, he said his secretary would soon return our adoption documents to us, which she did. We just sat there frozen with anguish; heads hanging low. We were keenly aware that this was our very last hope. Mike and Joyce would now have to return to Ohio with empty arms.

  Before I finish my cliffhanger though, let's pick up on Charles' adventure. Like my minibus trip home from the police station following my arrest, Charles had no money except for what it took to purchase a train ticket to Beijing. I arranged to have some money sent to him in Beijing via Western Union, but in the meantime he had no money to eat or get a hotel with. This dear disciple had more faith than his mentor to believe this huge mountain could be moved, but Charles was going by faith all the way to Beijing to move it. As I mentioned before, Charles grew up in a humble, rural village in Guangdong province but he, a political and social nobody, was now so bold as to believe he could get an impromptu meeting with the very important federal official who Charles was told would be able to authorize the adoptions.

  Personally, I could not help but have doubts he'd even get in to the intimidating government building which housed her office. But Charles did get in by the hand of God. He even got an invitation in to her private office. He had with him the adoption dossiers for all three couples. Charles met and made his appeal to her wearing just his common shirt and pants, but with the Spirit of God and his captivating charm. What could possibly be wrong with any of the paperwork for these wonderful, loving couples? Even much worse than the lame excuse given to my couple Mike and Joyce, she refused Bill and Jane's adoption because they'd adopted a child from Taiwan who had heart problems. She imagined that Bill and Jane wanted this new Chinese adopted child to provide "body parts" for their other adopted child who had health issues. True story! Of course Charles was aghast. He could not believe this woman who was in such a high position would even think such a thing. Once he quickly regained his composure, Charles did his very best to refute this line of thinking by restating how truly wonderful and loving this couple was. She didn't want to hear it. Once Charles reached the edge of being rude, he stopped and thanked her for giving him the opportunity to state his case. Somewhat discouraged Charles left to try to find some way to get a meal and a place to sleep. He really hadn't eaten since leaving Chengdu more than a day earlier and the only sleep he had was sitting in an uncomfortable wood bench seat on the train. With God's help, Charles did find someone to buy him a meal, but as far as sleep, he was forced to sleep outside. The next day he was able to pick up the money I sent via Western Union, but what was he to do about the adoptions?

THE GLORY – Returning now to my situation, I was sitting the waiting area with Mike and Joyce in the American Consulate in Shanghai completely discouraged. Making sure everything was there, I began hopelessly thumbing through all the documents which had taken several months to complete. When I came upon their marriage certificate, I looked at it in complete disbelief. With a shaking hand, I handed it to Mike and Joyce. It had the United States Consulate Seal on it certifying it to be authentic. In other words, it was the exact "impossible" authentication we had come there to get. Wait! What? Who? How? Why? We were completely baffled. We didn't dare go back to the secretary to ask what happened. We had our miracle and we weren't about to question it. This was a miracle from God, which meant this couple who had never been blessed with children, but were desperate to take their baby home, would indeed go home with their beautiful, tiny, miracle baby girl named Maggie Mei in their arms.

As for Charles, he was finally able to eat a good meal and get a good night's rest. The new day gave him renewed faith and energy. He was going to go back to the government lady once more.

So much was at stake; he simply couldn't face those three couples again without doing anything and everything he possibly could. Besides, *"with God all things are possible"*. Charles went back to that office and again, the woman invited him in. With charm, faith and a great deal of the Holy Spirit, Charles got what he went there for. All three adoptions were approved. He returned to Chengdu and all the adoptions moved forward to completion, as did my adoption in Changzhou. Altogether it took close to four weeks of tribulation. To God be the glory, great things He has done. Little Maggie Mei's adoption, was accompanied by baby girl Annalise, daughter Andrea and baby Chang Mei. I hope all these girls somehow came to understand the great miracles God did on their behalf to accomplish their adoptions; Maggie Mei in particular.

Ruth kept our girls busy with their camping in the Hong Kong Girl Scout program and Adrianne at a week of Christian Camp. She had a big 10th birthday celebration for Stephanie that I regretted missing. Ruth took them skating and bowling. She took them often to the local Happy Dragon water and bicycle park nearby us. Ruth did her best to keep them occupied so they could get their minds off what I was going through. Toward the end of the long ordeal with all the adopting couples, my calls home were filled with Ruth and my daughters crying to go home. I was not strong enough at that time to encourage them. As I mentioned earlier in the book, we had a one week rule that should any of our family feel they could no longer live in Asia, therefore, would we be returning to Kansas?

After just completing the adoption of Maggie Mei, I want to insert the divine journey Mike and Joyce took to be adopting a baby in Changzhou, China. I'm going to quote Joyce's own words from a letter she wrote to us a year after their adoption. Her testimony is quite long, but I share it because it powerfully shows how God moved just to bring this precious couple to adopt their little girl. Although every couple we assisted does not have a story so dramatic, it is representative in some ways of the testimonies of God working in the lives of many of our couples. Because I know this couple fairly well, I have no doubt whatsoever the testimony she shares is true and accurate.

Joyce wrote me the following letter. "The first knowledge I had of God's plan for our lives concerning adoption took place in the late summer of 1985. The Chinese, missionary, Nora Lam, was scheduled to speak at our Assembly of God church. Excited about

Nora's coming and wanting to know more about her life, I was easily absorbed by her biography (and movie), "China Cry". One evening, while reading the part about Nora's work with an orphanage in China, I clearly heard these words "you will have one of these children". Astonished, I lowered the book to see if my husband Mike, who was sitting across the room from me, had also heard what I knew in my spirit to be the voice of God. It was obvious that he had not, since he was still engrossed in the material he was studying on aviation. I was overwhelmed with this news as Mike and I have been married for 10 years and had accepted the fact that we were to be childless. Although I was ecstatic and wanted to share this revelation with him, it was such monumental news that I felt it would be best to keep it to myself until I had further confirmation from God. I didn't have to wait long, as a series of events led to the Lord's, revealing this wonderful news to Mike as well.

One day before Nora came to our church in September. I was praying about the service when I felt strongly impressed that the Lord wanted Mike to attend. Since he did not attend church with me on a regular basis at that time, I began praying that God would put the desire in his heart to hear Nora speak. Much to my delight God did just that, and off the two of us went on that glorious Sunday morning. I said glorious because several things happened that day which would change the course of our lives forever. Mike and I attended the second morning service. As we entered the sanctuary, I sensed that great and mighty things had already taken place during the first service. Our church was a very spirit filled place but in the years I attended, I had never felt God's presence so strongly. God's Spirit hung in the very atmosphere. It was like sweet, smelling incense, permeating the whole place. The church was alive with quiet testimonies of healings and revelations which had occurred in the first service. The excitement was mounting as people were eager to discover what the Lord was going to do. As I sat, prayed and waited for the second service to begin, never once did I consider that God had something personal in store for our lives that day. I was elated just to have my husband with me and have the opportunity to hear in person this great saint of God. Nora's excitement and fervor for the Lord was apparent as she hurried to the altar. What a humbling and convicting experience for me to see and hear this woman who had been so physically and mentally abused by her enemies because of her faith. Nora was so alive and excited to serve the God for which she had been so persecuted for.

After hearing Nora's testimony, the congregation was in prayer as Nora shared with us that the Lord was saying to her that there were five people present who were here to help build underground churches in China by donating $5000 each. As I prayed with the congregation for the five people who would hear God speaking to them and act accordingly, my own husband was the first to raise his hand! If I had not been seated, I feel quite sure that I would have fainted. Mike was the last person in that church I would have thought would make such a spontaneous decision. The Lord would have to be involved in such a financial undertaking since I knew we did not have the money in one lump sum to make such a gift. Mike had been planning to buy an airplane, and I knew for sure that Mike would not have committed himself to any amount of money, especially an amount so large, unless he had heard directly from God. I was later to learn that indeed was what happened. He heard the voice of God inwardly, saying, 'Do not miss this opportunity'. He had responded swiftly, and within a few seconds the other four people had raised their hands as well.

Nora then said, 'Let us move along quickly, God has revealed to me there are people here today He is going to heal. The Lord had already touched us personally, but it was to become more, for Nora then spoke with a word of knowledge to say "There is someone here in the audience with a tumor in her right breast, and God is going to heal you today'. Tripping over my husband's legs and feet, I made my way out of the pew and hurried to join Nora at the altar. I tried to remain calm as I stood before her, but inwardly, my heart was pounding with excitement. What was God doing for me? I wanted to fall prostrate before him, to cry, to sing, but instead, I only stood as Nora asked if I had a tumor in my right breast. When I replied that I did, she said 'me touch?' I took her hand and placed it on the tumor. I have been agonizing over this since my doctor who had located it during a routine examination a few weeks earlier. Nora then asked if that was my husband with me, and said for him to come and stand beside me. Mike was there beside me in an instant.

She continued responding to God's leading by calling out others to come forward for various healings. When everyone had come forward, she came back to me and said, sister, God has told me you are healed, and that I need not do anything else, 'now you touch!' When I did, the tumor was gone! What a day! I knew beyond a shadow of a doubt that God had healed me, and all I wanted to do was praise him. Nora began to pray for all of us gathered there, and when she did we all fell to the floor as we were slain in the Spirit by the power of God. God touched Mike's life in a very special and profound way that day, as he was also slain in the Spirit. Mike always gives that date as the day he knew God was real and more powerful than anything in his life he had ever known before.

After the service was over, Nora located Mike and invited us to attend a minister's conference in California. Our pastor was also going to be attending. When we asked for the date of the conference, my heart jumped once again. Nora said the exact date that I had an appointment with the surgeon at Ohio State University hospital for a breast biopsy. I rescheduled the appointment with the surgeon for a later date. After we returned from our trip to California, I had a thorough examination. My surgeon verified to me that there was now no sign of a tumor. Praise God! I was able to share with him what had happened and left him with a copy of Nora's book "China Cry". We attended the conference with our precious pastor, and that in itself was a wonderful time of fellowship. After the conference was over, Nora asked if Mike and I could remain until the following morning and have breakfast with her. She said that the Lord has been speaking to her about Mike, and that she had some things to share with us about our lives.

The next morning as we sat at a table with Nora, she began to share things about Mike's life and about him as a person only God could have revealed to her. She said, Mike, there is something that God wants you to do. He wants you to adopt a little girl. There it was again, the word from God I had hidden in my heart. I told Mike that this was truly from God, because he had already wonderfully revealed it to me. Nora said she would be happy to help us right away in adopting a little girl from China. What age child do you want? All of this was a little much to digest over breakfast, so we told her that we would let her know when we were ready. Later I felt as though I could've flown home without an airplane. Much to my surprise and disappointment, Mike shared with me about two weeks later that he was not ready to adopt. He stated that when he knew that God was speaking to him personally about it, then he would be ready. My spirit plummeted! After the high from having been healed, and the excitement of knowing I was going to be a mother for the first time in my life, I felt devastated. In time and through much prayer, I once again trusted God to bring this miracle child to fruition. After all, this was God's idea to adopt, not ours. I may not have felt so strong in faith at the time if I had known it would be seven years before we would have the child God planned for us in our arms. Although, I didn't doubt the miracle would come to pass, one day, when I felt especially troubled about it, I cried out to God, 'How is this adoption going to take place?' Immediately the reply came to my spirit, 'through an Assembly of God missionary.' There, I had the answer, but who was he or she and where were they? I waited and prayed.

One Sunday morning a visiting evangelist spoke at our church. After his sermon, many were gathered at the altar, to be prayed for, when he suddenly stopped and called out, there is a woman in the audience who has been praying for a baby. Please come forward. Second Corinthians 13:1 had truly been fulfilled *"on the testimony of two or three witnesses a fact will be established"*. As the evangelist laid hands on me, he began to prophesy that God has not forgotten His promise to me. The door was now open! Exactly what the Lord had promised would indeed come to pass. I was later to learn that at about the same time this message was given to me, the Ryels had gone into China. That was the open door for Maggie's adoption to take place. The Lord was faithful as time passed to place the desire of adoption in Mike's heart. He agreed for me to contact Nora to see if she could still help us.

When I reached her office by phone, the secretary informed me that Nora was no longer involved with adoptions, but she was able to give me the names of two organizations which dealt with Chinese adoptions. Could one of them be an Assembly of God missionary? You bet!! Those seven years of waiting were obviously necessary for us to receive one particular child. Not only had Maggie not yet been conceived at the time when the Lord first revealed his plan to us, but her parents may well have been young children. Each day that I spend with our precious daughter Maggie Mei, brings more certainty of the importance of waiting on God. He has blessed us above beyond anything we could ever have imagined possible and we give Him all the praise, and glory, Bless His Holy name forever!"

As we learned more about the changes in the adoption law, logically it appeared at some point Beijing would cut us off from doing adoption facilitation. Going forward, Beijing would only work directly with American licensed adoption agencies, and with no one working independently. We simply could not financially make it in Hong Kong without the subsidy of doing adoptions. Our one year contract for our apartment was soon set to increase from $1000 to $2000 per month due to the outside being painted and all the windows replaced. The cost of Charles spending an extra four weeks in Chengdu plus the trip to Beijing added to the additional two weeks I spent in Changzhou plus travel to Shanghai put us a few thousand dollars over budget. We could not in good conscience pass any of these additional costs on to the couples since they themselves had gone way over budget and missed work. Once the adopting couples returned home, Ruth and I had to seriously assess our options. We still had a number of couples who had completed all their paperwork and several others who were very near ready. The Emmaus Learning Center planning and implementation continued without us. Heather didn't want to return to America so she was praying that God would open a door for her to be able to stay. Our dear Heather was staying with us at the time when we invited a young couple we knew, Pete and Lauren Snyder and their two children for dinner. As we fellowshipped, the Snyders began talking about their need for someone to help teach their children, and perhaps just as important, an American friend to keep Lauren and the kids sane. They would be living in the midst of a fairly large inland Chinese city where there were no others that they knew of from a western culture. They and Heather really hit it off and quickly worked out all the details. God does answer prayer, but all too often He does so at the last minute. As you probably know, it's called a test of faith.

As we slowly made progress with our plans to return to Kansas, we still had a large number of adoptions in process. I sought Gods will as to what to do with all the couples I'd begun helping. First I contacted the twelve agencies in the United States I'd been in communicating with. After telling them what had transpired, and what my family's plans were, I sent them all the details for how they could contact Beijing and Chinese orphanages themselves. I made sure they had a clear understanding of what documents were needed for an adoption to be processed correctly. I then got with Alvin

Cobb to see if he might have any ideas. He suggested I contact Dwyatt Gantt whom I've referred to a few times previously in the book. Alvin set up a meeting where Dwyatt and I hashed out all the details of doing adoptions at Alvin's apartment. Dwyatt no longer had his agency placing English teachers in China and was seeking God for his next step in ministry. And, he already had contacts all over China as well as one in America who was qualified to operate an adoption agency. Answered prayer for both of us! I handed him most of the open files for couples who'd begun their adoption process with me and gave him everything he'd need to know about handling adoptions in China. Just as we were getting ready to leave Hong Kong, our Chinese orphanages began contacting us again, asking if couples could come to China to adopt. They had several children ready. They assured us that everything would go smoothly. So I set up those last several adoptions for Charles to complete while Dwyatt put together the network for future adoptions. After careful thought and giving warning to the couples who were waiting, we restarted sending orphanages completed adoption dossiers for several couples. This still did not negate the fact that Beijing would very soon block me from being a facilitator. There came a time when I was notifying all our couples, which at that point numbered nearly 40, that we were not going to be able to help them but Dwyatt would soon be up and going. All of this number had not gotten all of their paperwork done, but were simply in process. One of the couples who was ready was Richard and Nikki. After all the craziness we experienced with the previous

Mike and Joyce upon returning home with Maggie Mei

four adoptions, things started to settle down. Richard and Nikki had been in contact with us for several months and had at one point been totally denied by the orphanages, but we didn't give up. When the Chinese adoption law changed we thought it would even become less likely. This mom would just not give up her fight of faith. Because Richard and Nikki became so close to us throughout their struggle to adopt and because they were the last couple who adopted through us, we grew very connected to them. When they first arrived in Hong Kong the first words out of Nikki's mouth was that God had spoken to her that their adoption would go smoothly with no delays, and they would return home on the exact day of their scheduled departure. I however was doubtful after what I had just endured, but I kept my mouth shut. "It would take a miracle" I thought.

Their adoption process did go smoothly but they were alarmed when they first held Natalie because she seemed lifeless. They didn't know what was wrong, but it seemed their infant child wasn't healthy. Medical personnel at the orphanage examined the infant but could find nothing wrong. After a couple of days Natalie began acting normally, they came to realize this poor child had not been held or cuddled since being born. Love and care had never been shown this child. A mother's love brought Natalie back to life. This was the only time we had seen this happen with any of the babies, but we were told it was not so uncommon. Most good orphanages when it's discovered a child will be adopted would place the baby with a local caregiver to be nurtured. This adoption was not coming from any of the orphanages we dealt with before. Natalie's came from a small town near the provincial capital city of Nanjing. When we met Richard, Nikki, their other two children and their baby in Hong Kong, Natalie was very responsive and full of life. And yes, they returned home on the exact day of their scheduled departure, just as God had told Nikki.

As you've read this chapter you discovered we planned to move back to America, but you may have had the thought that perhaps we were premature in leaving, we should have stuck it out longer. We should have pressed through in faith. After all, God has done so much to provide for us up to this point, so why throw in the towel? God would surely provide your needs and make a way to further your ministry. These are all valid questions. Sure, we'd been through a great deal of trauma and were facing financial mountains.

But neither the trauma nor the lack of financial provision was the deciding factor for our decision to leave. Unlike our mindset of total faith following all the tests and trials we had undergone to that point, we simply no longer felt Asia was our home. Our heart was no longer in it and we simply felt God calling us back. Just as sure as I was that God called us to China, I was certain God was calling us back to Kansas.

As we were leaving Hong Kong, two more couples were in route to adopt. Charles of course was now in charge, we just couldn't be there to greet and connect them personally with Charles. He continued to facilitate adoptions for several couples who had finished their paperwork, including Joe and Deanne from Illinois. Altogether we completed forty adoptions. Although we'd begun relationships with orphanages in a few other cities, our many adoptions were facilitated from five Chinese orphanages. To God be all the glory, honor and praise

No humility, No honor!

23

It's Not Your Fault

September 2nd, 1992 at 1:00am we arrived at the Wichita Kansas airport and were greeted by a host of joyful faces. There was jumping! There was dancing! There was hugging! And there was kissing! There were enough pictures taken to fill a large photo album. The Ryels were home! At one point our most faithful of all friends, Deby Taylor, placed a key into Ruth's hand. The church had not only provided us money for our return flight, they'd rented us a furnished and decorated house to live in. Food would be in our refrigerator and food for our cabinets was coming very soon. We'd had no idea where we were going to live, but God through His people provided. Of course we couldn't wait to see it, so we and half the crowd made their way up to Valley Center late that evening to see our new place. We couldn't have been more thrilled. Our ministry's best friend Deby Taylor, Pastor Joe Voss and all our ministry supporters had stepped up in amazing ways and we were so humbled and thankful for all they did to get us home; even giving us a great new start for our lives.

THE VERY LONG FIGHT – We'd had a bit of reverse culture shock on previous visits home, but this was a great deal different. Coming home before, we were missionaries, but now what were we? Before, we had great plans and aspirations for our missions call, but now what was our purpose? Before, we had a great many disciples, home churches and scores of adopting families which God was using us to bless. But now all of that was 8000 miles away. It seemed we were now just nobodies with nothing important to say or do. Before we had an important calling, but now we had a lovely church pew on Sunday mornings.

What I desperately wanted to hang on to after returning home was for God to somehow still use me in missionary ministry. For several months I continued to send out newsletters, but instead of our ministry called "China Light", I called it "World Missions Network". I envisioned this new ministry was for the purpose of raising money for independent missionaries I personally knew. They were doing a great work and sacrificing a great deal for God's

Kingdom, yet they struggled getting the financial support needed to accomplish all they were called of God to do. Each month I would highlight a particular family and their awesome ministry. All financial gifts sent to me would be put together and sent directly to them. I don't recall anyone sending me much money, but I did get a letter from one of my supporters. She kindly spoke an inconvenient truth and explained to me that they would not be sending any money for these missionaries I was promoting because they didn't know them. They supported me because they knew me. Her intentions were good, but it was the beginning of a clear message that my missionary ministry was over. I now had to simply focus on pursuing life in America. Perhaps at some point in your life you've also experienced these kinds of feelings. To let go of a career that meant so much to you, and then start over is very difficult. Those who serve in our military certainly face this every day when they are released from their service.

From the beginning, Ruth and I would be asked by friends and acquaintances the question "how was it in China?" To answer such a vastly broad question was impossible. I only had about ten seconds to put in words all I'd experienced the past five years before I was interrupted to listen to what important things were going on in their lives. In fact, it wasn't long before Ruth and I stopped wanting to say anything at all about our missionary adventures, especially with new acquaintances. It just didn't seem all that important anymore.

To no fault of theirs, our precious church and all those who we absolutely knew loved us, I felt very useless and alone. Then, approximately one month after returning to Kansas, my dad was diagnosed with stage four, aggressive lung cancer. After a short battle, my sweet daddy died on March 14th of 1993. I slipped farther and farther into chronic depression; a condition I would fight in many ways, off and on, for the following 30 years. Although I desperately tried and wanted to be, I can't say that I was near the quality of husband to Ruth or the great dad I desired to be for my precious girls.

If you happen to engage with a missionary who has just come off the mission field, do not ask what it was like. If you'd read their newsletters, you know something of what it was like, so make a special effort to get together and ask about specific things you remember them talking about. If you seldom or never read their newsletters, set aside a special time to let them open up about it; that is if you truly care and aren't just making casual conversation. In any case, you need to realize they could very well be feeling lost. You need to realize they might even be in great pain. In China I became deeply broken. In America I would remain deeply broken as a minister of the gospel, as a person and as a man. Ruth and I pressed on though. The highlight of our lives early on was being invited to a couple of adoption reunions in Ohio. Three of the couples we assisted were from the same area of Ohio and hosted two reunions. It was wonderful to see so many of the families we facilitated adoptions for. The photo below shows the adopted children who attended one of our reunions.

Some of the children at one of our reunions

    A photo was taken which I've not been able to locate, of Ruth and I surrounded by all the Chinese children at the reunion. Ruth and I couldn't help but recall the prophetic dream our friend Joann Westfahl had of what we imagined as similar to that photo. Mike and Joyce were there with little Maggie Mei at the reunion, which was very meaningful to us in a healing sort of way. We had to make a living, but having chronic depression infects everything you try to do: relationships, stability in jobs, stability in your church and your self control. Among all the jobs I had during these 30 years, we were given the chance to be fulltime Children's Pastors but it lasted only a year. We also accepted the job as the Pastor of the Church Triumphant in Short Gap, West Virginia, but it was only six months before we were made unwelcome.

    Please understand I have no interest in gaining sympathy or casting blame by what I've shared; so what is the point of expressing the after effects of our time in China? It's for three reasons. First, it is to alert The Church that returning missionaries may be carrying deep wounds and scars. Though there are similarities of what returning missionaries might feel to what returning soldiers feel. I absolutely do not want to compare the level of trauma typically endured by our military, to that of myself or most any missionary. In both cases however, you might see them struggling in various ways. So what can you do to help returning missionaries? Give them something meaningful to do in ministry; particularly something involving missions, teaching or evangelism if those were the skills and anointing they expressed on the mission field. These men and women are often warriors who have been engaged in serious spiritual warfare. They may have open, infected wounds. Don't just sit them in a pew. Show them on-going honor and lots of love. Their hands have been trained for war, so give them another battle to fight. You may be inclined to give them rest, just don't let them sit very long or they'll become hopeless. Spend time with them regularly and listen to what their specific needs might be. Maybe they need counseling, but maybe they just need prayer and good friends to listen and encourage them.

Second, I share my struggles for those who have experience as a missionary, or pastors who've also been broken in battle. You are not alone! Reach out to people who've been there for you in the past. Be brave and honest with them. Continually seek out people to share burdens with. Stay close to your spouse and children and do not allow your spiritual enemy an opportunity to tear you down with depression or bitterness. You'll get through it with God's grace and the help of your Christian brothers and sisters.

Third, even though my family has lived through all of this with me, they've only seen it from their own perspective and not mine. I wanted them to have a written record of all our battles both in China and after China. I want them to know that through everything, I fought with ALL my strength to love and provide for them the very best I could. My heart's desire was to always be the strong Christian husband and dad they deserved. I deeply regret any failings my ongoing depression created.

THE GLORY – For me the glory; my complete freedom from shame was exactly 30 years in the making. In the fall of 2022 Ruth and I drove to Bentonville, Arkansas to enjoy a concert by a few of our favorites Christian artists- Kari Jobe and Cody Carnes with the Bethel worship team as well as Chris Tomlin. Kari opened the concert but near the end of their set, she and Cody sang one of their songs which we loved, "The Blessing". Ruth and I have taken part in a great number of powerful worship services and concerts over the years, but when they sang "The Blessing" it was beyond anything we'd ever before experienced in corporate worship. I can only describe it as heaven opening up like a flood gate. The Holy Spirit drowned the crowd, but then became a spiritual wave machine moving back and forth throughout the crowd of believers as we all stood for worship in this lovely open air venue. This experience will never be forgotten, but even less likely to be forgotten was the result of the personal anointing I experienced that night.

After returning home to Branson Missouri and going to bed, I was still sleeping when God spoke to me saying "It's not your fault". Again He repeated "It's not your fault! Even though I was still asleep, I knew it was God's voice in my Spirit and instantly knew what He meant. His words were a healing medicine for the deep shame placed there in 1992 when I played a role in putting those four panicked and hurting couples through their pain and trauma. I woke that morning feeling healed and in complete peace.

A few days later while attending a Sunday service at our church "The House of Mercy" in Branson West Missouri, God gave me more understanding. Our pastor used the words in his sermon "no fight, no glory". He was talking about how God sometimes takes us through terrible times in our fight of faith, but without those fights we never see the glory of God's great miracles which so often occur thereafter. As the pastor preached, God spoke to me again by the Holy Spirit saying "It was Me! I did it!" I began to cry. It was the cry of a captive set free! This was the second line to what God had said to me in the night just days before. It was the completion of my healing and it truly set me free. The blame I had taken on myself wasn't my mine to take because it was God who did it. God orchestrated all of it to ultimately show His awesome power. Even in those devastatingly difficult days, God was still at work using Charles and I, just not in the way we wanted or were accustomed to. To say it a bit differently, had everything gone smoothly for those four couples; there would never have been the absolutely astounding miracles. Our faith would not have been tested to work patience and trust in our lives. I don't know if any of those four couples or their adopted children will ever happen to read this book, but if they do, I want them to know what great things God did on their behalf, even though they may not have been very aware of it at the time. As for me, God certainly could have freed me of whatever was causing my depression, guilt and shame long ago. I prayed so often for Him to do so, but He didn't. Like Job, I still trust Him. His timing is always perfect.

To give you just one of a great many scriptural evidences for my thoughts, I site John 9:1-3 *"As Jesus was walking along, he saw a man who had been blind from birth. "Rabbi," his disciples asked him, "why was this man born blind? Was it because of his own sins or his parents' sins?" "It was not because of his sins or his parents' sins," Jesus answered. "This happened so the power of God could be seen in him."* Indeed, the bible is full of God's deeds which were preceded with chaos, suffering, injury, pain and even death; Jesus' life, death and resurrection being the greatest example.
☐☐THE GLORY voiced in this book is not and was not my glory, my victory, or my strength. Every time "THE GLORY" is mentioned in this book, it was most certainly God's glory being spoken of. *"For without Him, we can do nothing." John 15:5*

No suffering, No discipline!

■ FAMILY FOCUS

BG site of Chinese adoptees' reunion

By KAREN NADLER COTA
Family Focus Editor

Nancy and Jack _____, of Bowling Green, married eight years, had been trying to have a baby for seven of those years.

Bonnie and Randy _____ members of the same church as the Hollisters, knew their pain only too well. They were also childless after several years of marriage.

Wendie and John _____ had wanted a large family but couldn't have children of their own. After adopting three children in the U.S. and Columbia, they yearned for a fourth child to complete their family.

For these three local couples and more than 30 others around the U.S., the answer to a multitude of prayers came in the guise of Randy and Ruth Ryel, U.S. missionaries to China.

The Ryels had a first-hand look at one of the sad byproducts of China's current one-child-per-family policy. In China, sons are greatly valued; daughters generally are not.

Some Chinese couples whose first child is a daughter end up leaving her at an orphanage so they can try again for a son.

The Ryels knew that in America the opposite is true: there are not enough babies for all the couples who want to adopt.

They began to wade through the bureaucracy, cultural misunderstandings and international logistics to try to solve both these problems. The end result was 37 adoptions of little girls who could otherwise have expected to spend their entire childhood in orphanages, if they survived to adulthood.

The U.S. couples got a long-awaited chance to thank the Ryels personally for their little "China Lights" this past weekend as they converged on Bowling Green for a giant reunion. It was also the first time many of the couples had met each other.

"There are 17 families here today," said _____ during a group picnic Saturday at Bowling Green City Park. One couple came from as far as Minnesota and the Ryels had made the trip from Wichita, Kansas, where they are presently living. "They're back from China permanently," she added, so the Chinese adoption connection has ended.

Most families arrived in town for a welcoming reception Friday night. By Saturday the couples felt like old friends and the children —most of them toddlers — were enjoying all the attention.

"We've been planning this for two months," noted Mrs. _____ whose daughter, Leah, is 2. She, Mrs. _____ and Mrs. _____ got together several times to work on the reunion and to put together an album for the Ryels, containing a letter from every adoptive family and a photo of each child.

Jack and Amy _____ of Louisville, Ky., married 15 years, were thrilled with the chance to introduce their daughter Lucy to fellow Chinese adoptees.

The couple adopted Lucy at about one year of age. They had traveled to China with two other couples, from Pittsburgh and Minneapolis, who were also hoping to adopt with the Ryels' help.

Lucy had been abandoned at the

*We Welcome with "OPEN ARMS"
Our Little "CHINA LIGHTS"!!*

240

BG toddlers adopted from China
Three of the 17 adoptive families at this past weekend's gathering are from Bowling Green. Pictured are local proud mothers (from left) Bonnie ▅▅ with Hannah; Wendie ▅▅ holding Abigail; and Nancy ▅▅ with Leah.

state orphanage and when they first met her "she couldn't crawl or do much of anything," her father recalls. By the time she had been with the ▅▅ two months she had bypassed crawling entirely and was already walking.

Lucy is now somewhere between 2 years and 28 months of age. The orphanage did not know her birth date.

She is obviously bright — able to count to 20, and curious. "She's real proud of her Chinese heritage," ▅▅ said. "She'll see Connie Chung on TV at night and say 'She's Chinese!'"

The ▅▅ have since adopted a son, 5-month-old Jack, from Tokyo, Japan.

While each of the adopting couples' stories had similarities, there were also differences. The length, complexity and cost of the adoption process tended to increase over time.

"We were the second couple to go (to China) in the whole program. We were there just 2½ weeks. It was very easy," said Diana ▅▅ of Michigan City, Ind. She and her husband, Robert, brought home Kirsten, who will be 3 next month.

The children's health also varied. A couple from Naperville, Ill. recalled their daughter Kathleen, 1, was "subdued" and weighed only 9 pounds when they got her, at nearly 3 months of age. She quickly gained weight and interest in the world around her after coming to the States.

Currently, China has put a temporary halt to foreign adoptions in an effort to fix problems that have cropped up, including financial exploitation of would-be parents by some adoption brokers.

So the couples who met in Bowling Green over the weekend feel doubly blessed that a window of opportunity opened for them when it did.

"It's been fun," ▅▅ said of the reunion. "The people want to do it again, at least every other year."

BG couple tells adoption story

By KAREN NADLER COTA
Family Focus Editor

For Nancy and Jack ▅▅, adopting a child from China made a great deal of sense.

"I had always wanted a little Asian girl, so when we decided to adopt we checked into agencies that handled Asian children, and this one (handled by missionaries Ruth and Randy Ryel) was the only one currently doing adoptions," said Mrs. ▅▅.

The couple started the adoption process in April 1991 and flew to China in November of that year. There they were introduced to their daughter, Leah, now 2.

"We were gone a total of two weeks in China. It was a very easy stay. The people at the state orphanage in Changzhou, near Shanghai, were so helpful."

Leah made a relatively smooth transition to life in the U.S. Mrs. ▅▅ mother came to stay and help out for the first couple of weeks and friends from church brought meals.

All seemed to be going beautifully until New Year's Eve.

"She just appeared to have the flu, vomiting, very pale," said Mrs. ▅▅. "By 2:30 in the afternoon we were in the emergency room and she was in shock."

Leah was transferred from Wood County Hospital to Toledo Hospital where she spent two days in the intensive care unit before being Life Flighted to Children's Hospital in Ann Arbor, Mich., for two more weeks.

Doctors said a virus had attacked Leah's heart. "Two mornings in a row we were told she wouldn't make it until night.

"That was just tremendous. After going all that way, the devastation that we might lose her!

"But she's fine now. No heart problem."

Adoption Couples

Throughout the book you'll have noticed I mentioned many of our adopting couples, and even highlighted many of their stories. We left Asia before I was able to complete all of those I'd been diligently working on. A few of these couples were assisted by Charles alone after my family returned to the United States. Others, as I mentioned in the book, were passed along to Dwyatt Gantt for him to complete. At first he began as an organization known as "China's Children". Later he changed the name to "Children's Hope International" when his adoption program began reaching other countries. Since those days, his ministry has completed many hundreds, perhaps thousands of adoptions, not only from China, but from many other countries as well. It's truly astounding to me looking back over my life how God did so much with so little. But I guess this is truly the message of the entire Bible, and part of the reason that it's declared to be "The greatest story ever told!"

Peter and Pattie adopted Annalise
Robert and Dianna adopted Kirsten
Frank and Colleen adopted Tricia
Jerry and Susan adopted Lindsay
Andrew and Laura adopted Rhiannon
Kim and Carolyn adopted Sarah
John and Denise adopted Leah
John and Joyce adopted Rachel
Larry and Susan adopted Mollee
Paul and Louise adopted Sarah
David and Cathy adopted Angie
Ken and Brenda adopted Joy
Don and Diane adopted Elizabeth and Sarah
Jack and Nancy adopted Leah
Alan and Denelle adopted Meredith
Steve and Kim adopted Stephanie and Sarah
Michael and Penelope adopted May-Anne
Delbert and Laura adopted Katharine
Joe and Deann adopted Kathleen
Richard and Patti adopted Elisabeth
Richard and Donna adopted Lianne

Frank and Ruth adopted Mariah
David and Cathy adopted Amanda
John and Amy adopted Lucy
Sylvester and Deborah adopted Sarah
Bill and Jane adopted Andrea
Robert and Patrice adopted Annalise
Mike and Joyce adopted Maggie Mei
Richard and Nikki adopted Natalie
John and Wendie adopted Abigail
Gordan and Colleen adopted Michelle
Donald and Mai adopted Lian
Randy and Bonnie adopted Hannah
Jim and Susan adopted Caitlyn
Mike and Patricia adopted (I was never told her name)

Copyright © 2024

No part of this publication may be copied, reproduced in any format, by any means, electronic or otherwise, without prior consent from the copyright owner and publisher of this book.

Made in the USA
Columbia, SC
03 February 2025